An Imaginativ

CW01594310

The author

Margaret Bryer qualified as a social worker. She worked from 1967–1981 for the London Borough of Wandsworth, first as a Child Care Officer, then a Senior Social Worker and finally as Principal Officer of the Adoption and Fostering Unit.

From 1981–2001 she worked as an independent social work trainer and consultant in Child Care. This brought her into contact with many local authority departments and voluntary agencies, and with the panels of Guardians ad Litem in Oxfordshire and Berkshire.

From 2002–3 she lived in Geneva and worked as a volunteer caseworker at the ISS General Secretariat. On her return to the UK she joined the Board of ISSUK from 2004 to 2009, and then the Board of CFAB until 2011.

She has written this history of ISSUK from an independent point of view. While the history is based on records, the interpretation of those facts expressed in the book are those of the author, or of the person quoted.

An Imaginative Co-operation

The History of International Social Service of the United Kingdom 1955–2009

Margaret Bryer

etica

Published by
Etica Press Ltd
147 Worcester Road
Malvern
Worcestershire
WR14 1ET

© M Bryer 2015

The moral right of M Bryer to be identified as the author of this work has been asserted by the author in accordance with the Copyright, Designs and Patents Act of 1988.

A CIP Record for this book is available from
The British Cataloguing-in-Publication Data Office

ISBN 978 1 905633 22 7

All rights reserved. No part of this publication may be reproduced, stored in a retrieval system, or transmitted at any time or by any means electronic, mechanical, photocopying, recording or otherwise, without the prior written permission of the copyright owner and of the publisher.

Text design and typesetting by Etica Press

Cover design by Jonathan Doyle

Printed and bound in the UK by Berforts (Stevenage)

Contents

Foreword

In 2009 the Board of Trustees of the International Social Service of the United Kingdom, commonly known as ISS UK, made the decision to change the charity's 'public name' to "Children and Families Across Borders", with the acronym of CFAB, whilst remaining as the UK Branch of the ISS network. This change came into effect on 1st January 2010. I was the Chairman of the charity and Margaret Bryer was one my fellow Trustees. In 2011 the Board discussed the idea that a history of our Branch, from its foundation in 1955 until the time it ceased to be publicly referred to as ISS, be commissioned. We were extremely grateful that Margaret Bryer volunteered to write this history.

What Margaret has produced is a tribute to her dedication to what has indeed proved to be a time-consuming task. Even more, this history acknowledges the immense contribution of all those many people who, over a considerable number of years, have ensured that our charity does all in its power to deliver its primary purpose as:

> "an independent charity and part of an international network, which acts to promote and protect the rights and welfare of children, individuals and families, whose personal circumstances require inter-country liaison".

In much the same way as indicated throughout this historical record, CFAB has changed and adjusted since 2010 to meet the different circumstances that it confronts in its continuing determination to protect children and unite families across borders, whenever there is a UK element to the individual cases. I am sure our predecessors would be happy to know that in 2014 our charity is flourishing, and continues to focus on providing our unique social welfare service to vulnerable people across the globe.

Douglas Lewis CBE
Chairman ISS UK (2004–09)
Chairman CFAB (2010–14)
International President of the ISS Global Network (2014–)

Acknowledgments

I could not have written this book without the experience of being a volunteer in the ISS Geneva office, and a Trustee of ISSUK. I would like to record my appreciation of all the people I worked alongside – for friendship and some wonderful conversations – for the interest and stimulation of the work, and the struggles to overcome challenges. It has been a privilege to be part of such a caring and committed organisation.

Many people have helped with the writing of this book. I should like to thank Audrey Moser, Heloise Kareem, Tom Luce, Sheila Poupard, Charles Marshall, Doug Lewis and Chris Platt, all of whom I was able to interview, and from whom I learned so much. Special thanks are due to Chris Platt who, over many months, provided me with desk space when required, and found all the various documents that I needed. Thanks too, to Jean Ayoub and the staff of the General Secretariat in Geneva, for giving me access to the archive there.

There is so much fascinating material that I had to be very selective. Unfortunately, there were also many gaps in the archives, and so some sections are scantier than I would have liked.

I am grateful to those who have read the draft manuscripts and made many useful comments; namely Liz Grimsey, Heloise Kareem, Doug Lewis, Chris Platt, and my husband David and son Nicholas. It goes without saying that any errors are my responsibility alone.

I am particularly grateful to Ali Sattaripour for making the publication of this book possible.

Margaret Bryer

September 2015

Introduction

This is the story of a charitable organisation – and also a professional social work one. It is a record of the 55 years from the opening of a Branch in London of International Social Service (ISS) in 1955 to the end of 2009. At that point the organisation changed its name (but not its purpose and function) to Children and Families Across Borders (CFAB). But these 55 years are only part of a much longer story.

The threads that run through this story are the movements of people across continents and national borders, separating family members one from another; the social problems that arise from such migrations, and the responses to those problems. The unique contribution of ISS to this has been the development of a network of social welfare agencies across the world, so that problems that arise when families are separated can be addressed from one country to another. In addition to all the work with individuals, there have been some fascinating projects set up to help specific groups of people. These projects have nearly all been time-limited, and one of the purposes of this booklet is to record this work, so that those who are now involved with the organisation may understand the richness of the background. The story also traces how the organisation has been funded over the years, and shows the contribution of so many people to the survival and success of the charity.

The Mission Statement of ISSUK was written towards the end of the period covered by this history, but it encapsulates the work of the charity throughout this time. It states: **"ISSUK is an independent charity and part of an international network, which acts to promote and protect the rights and welfare of children, individuals and families, whose personal circumstances require inter-country liaison".**[1]

1 Agreed by the ISSUK Board of Trustees 26.1.05.

In researching the origins of ISS I have read books, documents, letters, reports and websites, and have talked to some of those involved. This is a personal view of how the many strands of this story interlink. As with the history any organisation, that of ISS contains many different elements, and the reader will find examples of great achievements, but also of setbacks and problems. Some of the lessons to be learned come from the evidence of how such difficulties were tackled.

The names of the different parts of the organisation have changed over time; for example, ISSUK itself started as the British Branch of ISS, then changed to International Service of Great Britain (ISSGB) in 1957, and only changed to International Social Service of the United Kingdom (ISSUK) in 1991. In general I shall keep to the names used as they come up in the story, but when referring to the whole period in Britain or the UK I shall use ISSUK. (When referring to the wider organisation I use ISS.) I have sometimes found discrepancies in dates, and this may be because one source quotes the beginning of a discussion or process, while another source gives the date of completion. Occasionally the date given for the start of ISS in the UK is given as 1953, because that is when the name was first used, but the generally recognised date is 1955, when the organisation became fully independent.

The usage of titles and names has changed during the period covered: in the first years of ISS in Britain all reports give titles and surnames and rarely give first names. (Indeed, I have not always been able to discover the first names of some people.) Gradually first names were used, earlier for staff than for trustees. However, in order to be consistent, and in keeping with modern practice, in the earlier chapters the first mention of each person gives the title, first name and surname (with married and titled women the first name is in brackets), and then after that I generally use only the first name and surname.

Terminology has changed too, and for example, the term "Chair" is now more commonly used than "Chairman". However, I have stayed with the term "Chairman", irrespective of the gender of the person, because this was the term used throughout almost all the period of this history.

The first three chapters will trace back to see how the ISS came into being, first internationally and then in Britain, and demonstrate how the structure, principles and methodology were established, as the basis on which the organisation continues to develop the work in response to current needs.

The following chapter sets out the context within which the ISS operates, and the factors that have influenced the three central themes of this story; a voluntary agency as part of an international network; the social work carried out by the agency, and how this work is funded. After that the story will broadly be told chronologically, decade by decade, but sometimes it is best to follow one subject through to a conclusion, even though this may take it out of the time scale. This is particularly so in relation to the various projects undertaken. In each decade more or less the same themes are covered, so that any developments of these can be traced, chapter by chapter; firstly, there are descriptions of major world events that affected the work; then a section on legislation, including International Conventions and British law. These are followed by a bit about the ISS headquarters and ISS GB/UK within the network. Regarding the British Branch, there are sections on governance, staff, finances and fund-raising, and links with other agencies. Finally, but centrally, there are descriptions of the casework and special projects, which are set in the chapter of the decade in which they started. In order to illustrate the work, I have included some very brief case histories. All these case examples are taken from work done by ISSUK workers. The stories are real, but the details have been changed for reasons of confidentiality. These examples can only touch on the main elements of each case, and do not portray the very complicated and drawn-out situations that frequently arise.

Arranging the material chronologically seemed to be the best way to show the development of the organisation, although this has inevitably led to occasional repetition. Those readers who wish to follow one theme, such as governance or fundraising or casework, may use the index to find the relevant sections.

There is more information about the later years for two reasons: firstly, because much of the material of the earlier years is missing. It seems that there may have been somewhat over-enthusiastic clearing-out when moving to new offices. Luckily, some of the earliest correspondence has been kept in Geneva. Secondly, there is inevitably much more information about the later years because I, and those I talked to, were closely involved with ISSUK during those years. So the story of the last two decades includes a lot more detail about the ups and downs of the organisation, but above all it demonstrates the determination and energy that went into keeping the charity going through very difficult financial times. It is hoped that this will be of particular interest to those who may have to face similar problems in the future.

Hundreds of people have given time and skill to the work of ISS in Britain and it is impossible to name them all. I shall highlight the contributions of a few of the most outstanding ones, showing the range of life experiences that they brought to the charity. Lists in the Appendix gives the names of the main post holders, and many of the Trustees, staff and volunteers who worked for and with the organisation for ten years or more. Similarly, there is no room to list all the many Trusts and individuals who have given money to the organisation over the years, but in the Appendix you will find the names of Trusts that have most consistently or most generously supported ISS.

The Appendix also includes a list of acronyms, a list of all the national branches of ISS, a list of the countries with whom ISSUK worked in one year of each decade, a list of countries taking part in the annual Spring Fair, and a list of the main legislation affecting the work.

Chapter 1

The background history

In a sense, any starting date is arbitrary, because there have always been groups of people who have put themselves out to help travellers and migrants. But we can trace the origins of ISS directly back to 1855 – one hundred years before the formation of ISS in Great Britain. In that year in London two women independently decided to do something to help vulnerable women who were far from home, and they focussed on two groups in particular; nurses travelling to or from the battlefield hospitals of Turkey and the Crimea, and the large numbers of young single women travelling to the cities in search of work. Mary Jane Kinnaird established the London Young Women's Institute, for Nightingale's nurses and other working women, with residential accommodation at the North London Home in Charlotte Street. Later she opened other boarding houses near ports and railway stations, so that travelling women could have somewhere cheap and safe to stay. Meanwhile, also in 1855, Emma Robarts set up a Prayer Union in Barnet, London, which she later called the Christian Association of Young Women – with the purpose of not just praying with and for young women, but also offering help in a number of practical ways.[2]

The two women met in 1877 and together formed the Young Women's Christian Association (YWCA). (This was to be in line with the YMCA which had been founded in 1844.) Meanwhile, in the USA similar groups were established in Boston and New York in the 1860s, and by the 1890s there were branches in several other countries.

In 1894 representatives from the UK, USA, Sweden and Norway formed the World's YWCA. It was to be "a global

2 From Encyclopaedia of Protestantism.

network of women and girls working for justice, peace, health, human dignity, freedom and care for the environment".[3] Four years later there was an International Meeting in London attended by 326 representatives from 17 countries, and from then on the Worldwide YWCA flourished in a growing number of countries. The headquarters moved from London to Geneva in 1930. (There are now branches in more than 120 countries.)

So the scene was set for a global network of agencies all having the goal of helping young women, especially those who were away from home. The focus soon widened to include women with children, and then families. We are concerned here with the needs of those crossing national borders.

In the main, people migrate for one or more of these three reasons: escape from conflict or persecution, flight from famine or disaster, and pursuit of greater opportunities. In the last decade of the 19th century most migration was driven by economic necessity. "Central to the thousands of stories of migration at that time was economic need. Men, against terrible odds sometimes, would journey far from their homeland in the hope of finding work, saving money, and then sending for their family to join them. The hoped-for reunions were seldom straightforward. Some wives would never hear from their husbands again. Others would endure a wait of ten years or more, then an arduous journey to the new country, only to find rejection at the port of entry because of legal or health-related complications. All were vulnerable to exploitation by unscrupulous steamship companies. And nothing in their old lives could have prepared the émigrés for all the new situations, rules and regulations that they would experience upon arrival on an unfamiliar shore."[4]

"Throughout all this human ebb and flow, thousands of children were involved, with problems of care and assistance, conflicts of citizenship and nationality, guardianship, and clashes of civil and ecclesiastical laws".[5]

3 World YWCA website.

4 A very personal service – a history of ISS Australia's first 50 years of service 1955–2005: B Pertzel, 2010.

5 Young People in Migration – Keynote Speech by A Moser at International Council 2000.

The Aliens Act 1905 (which superseded previous Aliens Acts and Naturalisation Acts), was important because it was the first legislation to introduce powers to deny entry to immigrants considered "undesirable". Then the British Nationality and Status of Aliens Act 1914 granted British nationality to citizens of the UK, Commonwealth and Colonies, based on allegiance to the Crown. It concerned the naturalisation of aliens, and the status of women and children where one parent was an alien. Also in 1914 the Aliens Registration Act and the Aliens Restriction Act were rapidly passed at the beginning of the war. For the first time, every person entering the country had to produce evidence of identity, and from 1915 photographs were required in passports. All passports were now endorsed with red stamps on arrival and black stamps on leaving the country (the embarkation stamps were abolished only in 1998). The organisation of the Immigration Service was set out in the Aliens Order 1920.

In 1914 there was an international conference in Stockholm, under the auspices of the World's YWCA, at which a resolution was passed to set up a study of the problem of migration. "Out of a dawning awareness of the unnecessary waste and tragedy in the lives of transplanted people, there grew a determination to discover the means by which migration might become a less destructive experience, and, if possible, one of real value."[6]

However, World War 1 intervened, leading to the break-up of the Austro-Hungarian and Ottoman Empires and these events, together with the Russian Revolution, caused chaos across a huge area. An unprecedented number of refugees criss-crossing countries and continents was overwhelming all existing procedures and facilities. "In spite of the fact that the lack of communication during prolonged separation had weakened many family ties, there was a great human flood ready to surge toward reunion through the ports long closed by hostilities. Facilities everywhere were inadequate and there was grave danger of epidemics … thousands were buying tickets for the 'land of promise' without the remotest notion of any legal complications."[7]

6 International Social Service – a History 1921–55 by R Larned 1960.

7 Ibid p2.

In 1920 the World's YWCA convened at Champéry in Switzerland and delegates recognised the need for co-ordinated action between countries to ease the passage of those travelling to unfamiliar lands, and to reduce the numbers of migrants being refused entry to the country to which they had gone. It was decided to establish a Standing Committee on Migration in 1921, based in London, and to set up a thorough study of the situation, and to establish methods of co-ordination of effort. An American social worker with US YWCA, Mary E Hurlbutt, was commissioned to do a six-month survey of migration from Germany, Poland, Czechoslovakia, France and Switzerland. Her seminal report "the Welfare of Migrants" was published in 1921. It highlighted the enormous problems for migrants: lack of resources, lack of information, confusion and desperation and exploitation. It made a strong case for greater protection for migrants. Not only did this report inform the work of all branches of the World's YWCA, but it was also put before the International Emigration Commission set up by the International Labour Office (ILO) and so reached a wider audience. Mary Hurlbutt later became Director of ISS from 1926–30.

The seven members of the Standing Committee on Migration laid down the following principles and aims:

- "outposts would be established at the crucial points of migration, to give migrants the best possible service, and records kept in such a form as to provide a basis for study.
- the service should be developed in co-operation with all agencies interested in the welfare of migrants and should be without discrimination as to nationality, race, religion or political affiliation.
- although willing to take a certain amount of responsibility for initiating the work, the World's YWCA would definitely aim to relinquish control as soon as practicable to an independent, representative and co- operative body"[8]

Service Bureaux were set up in several strategic cities: Prague, Warsaw, Paris, Cherbourg, Le Havre, Antwerp, Athens, Constantinople/Istanbul and Ellis Island in New York. "Personnel

8 Ibid p4.

was selected not alone on the basis of appropriate experience, nationality and requisite languages, but a disposition to appreciate and respect, not merely tolerate, cultural and religious differences. Headquarters in London kept all the Bureaux informed on laws and procedures through a news-clipping service and information bulletins."[9] Most Bureaux were attached to post-war units of the YWCA, but some, such as the ones in France, were independent. In the USA the work of the YWCA was carried out through International Institutes, set up in cities with large foreign-born populations. From the start all the Bureaux sought the co-operation of local agencies and communities.

Whilst governments struggled with the immense needs of the shifting tide of peoples across Europe and beyond, the Service Bureaux were able to set up the basic structure that continues today, that of concentrating on individuals. Sometimes it was just information that was required, but grants or other practical help could also be given to certain groups of needy people at a point of crisis. However, most cases concerned the efforts of people to find and get in touch with relatives – often with little to go on. The methodology was simple – to send and obtain information by means of letters – but to do so via the auspices of knowledgeable local organisations. If information was obtained, it might lead to the reuniting of families, but if this was not possible, it could end the pain of uncertainty.

Those planning to travel abroad to find work often needed help with the bewildering and changing details of what was required. In 1921 the USA introduced its first quota system with little warning, which had a catastrophic impact on would-be migrants. Some were turned back at the port of exit, finding that they suddenly required visas; others got as far as Ellis Island before being turned away. These people had given up their homes and livelihoods and had nothing to return to. Provision was rarely made for dependents, many of whom were left in the countries of origin, and so they also turned to the Service Bureaux for help.

There was an added difficulty for the thousands of displaced people who had become stateless. Although some countries had

9 Ibid p5.

issued passports for many years, they were not in common use until the First World War After the war countless people found themselves without these essential documents – and many thousands of refugees had not just lost their passports but had also lost their right to have one. These stateless persons could find themselves stuck, often in a country of transit. The largest group of people deprived of their nationality was Russian – those fleeing after the Revolution. There were also estimated to be 200,000 Armenians who had fled the genocide in Turkey. So the High Commissioner for Refugees at the League of Nations, Fridtjof Nansen, devised the Nansen Passport in 1921, to be used by stateless refugees and honoured by national governments.

Differences between national laws proved stumbling blocks for many, particularly for those women married to foreigners. Years later, ISSUK would set up a special project to help such women, and this is just one example of how the seeds were sown in those early days for the future work of ISS.

The Minutes of the Migration Committee (as the Standing Committee on Migration was now called) give an insight into the breadth of problems covered in that period. As well as the main problems of divided families, there is the first mention of exploitation of people, which is, of course, a sad feature of migration. It was reported that work would be done with shipping companies, to try to improve conditions for passengers, and ensure that companies kept to their legal requirement to return those people refused entry. In 1921 YWCA took part in a conference organised by the League of Nations Health and Welfare Section on the subject of "The White Slave Trade" – ie the trafficking of women. In fact they had to urge that there should be some women delegates to the conference. A statement called for "legislation for the protection of women – not against individuals but against the causes."[10] So it became clear that, as well as focusing on individual cases, the organisation also needed to make its voice heard by contributing to debates about changes in laws and procedures in order to help all migrants. It was recognised that help and information had to be available before

[10] Minutes of the Migration Committee of the YWCA July 1921.

would-be migrants left their home countries, in order to limit the numbers being turned back on arrival elsewhere for lack of entry permits.

The committee tackled some moral questions that still seem apposite today, although the wording would be different now. In October 1921 the Minutes record that the following questions were posed:[11]

"1. Does it concern a Christian woman that her fellow countrymen migrating should be prepared to be good guests in the country to which they are going?

2. How far is a Christian woman responsible for making guests feel welcome in her own country?

3. How far is a Christian woman responsible for the way in which people of other nationalities or race are spoken of in newspapers or magazine articles, in public speeches and places, in school histories and geographies or in every day conversations?"

In 1922 a report posed the question "how far should human suffering be taken into consideration in new migration laws?[12]

In 1923 the Migration Committee of the World's YWCA recognised the need for a permanent programme. The YWCA had been founded by Protestants and, although its work was always non-discriminatory, it was perceived in some countries as being biased. So it was decided to set up an independent and internationally governed organisation. There was some discussion about putting the new organisation directly under the auspices of the League of Nations, or under the Emigration Section of the International Labour Office. But in the end it was decided that it would have more freedom if it was completely independent.[13]

11 Minutes of the Migration Committee of the YWCA October 1921.

12 Report of Conference of YWCA Migration Bureau March 1922.

13 Minutes of Migration Committee of the YWCA June and October 1923.

Chapter 2

From International Migration Service to International Social Service 1924–46

In May 1924 at a meeting of the World's YWCA in Washington DC, the decision of the Migration Committee was ratified, and on 1st October 1924 the International Migration Service (IMS) was established. Although this remained the official name of the organisation until 1946, the first mention of the name as International Social Service was at a meeting of the Committee in September 1924, and this name soon came into common usage. Most reports of the history of ISS date its start to 1924 (although sometimes the date of 1921 is given, ie: when the first Migration Committee was set up). I shall use ISS rather than IMS from now on. The name in French is Service Sociale Internationale, so the acronym became ISS-SSI. French and English, and in due course Spanish too, became the official languages of the organisation.

The Migration Committee was re-appointed as a Provisional Organising Committee in London, under the Chairmanship of Lady (Dorothy) Gladstone. During the next four years the name changed to The International Migration Service Committee, then the International Committee of the IMS, then the Executive Committee of the IMS and finally, when it was based in Geneva rather than London, it became the International Council of the IMS. The members of the Executive Committee formed the nucleus of the first International Council, but it soon included seven nationalities: British, American, Czechoslovak, French, Greek, Polish and Swiss.

The initial funding of the new organisation was a big issue. The World's YWCA had almost run out of funds, as it had depended largely on American post-war funding, and all European money was channelled into post-war reconstruction. In the event, the success of the development of IMS was almost entirely due to the determined efforts of four young members of staff of the American YWCA. They set out to fund-raise in their spare time, calling themselves "The Committee on the Universe". They began by pooling their own meagre resources, and had enough to survive for one week. An appeal to a philanthropic foundation brought enough funds for three months. Using every possible contact they gradually built up a support base and raised enough to carry on. They approached two types of potential supporters: "people who could see the need for casework across frontiers, and people who were interested in forging links between countries and could appreciate the need for an international network at the level of service to families and children."[14] Progress seemed slow and reports show how they lived on a shoe-string – files were kept in orange-boxes. But it was during those three months that the basic structure of the new organisation was established.

At the first meeting of the Council, which lasted for 3 days in September 1925, members worked out the details of the organisation, which was to have a central Headquarters linking together a network of different national units. The aim was to build more than just a loose federation, by achieving a workable balance between national sovereignty and international co-operation. Ruth Larned wrote: "the concept of constant interdependence meant a combination of individual strength and mutual reliance. It implied some subordination of purely national interests in every Branch in favour of a constant awareness of all the others, a weighing of Branch developments in terms of the whole, a pooling of the experience of each for the benefit of all – in short, the practice of thinking internationally".[15]

The aims of the new organisation were:

"1. to render service through co-operative effort to individuals and families whose problems have arisen as a

[14] International Social Service – a History 1921–55 by R Larned 1960 p14.
[15] Ibid p17.

consequence of migration, and the solution of which involves action in more than one country.

2. to study from an international standpoint the conditions and consequences of migration in their effect on individual, family and social life."[16]

The Constitution was signed by Lady Gladstone on 4th September 1925 as President of IMS. Miss Ruth Larned had already been appointed as the first Director. She had been International Migration Secretary of the World's YWCA (and later became Director of the American Branch of ISS).

The Structure of IMS/ISS

The Council had overall responsibility for the policies of the organisation but day-to-day running was the responsibility of the International Director at Headquarters.

The Headquarters

It was realised that the centre had to be in Europe, where most of the Bureaux were, and so in 1925 the headquarters was set up in Geneva. The role of the HQ was to support and develop the individual national units; establish common principles, policies, procedures and practices in so far as was practicable, and co-ordinate the way in which these were used, so that the whole network would have a recognisable ethos. The Headquarters staff also represented the whole organisation at a international level.

There were the following four distinct types of national units:

Branches

The Bureaux in Europe and the Near East became Branches of the ISS. All Branches were autonomous, non-governmental social welfare organisations. Their Statutes had to conform to ISS principles and aims and international legislation, but otherwise they worked under local laws and practices. Each developed its own character, influenced by the particular experiences and needs

[16] Constitution of International Migration Service 1925.

of the population. At first there were 6 Branches – in Poland, Greece, Czechoslovakia, France, Germany and the USA.

Every Branch formed a national committee, and employed and trained national staff. The new Branches had to find ways of becoming self-supporting, by obtaining funds locally. They had to make an annual payment to the Headquarters.

Affiliated Bureaux

In some countries there were no independent social welfare agencies to become Branches of ISS. Instead, one of the governmental welfare departments would assume responsibility for ISS work in the country. These Bureaux, like the Branches, were members of the ISS, could use the ISS name, were represented on the International Council, had access to all the resources of the Headquarters and Branches, including training, and were required to make contributions to the budget of ISS Headquarters. But they were not autonomous, and could not make independent decisions.

Delegations

From time to time ISS would itself set up and fund a delegation in a country. This was generally in a country that was moving towards the establishment of a Branch, but was not yet in a position to do so. For example, when the States introduced a quota system, many who had hoped to go there went instead to South American countries where foreign workers were welcome, and this led to the setting up of Delegations in Argentina and Uruguay.

In general, references to Branches will also include Affiliated Bureaux and Delegations. Sometimes the term "Units" is used for all three categories together. And the term "network" is used when referring to every agency, including the correspondents.

Correspondents

From the beginning the ISS staff in each Branch made contacts with local welfare services, voluntary agencies and diplomatic missions in the countries to which they referred cases, or from whom they received referrals. Gradually some of these links were formalised into a network structure. An agency in a country without a Branch of ISS that agreed to work on cases referred to them, with a common approach, was regarded as a partner – termed a Correspondent. But Correspondents could not use the ISS name, as the ISS work was only a small part of their remit. Once a link with a Correspondent was established, that agency could be used by all the Branches. And the Correspondents could turn to the ISS when they needed help from abroad in relation to international problems of their own clients.

Sometimes more than one correspondent would be used, if there was no over-arching welfare service. In countries with well-organised social services the task was to select the agency best equipped to handle a particular need – child care, health, family welfare or official assistance. When requests for service led into areas where organised social care was unknown, the only way to communicate was often through leading members of the community. "In the constant effort to apply casework principles to inter-country service, the Branches and Headquarters showed great ingenuity in finding reliable assistance."[17]

Principles

At that first meeting of the Council in 1925 some basic Cardinal Principles were set out, and these have remained essentially unchanged.[18] They state that:

- Service should be given irrespective of the nationality, race, religion or political persuasions of those served.
- The Branch Committees and staff should be predominantly indigenous to their countries.
- Each Branch, in planning its programme to meet the needs of its country, should constantly recognise its obligations to the whole network.

[17] International Social Service – a History 1921–55 by R Larned 1960.
[18] Ibid p16.

- There should be common policies, methods and standards of service, with emphasis on quality.
- To keep the service programme in balance, each Branch should report its tentative plans and its budget for the coming year for consideration and approval by the Council.
- The findings growing out of service should be studied with a view to identifying problems requiring national or international action.
- The support of the ISS should be borne by the Branches, with each contributing according to its means to the support of Headquarters.
- Subsidies from Headquarters must be regarded as only temporary assistance in starting a new Branch or for special aid in an emergency.

Methods and standards of work

How was this cross-border work achieved?

The task was to take a referral from an individual or agency in one country and transmit that referral to the agency in the other country, in a manner that would be understood and would elicit a response, and once a response was received to convey it to the referring agency. The job of a postman you might say! But the reality has always been extremely complex.

"Since the ISS works with social agencies in many countries whose languages, laws and cultural patterns differ, great understanding and imagination are called for in the process of communication. Skilful letter writing at both ends of a case must provide clear statements of all the pertinent facts, must bridge differences in attitudes, and give sufficient interpretation of possible alternatives to make them intelligible in another setting. Time must be allowed for exchange of ideas so that satisfactory solutions may be reached together. Obviously this is no mere forwarding of letters, but rather 'conference by correspondence'."[19]

19 The story of International Social Service – a Digest – Larned 1960 p16.

Early on the staff recognised the need to have common methods of work, and these developed gradually. All referrals that were not directly from one Branch to another, were channelled through the Geneva office – a cumbersome process, but essential in enabling standards to be set and monitored. The staff in Geneva would get to know new Correspondent agencies and spend time making sure that they understood the philosophy and principles underlying ISS's work, as well as the detailed processes involved in sending, receiving and responding to referrals. The staff would ensure that referrals were written in a consistent way, and would also monitor the work going to each country and could prioritise cases if necessary. This protected the Correspondents from referrals coming to them from a number of countries, in different formats, and probably all urging a quick response!

There are three main threads to the work – knowledge and experience of the laws and procedures in each country; sensitivity to cultural issues; and social work skills in dealing with complex personal problems. The 1920s was a period of great development in the professionalisation of social work, moving away from a charitable exercise giving relief to the needy, into a better understanding of the dynamics of human behaviour and the complexity of social problems, and thus to the development of strategies for dealing with them. There was recognition of a new body of specialised knowledge and skills, and social work training courses were set up. This was, of course, happening in several countries and ISS was able to disseminate some of the knowledge and experiences of individual Branches.

Training

In order to develop the necessary standards of service in spite of the great differences in the understanding and practice of social work in different countries, ISS HQ set-up three-month training courses, co-sponsored with the International Committee of the Red Cross, the League of Red Cross Societies and the Carnegie Endowment for International Peace.

The first took place in Paris in 1934. "Associates" from other European countries, such as Hungary, Norway, Sweden and

Romania attended and continued to co-operate with HQ until the war made it impossible for some of them. In addition there were transfers of staff between Branches and HQ. Regular conferences and training courses have been provided by ISS HQ and Branches ever since then – for staff, workers from Correspondent agencies, and a wide range of statutory and voluntary agencies.

Financing the service

Funding was always a concern of all parts of the ISS, as Branches had not only to pay for themselves, but also contribute to the costs of ISS HQ. Some Branches were able to obtain government subsidies, provided that they could remain free to operate as a voluntary social agency, and most obtained grants from voluntary organisations, trusts and individuals. In the early years the main burden of funding the Headquarters and supporting the poorer Branches fell on the American Branch.

The records show that there were many times when Branches struggled to keep afloat financially. And at times it looked as though the service would not be able to continue. There were many pleas from international and national organisations to keep going because the service was much appreciated, and so, with salary cuts and other retrenchments, somehow every crisis was survived. The trouble was that the reasons for the financial squeezes, for example, the depression and then the war, were the very factors that inflated the need for the service.

The issue of paying for services has always been contentious. There was always a basic understanding that the service between Units of the ISS should be provided free – theoretically a reciprocal service, but of course, this never worked out fairly, and Correspondents in some of the poorest countries were expected to provide a free service to some of the wealthiest countries. Furthermore, there were different approaches to the issue of asking agencies or individuals to contribute towards the costs of a service that they had requested. (Much later on, charges were introduced by many Branches.) It was sometimes necessary to send funds overseas, for example to pay the fares for a wife to travel with her children to join her husband who had migrated ahead of them, and if there was no other way, ISS took on the task of transferring the money. But nothing was simple when it came to the transfer of monies from one country to another. Larned described the problem well:

"The ISS has always felt that the cost of any plan for relatives in another country should be assumed, if possible, by the person requesting the service, thus counteracting the dulling effect of distance and separation on the sense of family responsibility. But to make such plans between countries, through at least four different offices, ie two Branches and a local resource at either end of the case, presented unexpected difficulties besides the obvious ones. For instance, the moral obligation to account for the thousands of dollars deposited in one country for use by relatives in another, all down to the last drachma, zloty, or franc, was not a simple task, especially with the rapid fluctuation in exchange rates. An elaborate system of accounting had to be set up which all the Branches could use together. That such problems were met and solved was again proof of the undismayed approach of ISS and its determination to find ways to stretch social case work far beyond national boundaries."[20]

We can see from all these stories how the bedrock of ISS work was set in those early years. Most of the problems that have been faced over the years, and in numerous countries, can be found in the early history of the organisation. As different conflicts, man-made and natural disasters and personal crises have caused people to seek a better life elsewhere, so the structures for helping them have changed. But the fact that the core approach of ISS Branches has changed so little bears witness to the effectiveness of the ways in which those Branches were established and the work was developed.

Branches in the 1920s and 1930s

Here are brief sketches of a few of the activities of different Branches in the 1920s and 1930s. With regard to migrants, countries were predominantly identified as countries of exit, or transit or entry.

[20] International Social Service – a History 1921–55 by R Larned 1960 p32.

The Polish Branch was authorised by the government to arrange interim protection for children travelling to join parents elsewhere. It organised the fostering of malnourished children and helped with their education, so that they were fit and able to understand and master the tests and medical examinations that were administered by the US Immigration authorities; failure of which meant refusal of admission. And ISS staff were able to contribute to submissions to the US authorities to get the entry tests revised in order to be more relevant to those from other countries and cultures.

In another "country of exit", the Director of the Czechoslovakian Branch was asked to represent his government at an International Migration Conference in Rome in 1924. This is the first record of such an advisory role to a government, but it was repeated many times in different countries. The Czech Government was overwhelmed by numbers seeking to move abroad. In 1926 for example, there were 40,000 applications for passports, while the quota for entry to the USA of Czechs was just over 3,000 per year. ISS staff worked in barracks set up for would-be emigrants and, as result of what they learned, urged for international co-ordination of laws on citizenship, migration, divorce, guardianship, and support for dependents in other countries. All these issues have been familiar to ISS staff ever since.

Greece was a country of exit, transit and entry. The transfer of populations with Turkey in 1923 led to more than a million people being relocated, and when the Branch was established in 1928 the political situation was precarious, there was widespread unrest and the Branch perhaps had the most difficult time of all, until it had to close at the beginning of World War II, but the staff persevered because of a belief in the unique role of the casework service they could offer, which was additional to the practical relief being offered by other agencies.

As a "country of transit", France saw thousands of migrants a month passing through Paris and the ports and the French Branch was instrumental in providing services of information – eg translations of official notices into the dozens of languages spoken by immigrants – and in making sure that practical help and facilities were available too. But there was also a huge need to help the many who failed to move on, due usually to lack of appropriate documentation, and the thousands of immigrant labourers brought into the country to work.

In 1928 a Branch was set up in Germany, where social casework was already quite developed, and there was plenty of work in the 1930s as so many fled from Germany, and families were often separated in the confusion.

The American Branch, which had formally opened in 1924, dealt with the issues arising in a "receiving country", both in relation to problems of settlement, and the myriad problems of disunited families. "If ever a link with Europe was needed by distraught people throughout the United States, it was in those days when US immigration policy so suddenly changed, and when so many families were thwarted in their hopes of reunion."[21] The Branch carried out several studies: firstly of the social consequences of migration and the effects of American immigration law and quotas, then in 1926 a study of deportations, and later a socio-legal study. The role of ISS was to present to Senate Committees, Government departments and the legislature such findings as were pertinent to them, and germane to discussions on changes to laws on immigration, divorce, maintenance and so on.

A Swiss Branch, separate from the Headquarters, was formed in 1932. A study was undertaken by University students, under the guidance of the ISS staff, into the causes and results of repatriation – mostly as a result of the depression and unemployment in the country to which the people had migrated. Valuable lessons were learned about the importance of carrying out social enquiries prior to people moving. Many who were struggling in a new country harboured beliefs that life would be easier in the country of origin, only to be badly disillusioned. (Counselling those seeking repatriation would later become one of the projects of ISSUK.)

[21] Ibid p32.

World War II

As well as causing large-scale dislocations of peoples, the war also fundamentally affected the work of ISS Headquarters and Branches. The ISS managed to function during the war across some national boundaries, and the bonds between the constituent members of ISS held firm, despite the part played by each country in the fighting.

In 1940 ISS USA worked with the USA Committee for the Care of European Children, to bring evacuated children over and find foster homes for them. About three thousand British children travelled to the States under this scheme. The Swiss Branch played an important role with the many displaced people who arrived in Switzerland during the war, and was given responsibility for finding placements for several thousand refugee children. The Branches in Greece and Czechoslovakia as well as Germany were forced to close, and staff of other Branches had to work under increasingly difficult conditions. The former Director of the German Branch continued without pay to help clients to escape and managed to keep in touch with ISS Headquarters. Several ISS staff were imprisoned; others were in hiding, like the Director of the Polish Branch during the Warsaw Uprising. Communications were badly affected. Embassies and Consulates were closed in countries at war; aliens had to register and illegal immigrants were vulnerable to deportation, but with nowhere to go.

The story of the French Branch demonstrates the heroic efforts made to keep the service going. (Information in a report by Kay Luce: "The early history of ISSGB" 1992.) When the Germans arrived in Paris they took over the ISS office building, and there was no time to destroy records. But Mme Françoise Vignat evaded the guards and entered her office and transferred incriminating named records of Jewish clients to another category of "light cases" which were filed under numbers not names. Later on she returned and persuaded the occupying force that ISS work was non-political, and so they were allowed to resume some sort of service, sometimes working alongside the German Red Cross. To fund their work the President of the Branch smuggled money into Paris in her knitting wool! Towards the end of the war the

French Branch was operating from Lyons and was arranging for the emigration of Jewish children to Switzerland. Mlle Trillat (who later became Director of the Branch) was caught, imprisoned and tortured and only released when the war ended. After the war the French Branch played a major role in providing help and relief to the nationals of countries whose own agencies were no longer in France, and assisted in the repatriation of French nationals from abroad, including 1,200 French children being cared for in Switzerland, and the reuniting of over 900 Polish children who had been left in Poland when their parents went to France to work.

By the end of the war there were 4 Branches still in operation: France, Italy, Switzerland and the USA. Branches in Germany (1950) and Greece (1953) were re-opened. But the Branch in Czechoslovakia could not re-open and that in Poland had to close. The inter-relations between the Branches was crucial in easing the movements of so many people.

Expansion of branches

After the war there were constant calls to open new Branches of the ISS, and the HQ had to manage the expansion of the service, and not overload it, by considering in each country the following: the relative need in that and other countries for the service; the potential for a strong sponsoring committee to run the service and raise funds; and the willingness of government offices and public and private social agencies to take part. All these ingredients were necessary – for example, in Italy the need for the service had been obvious in the 1930s, but the attitude of the Fascist regime made it impossible, and so the Italian Branch was run from 1930 under the auspices of the Red Cross, and only became independent after the war.

Larned sets out the dilemmas for the Headquarters: "however important the choice of country in establishing a new ISS Branch, there was the further need to consider whether expansion of the service was more or less important than raising the minimal standard of service within ISS itself. In the few years of its existence it still had far to go in finding the way to do effective work with conditioning factors so different in different countries.

There was too, the question of balance between service and study which might point the way to improvement of conditions. Where should the emphasis be put if it was impossible to do all with the limited staff and means at its command?"[22]

During the next ten years the work of ISS expanded; and new Branches formed in Europe – in Austria (1950), the Netherlands (1950), Belgium (1954), and Great Britain (1955). Further afield Branches were opened in 1955 in Australia and then in Brazil, Uruguay and Venezuela. Delegations were established in Argentina, Japan, Korea and Hong Kong.

ISS staff worked closely with UN agencies, and in 1947 ISS was granted consultative status to the Economic and Social Council of the UN (ECOSOC) and was asked to organise a conference of NGOs who might help shape an international migration programme. ISS also worked with agencies such as United Nations Relief and Rehabilitation Association (UNRRA), the International Refugee Organisation (IRO) and the International Council on Social Welfare (ICSW). ISS staff worked in camps for displaced persons in Germany, Austria and Italy, in a programme aimed at providing a firm plan for each unaccompanied child, tracing where possible family members through the ISS network. Another group of referrals proved particularly controversial: problems arose when deciding what to do about those children who were well settled in foster homes in an alien country, and remembered no other family life, and yet whose birth families wanted them back under the Repatriation Schemes. The problems of re-adjustment would inevitably be huge, so who could decide what was best for each child? In most cases it fell to the Courts to make these judgements, and it was, and has remained, a central role of ISS to try to procure the necessary reports for Courts.

"The co-operation which developed between ISS and various UN agencies, demonstrated the way in which ISS has, since its foundation used the collective experience of its network to try to achieve better protection of children and of families involved in inter-country movement."[23]

22 International Social Service – a History 1921–55 by R Larned 1960 p42.

23 Young People in Migration – Keynote Speech by A Moser at International Council 2000.

International conventions and legislation

All this development of ISS went on alongside very significant changes in legislation and regulations affecting many aspects of people's lives.

The United Nations organisation was founded in 1945, replacing the League of Nations. Under its auspices many international Conventions were introduced over the years, covering a wide range of subjects.

The most significant document was perhaps the **Universal Declaration of Human Rights 1948**: "The General Assembly proclaims this Universal Declaration of Human Rights as a common standard of achievement for all peoples and all nations, to the end that every individual and every organ of society, keeping this Declaration constantly in mind, shall strive by teaching and education to promote respect for these rights and freedoms and by progressive measures, national and international, to secure their universal and effective recognition and observance, both among the peoples of Member States themselves and among the peoples of territories under their jurisdiction."[24] This Declaration carried moral rather than legal obligations, but these could be incorporated into national legislation.

The British Nationality Act of 1948 gave automatic right of abode in Britain to citizens of the Commonwealth nations.

The first European Convention was "For the Protection of Human Rights and Fundamental Freedoms" – more commonly referred to as the European Convention on Human Rights 1950, which was ratified by the UK in 1951.

The UN Convention Relating to the Status of Refugees of 1951 was a key instrument in defining who would be regarded as refugees, what their rights were and the obligations of countries to them.

One of the most intractable problems was still that of statelessness. Millions of people were uprooted by conflict, forced to flee or found themselves in another country due to changing borders. Without identity papers of any sort they were

[24] Preamble to the UN Declaration of Human Rights 1948.

in limbo and unable to move. And children born to stateless parents might find themselves with a different status – children born in Britain were automatically given British nationality, but in many European countries children took the nationality of the father and so would also be stateless. So two UN Conventions about statelessness in 1954 and 1961 were introduced. These were designed to reduce the number of stateless persons by persuading states to grant citizenship to more of them.

CHAPTER 3

ISS of Great Britain – the beginnings

At last we have come to the actual setting up of the Branch of ISS in London, as an autonomous body within an international organisation.

Britain had always been involved in ISS, because the International Migration Committee of the World's YWCA was based in London, and the British Chairman became the first President of ISS in Geneva.

The first mention of a possible Branch in Britain that I have found was in the Minutes of the Migration Committee in 1925, and in 1926 there were reports of an attempt to raise money in Britain. In 1926 the Minutes record: "The request for a Bureau in England has come especially from other branches, particularly the USA – there is considerable emigration from Great Britain to the USA – in 1925 17,000 emigrated and a significant number were deported back to Britain. People were convinced of the need for a Branch in Britain but there were simply not enough funds to establish it."[25]

It is not clear when there was first any formal arrangement for dealing with those ISS cases that concerned Great Britain. It may be that, from the early days of IMS, some cases were referred to the Charity Organisation Society (COS), which in February 1946 changed its name to the Family Welfare Association (FWA). The COS was a social work charity which was set up in 1869. Originally founded to bring together a whole lot of small alms-giving charities, and to develop ways of assessing need among the poor by more thorough investigations of family circumstance,

[25] Minutes of International Committee of IMS Sept. 1926.

it was soon in the forefront of promoting social work training and practice. It was also concerned with matters of international concern, including migration. "Early COS case-papers show that family caseworkers have from the beginning of their history needed to consult with agencies or individuals abroad".[26] Certainly, by 1946 the FWA was taking direct referrals from other ISS branches. For example, it was asked by ISS Germany to help with the problems of displaced persons.

In 1938 Miss Kathleen Luce (always known as Kay) was appointed as a social worker with the COS. When the COS became the FWA, she became the Casework Secretary for the FWA. In 1953 the FWA was designated as Correspondent for ISS in Britain.

After the war there was an increase in cases with an international component, including the problems of the deserted wives, girlfriends and children of foreign servicemen who had been stationed in Britain, and the FWA was designated by the Home Office as the centralising agency for dealing with such cases, trying to sort out paternity issues, and obtain financial support from the men. In addition there were many family problems arising from the large-scale emigration to Australia. Then there was the steady growth of immigration to the UK from the West Indies from 1948 onwards. The number of cases being referred directly to the FWA and to and from Geneva increased substantially, until the FWA was overwhelmed.

By 1953 discussions were taking place between Mr Bernard Astbury, the Secretary of the FWA and Mr William Kirk, the International Director of ISS in Geneva, about formalising the position of a British Branch, but still under the auspices of the FWA. Bernard Astbury set up the British ISS and Refugees Committee as a sub-committee of the FWA under the Chairmanship of Mrs (Frieda) Wheeler (later Lady Wheeler). It met for the first time on December 1953. Separate statistics were kept for the ISS cases from this time. Unfortunately no Committee records remain for that early period, but copies of some letters have been retained in the office in Geneva. It appears that things

[26] Referral Technique – Imaginative Co-operation – K Luce 1955.

were progressing slowly. On 2nd February 1955 Kay Luce wrote to Miss Dicy Dodds, the Director of Field Operations in Geneva, saying: "suffice it to say that for the moment we are not unhappy at the way things are going".[27] Dicy Dodds commented on this to Françoise Vignat of the French Branch: "in view of the British tendency to understatement, this seems indeed encouraging!"[28] Dicy Dodds probably did as much as anyone overseas to facilitate the setting up of the British Branch.

A note in a report by K Luce notes that "on 14th April 1955 the FWA Council made a definite decision to hive off the foreign and refugee work to an organisation to be known as the British Branch of ISS, backdating their decision to April 1st 1955".[29] And the first Annual Report of the British Branch of ISS states that the Branch began on 1st April 1955. After all this, there was great satisfaction when the Branch was established. "We shall be thankful to have the Headquarters service, and to use it much more widely than we have done in the past."[30]

New Branches were expected to adhere to the procedures set out by the HQ, and the new British Branch agreed but with two conditions: firstly, cases involving Commonwealth countries would be dealt with directly and not through HQ, and secondly, "cases between the UK and countries without ISS Offices, and which are not part of the British Empire, will be handled either through Headquarters or direct, as seems most appropriate. We should, for instance, continue to write to the Anglo-Egyptian Aid with regard to British residents in Egypt."[31] Apparently, later on there were problems with these conditions as ex-colonies gained independence and the British Branch was vulnerable to changing attitudes that it did not fully understand.[32]

By November 1953, Kay Luce was referring to the "necessity to increase the staff due to the increase of work which has arisen

27 Letter from K Luce to D Dodds 2.2.55.
28 Letter from D Dodds to F Vignat.
29 The Early History of the International Social Service of Great Britain. Article by K Luce 1992.
30 Letter from K Luce to D Dodds 31.7.53.
31 Ibid.
32 Interview with A Moser.

from our becoming the British Branch of ISS".[33] Kay visited the ISS in Geneva and France that year, to learn more about the organisation. In 1954 the Headquarters lent the British Branch the services of a Yugoslavian social worker called Danica (Dani) Adzemovic. She was a refugee from Serbia and spoke 7 languages, and was a great asset. At first the two social workers were given a separate room in the FWA offices in Denison House, Vauxhall Bridge Road, London SW1, while the typists remained in the FWA Casework Department. After ISSGB became independent, it remained within the building occupied by FWA but moved to separate accommodation.

Name changes

The changes in organisation are reflected in the changes in the notepaper used. Until October 1953 all correspondence was written on FWA paper, showing only the FWA logo. However, in November the paper has a three-part heading: on the left is the international logo of ISS and on the right is the logo of the FWA, while in the centre it says: "British Branch, International Social Service (The Administrative work is carried out by the FWA)".

In September 1955 the logo of FWA has disappeared and the central part says: "ISS British Branch, in association with the FWA". There was a suggestion that GB should have its own logo but clearly this was rejected because the Branch kept the logo used by HQ and other Branches. At the end of 1956 the name changed from ISS British Branch to ISS of Great Britain, and the words "in association with FWA" were dropped from the notepaper.

The Constitution

A draft Constitution of the British Branch of the International Social Service (ISSGB) was presented at the meeting of the Executive Committee on Thursday 14th July 1955. It was modelled on the Constitution of the FWA and included the following:

33 Letter from K Luce to D Adzemovic 4.11.53.

- "Clause 4: The Branch is established for charitable objects and purposes only.
- Clause 5: In particular it is established to carry out the aims of the Headquarters of the ISS as set out in its Constitution.
- Clause 12: The Executive Committee shall manage and control the affairs of the Branch
- Clause 16: It shall work in association with FWA until such time as the arrangement shall be terminated by mutual agreement."[34]

However, it took another 18 months to achieve an agreed Constitution. For the next year there was an ongoing debate about whether or not the Constitution was acceptable under British Charity Law. It was important that ISSGB could be granted charitable status, in order to obtain tax relief on all covenanted donations. However, because one of the stated aims of ISSGB was to carry out the aims of the ISS HQ, this was considered to be too generalised to satisfy British Law. Legal opinion was sought, and the advice given was that there were only two options: either ISS HQ would have to change its Constitution or ISSGB "should be re-constituted as an organisation separate and distinct from ISS but with power to co-operate with ISS for the purpose of assisting any activities of ISS which were charitable according to the law of England."[35] The matter was referred to ISS HQ and it was decided that the ISS Statutes could not be altered to meet the requirements of the British Inland Revenue.

This must have all been most frustrating for those concerned, but a new Draft Constitution was prepared in July 1956. After months of negotiation, the International Social Service of Great Britain was recognised by the Inland Revenue Authorities as a charitable organisation, provided that no funds for the British Branch were used for any purpose that was not charitable by English Law. Finally, this new Constitution was signed at the ISS Committee on 3rd January 1957.

In a letter to all ISS Branches, Dicy Dodds wrote: "We are glad that our British Branch has been able to arrange its legal

[34] Draft Constitution of ISS of Great Britain 1955.

[35] Legal Opinion of D McMullen, Lincolns Inn, 18.1.56.

status in such a way that it has proper official status as a national agency in Great Britain, while it shall of course at the same time continue to be recognised as an official Branch of ISS".[36]

The structure of ISSGB – Governance

From the start the organisation was the responsibility of a Committee of Trustees (it became known as the Executive Committee in 1958 and the Council in 1963). The role of trustees of charities has always been understood to be as follows: "the Trustees as a Board should collectively be responsible and accountable for ensuring and monitoring that the organisation is performing well, is solvent and complies with all its obligations."[37] This meant that they were responsible for setting policies, and ensuring that the structure, staffing and funding were suitable and adequate to enable them to be carried out. The Committee of Trustees was an Unincorporated Body which meant that the governing body had full legal and financial responsibility for the organisation's affairs, including any debts. (It was not until 2000 that it became an Incorporated Body.)

The Honorary Officers of the Committee were the Chairman, Frieda Wheeler, Vice-Chairman, Mrs (Olive) Hargreaves, and Treasurer, Michael Sadd.

There were ten other members of the Committee, who represented various interest groups: the diplomatic community, refugee organisations, other social work agencies, and those who might have access to potential funders. Several of them had been members of Council or Committees of the FWA. In due course Sub-Committees were established, to enable different aspects of the work to be considered in more detail than was possible in the main Committee.

The first President was Angela, Countess of Limerick. She, and all successive Presidents have always taken an active interest in the charity. Within a year there were also 6 Honorary Vice-Presidents – a title given to distinguished supporters, which most

36 Letter from D Dodds 27.12.56.

37 Good Governance – a Code for the Voluntary Sector 2005.

of them retained until their deaths. In following years, some of the Chairmen and Trustees were appointed as Honorary Vice-Presidents when they completed their term of office.

> **Angela, Countess of Limerick** 1897–1981. She served as President from 1955 until 1966 and then as a Trustee until 1981. "Her continuing interest and support had much to do with its success. She remained a most active member of Council until her death and was always available to give wise advice in times of difficulty.[38] The Times said in her obituary: "Angela Limerick had a great breadth of vision, an astonishing memory and grasp of detail, and a remarkable ability to establish close and lasting personal relationships after brief acquaintance; above all she had the gift of inspiring and encouraging others and bringing out the best in them."[39]
>
> For more than 60 years she worked for the Red Cross, starting as a Red Cross volunteer nurse in 1915 in the Voluntary Aid Detachment (VAD), falsifying her age because she was too young to serve abroad. She nursed the wounded in both French and British hospitals. In London in 1940, during the blitz, she was in charge of the local Red Cross branch and later she was Vice-Chairman of the League of Red Cross Societies for 15 years and Vice-President of the British Red Cross Society, and Chairman of the Standing Committee of Red Cross and Red Crescent for 8 years. Unusually, both she and her husband were made Companions of Honour.

Staff of the new ISSGB

Kay Luce had transferred from the FWA to become the Secretary of the Branch, although she did not have to move far, because ISSGB had offices in the FWA building. By 1960 she was called the Director rather than Secretary. Dani Adzemovic stayed on for a year as the one other social worker, and Miss Frances (Patty) Riddell Blount joined the team as a volunteer after a few months. To help them there were 2 typists. Mrs Gullick and Mrs Paschen, – 1 full-time and 1 half-time – and a half-time filing clerk, Miss Violetta Metaxa. All these clerical staff were shared with FWA.

[38] Annual Report – AR 1981.

[39] The Times April1981.

From the beginning, ISSGB depended greatly on the help of a series of volunteers to take on tasks such as establishing appropriate systems for filing and book-keeping, and with the fundraising. Two Polish volunteers helped with the refugee work.

Financing the new organisation

The FWA gave £850 to the fledgling ISSGB and also guaranteed to cover any deficit for the first year, but after that the new Branch was expected to be self-funding. As ISSGB were sharing some administrative resources with the FWA, overheads were kept to a minimum. The Buttle Trust made a grant of £1,000, to be shared over three years. From the beginning it was recognised that there would have to be a mix of funds, from individual donations, grants from Trusts and official bodies, and fundraising events

During this initial period, two of Kay Luce's main concerns were the recruitment of staff to cope with the work and finding the necessary funds. On the whole, the establishment of ISSGB seems to have gone remarkably smoothly.

Chapter 4

ISSGB – later ISSUK: The context; the work; opportunities, constraints and challenges

At this point it might be helpful to leave the history for a moment, and to give an overview of the context within which ISSGB operated. In this chapter I have described in broad terms the range of the work, and identified the most significant factors that have always affected the capacity and ability of ISS units to carry out their work. The structure of the organisation, and the international and national frameworks within which it operates, provide opportunities, impose constraints and offer challenges. Both the social work and the fundraising raise many issues, each of which poses some tricky dilemmas. These are mainly put in the present tense because they are still ongoing in relation to the inter-country work of ISS worldwide, and that of CFAB, and indeed of other agencies. Some of these issues had already been evident before ISSGB was formed and others will be discussed in following chapters.

The context has five main components: world events, being part of an international network, the legal framework, the professional framework and economic context. These are interwoven. For example, legislation is often introduced in response to one or more of the other factors. All too often the economic situation has delayed development of the work.

However, there is a further, vital component of the story, and that is the people. Throughout the period of ISS in Britain, perhaps the greatest resource has been the individuals – staff, trustees and volunteers, who have used their experience, time and skill to maximise the achievements of the charity. ISSUK has indeed been fortunate in the variety of people with wide international and national experience in relevant areas, who have played a part in the organisation. Often the only constraints on what they could achieve have been lack of time or money.

In the wider ISS network, all over the world people have worked, often against great odds, to help individuals to overcome their problems. The successes of the organisation demonstrate the commitment of all involved to overcome obstacles and provide the best possible service. But, in a rapidly changing world, new problems emerge all the time, and it would be unrealistic to imagine that the work could ever become straightforward.

World events

The events that affect the work of ISS may be sudden and short-lived, or much longer lasting. They may concern a small part of the world, or be widespread, such as economic recessions. While it is the role of governments and large international agencies to respond to the logistical problems caused by mass migrations as a result of conflict or disasters, there is a complementary role for the ISS in focusing on individuals and their problems. ISS staff respond to problems arising directly from migration, and also to problems that arise later as a result of family separations or breakdowns.

Being part of an international network

The initial organisational structures of ISS internationally and ISSUK are described in previous chapters, and alterations to these governance and staffing models are dealt with in later chapters, in the decade in which they took place.

The British Branch of the ISS benefits from being part of a larger organisation. The wide knowledge base of the combined ISS offices means that information and ideas can be disseminated around the network. It has more status and influence with other organisations than it would have as a solitary agency. The staff have to adhere to the methodology agreed by the whole organisation, but they have also played a part in setting the standards and developing the work. There are inevitable tensions in any international body whose members are independent agencies, and so the relationships established between staff in different countries as they work on cases together, and meet periodically to share experiences, and thrash out differences, are invaluable in strengthening the whole organisation.

The great strength of the organisation has always been its inter-country network, which offers an unrivalled opportunity to reach people wherever they are. Much depends on the legal system and the structure of child welfare and other social services of each country. When these work well an excellent service can be offered, but in many countries there are not adequate welfare services, and the agencies may have difficulties in taking on cases from abroad when they cannot meet the needs of clients within their own country. The inability to provide an acceptable service from some countries is one of the biggest constraints on all ISS offices. That is why the building up of the network is so important, and the investment of time by ISS staff in finding, training and supporting Correspondents has always been so important. When good relations can be established with local agencies, the staff of those agencies reap significant benefits from their involvement in inter-country cases, and are encouraged to establish a more reliable service. They are also helped to understand the problems that beset their nationals when moving overseas, in relation to immigration requirements, and so on. But severe shortages of resources of staff and money in Geneva have sometimes held back the development of the network. The question of how best to strengthen the network has always been one of the biggest challenges to the organisation.

In addition to the relationships within the ISS network, there are opportunities for links with many other international and national bodies. In Geneva the General Secretariat office is situated close to a number of UN organisations, and British staff and trustees have been included in the groups drafting some UN documents.

In Britain the main links have always been with Central Government Departments, the Local Authorities, Court welfare services and other voluntary social work agencies. The ISS can offer an international perspective to discussions.

However, creating and sustaining all these links is time-consuming, and at times of pressure on resources it is notable that some links have weakened, with the effect of reducing the profile and reputation of ISS, both internationally and in Britain, and it is then difficult to re-establish these links.

The legal framework

The legal framework may sometimes restrict agencies in what they can do, but at other times it will allow them to expand their activities. It is a challenge to keep up with changes in the large number of laws and regulations. In some instances it may only be one or two sections of a law that are relevant to the work of ISS, but these still have to be applied.

ISS works within an international and national framework of Laws and Conventions *(see Appendix for a list of the most important ones*). Most of these are mandatory, placing duties and obligations on agencies. Within the boundaries set by all the statutes, organisations can find imaginative ways of fulfilling their purposes. ISS has been involved in consultations about a variety of changes to legislation such as adoption, abduction and protection of children.

The international Conventions are produced by the UN, the Council of Europe or the Hague Conference. Each Convention is a multilateral treaty that sets forth minimum standards for international co-operation and protection, but is only binding if a country has both signed it and then ratified it. The Conventions may be amended by Protocols. The Hague Conference on Private International Law was formed in 1893 to work for the progressive unification of the rules of private international law, that is, to address the conflicts which arise when different jurisdictions are applied to a case. The fundamental purpose of Hague Children's Conventions is "to provide the practical machinery to enable States which share a common interest in protecting children to co-operate together to do so".[40] All these international legal instruments have to be formally incorporated into English law before the courts are obliged to apply them. Courts must take the Convention into account in interpreting Acts of Parliament and common law, but must ultimately follow the terms of the Act even if inconsistent with the Convention. "These standards must be optimised with the help of professional socio-legal services that, like ISS, are active in the relevant domains… In the sensitive field of children's and families' rights, what is especially needed is a personalised social follow-up process."[41] One part of the role of the ISS is therefore to understand all the issues and interpret them as required to the other parties. Another task has been to encourage the British government to ratify relevant new international conventions.

In the UK there are laws pertaining only to England and Wales and others for Scotland and Northern Ireland, but these are broadly similar on welfare matters. (In this book I list only the laws of England and Wales.) Throughout the history of ISSUK new laws have given greater protection to children and other vulnerable groups, including immigrants and refugees. Alongside each Law is a collection of Rules and Regulations, setting out details of how the law should operate. In some areas, such as adoption, there are many of these, with which the courts and agencies must comply.

Furthermore, ISSUK has always been subject to Charity Law which, until the Charities Act of 1960, was based on the Statute of Charitable Uses of 1601 which defined the categories of charitable purpose. These were: "for the relief of poverty, advancement of education or religion or other purposes considered beneficial to the community".[42] The Charities law of 1960, and subsequent laws of 1992, 1993 and 2006 expanded the number of categories and laid down requirements for charity governance, accounting, reporting and fundraising. Being a charity is particularly important for fundraising because of the

40 Hague Convention website.

41 The Activities of ISS and their Legal Bases 2007.

42 Statute of Charitable Uses of 1601.

tax relief on donations and because of the perception of charities generally as worthwhile organisations.

Since 2000 ISSUK has also been subject to Company Law, which dictates what information has to be collected and reported each year.

In the international context of ISS there are also the laws of other countries to take into account. The staff of the General Secretariat have always kept basic data on all the correspondent agencies and up-date it regularly, and make it available to all Branches, but it has still been necessary sometimes to consult the correspondents directly for more detailed information. Each correspondent agency is in the best position to provide detailed information about the laws and processes in its own country. Even in recent years, when the internet has provided easy access to quantities of information, it can still be important for the correspondents to interpret or clarify this information – for example in relation to the governmental responsibility for a disabled child. Whenever there are differences between the laws and regulations of two countries, it is generally held that the legislation of the country in which a child or family resides takes precedence.

Professional framework

Although the social work profession is at the heart of ISS, and is the focus of this section, many other professionalisms are required. In the office setting, the contribution of administrative staff is crucial. Fundraising and financial management expertise is centrally important. Regular legal advice has been essential. ISSUK has also benefitted from outside help with accounts, insurance and personnel matters.

The Social Work Service: the ISSUK social workers operate within the context of the principles, policies and procedures of the General Secretariat, and those of the British Branch itself, and seek to follow the tenets of accepted good practice in relevant fields of social work. This framework is broad enough to offer opportunities for imaginative solutions to be sought for problems. The work can be divided into three sections; general enquiries, case referrals and special projects.

1. General enquiries

ISSUK has been the first port of call for countless individuals and social work professionals, both in the UK and overseas, who have sought information and help. The role of the staff taking the initial calls is important, as they set the tone of the response. The number of enquiries and the range of topics concerning almost every country in the world is staggering. Many enquiries are straightforward and can be answered right away, but sometimes further investigation will be needed to find the necessary information. When the enquiry is not appropriate for ISS the caller will be referred elsewhere. And when the request is for a service in another country then it is deemed "a referral", and the enquirer is advised how to proceed. The development of the way in which enquiries have been dealt with is one of the most important achievements of ISSUK.

2. Case referrals

Kay Luce wrote: "Referrals come to ISSGB from a great variety of sources, – from other branches and agencies abroad, from central government departments, Embassies, statutory and voluntary social services, refugee and other welfare organisations in this country."[43]

Many requests for help come from individuals, who cannot by themselves find a solution to problems of a divided family. Peter Fry wrote: "ISS sets out to build bridges between countries; to make possible a dynamic communication between people so that they themselves can resolve their problems. While the team, consisting of local social workers and ISS units, make the bridge, we must never forget that this is only effective when we have enabled the people with whom we are concerned to find together a solution to their difficulties."[44]

However, the greater proportion of the referrals have at least one extra link in the chain – these are the cases referred by other agencies: usually social work agencies, the courts or diplomatic missions.

43 K Luce – article in Journal of Medical SW Vol. 15 No 3 June 1962.

44 AR69.

The ISS social workers are just a part, albeit a vital one, in a much longer process of helping individuals and families. They contribute to the decision-making process by providing crucial information from individuals or authorities in one country to those in another. Many of the cases involve the tracing of families or individuals, but this is very rarely just a paper exercise. The ISS social workers' task is also to help everyone involved in these situations to understand the legal, administrative, social and cultural implications of what is happening.

There are many issues arising from this work, and the main ones are: time-scales in obtaining reports, the quality of those reports, cultural considerations, confidentiality and how information is used. All these are relevant, even if sometimes one issue predominates.

The General Secretariat established a system of categorising cases, for the purposes of collecting statistics in a similar manner from all Branches and Affiliated Bureaux. The coding changed slightly over the years, and the following is the coding that was established in 2002. Each case is given one or more of a total of 47 problem codes, and these codes have been consolidated into one of the following categories. This list gives an overview of the range of problems dealt with. Aspects of these will be considered in more detail in later chapters, with reference to the casework and to special projects.

A. Adult Welfare: Referrals concerning adult placements, adult abuse; adult guardianship; and prisoners.

B. Child Welfare and Child Protection: Requests from concerned relatives or agencies for checks on the whereabouts, safety and welfare of children who have been moved across international borders. This includes children who have been abducted by a parent or other adult. They may also include those known to be, or believed to be victims of abuse and neglect;

   Issues of care, custody, guardianship, parental responsibility and maintenance obligations, following a divorce or separation or abduction of children;

   Placement of children in institutions or with families: kinship placement; assessment of overseas relatives as possible carers for children who cannot live with their parents; foster family placement, including Private Fostering;

Questions of contact between children, parents and other relatives.

C. Family Welfare: counselling in cases of marriage or partnership between nationals of more than one country; counselling about legal procedures and cultural implications. Issues of nationality of children; help with problems arising from separation and divorce; family mediation.

D. Adoption: Requests for Home Study Reports on potential adopters; assessment reports on adoptability of children; and applications for documentation that is required for adoption proceedings, such as birth certificates, health information, parental consent, references.

E. Tracing and Reunion – of known and unknown family members: Family reunification, re-establishment of contact, searching for roots by adopted persons, and those separated from birth families for other reasons.

F. Migration: settlement of migrants who have left their country of origin, and repatriation of those wishing to return to their country of origin or to a third country; work with refugees and asylum seekers including unaccompanied minors; issues of nationality and citizenship.

G. Health: Requests to obtain information about medical histories or medical resources; assessment of sick persons with view to possible placement; assessment of carers.

H. Legal: requests for legal information and assistance, and applications for documentation.

Issues of changes of name, nationality, legal rights.

I. Financial: All requests relating to maintenance payments, and financial obligations and rights.

J Other: Education and any other matters not included in other categories.

ISS social workers have a role to play at each stage of the process of obtaining information or assessment reports from overseas.

Taking referrals

Firstly, they work with those referring a case, explaining the complexity of working with the country concerned, and giving a realistic expectation of what can be achieved (and, if necessary, saying when no service is possible). They advise the referring agency about the form that a referral should take, following ISS guidelines, so that the referral will be couched in terms that are familiar to a correspondent agency. But sometimes referrals also have to adhere to the required guidelines of the referring agency, for example for a court report. The ISS worker may have to negotiate between two types of referral so that the required information is given to, and elicited from, the agency in the receiving country. The ISS workers in both countries will liaise to exchange information about the particular referral, and any specific issues that should be addressed.

Passing on the referrals

The referring social worker may only be concerned with one case in one system, but the correspondent agency has to cope with a variety of cases coming to it from many parts of the world. That is why initially the system was set up in which referrals to many Correspondent countries had to go through the General Secretariat, and this remained in place throughout most of the period covered by this history. Of course this had both a positive and negative effect. On the positive side: the case referrals often required translation – both into the language of the receiving country, and also into a format that would be familiar to the Correspondent. The worker in the GS who was sending all the referrals to a specific country would have some knowledge of the correspondent agency and the current conditions in that country, and so could judge when to stress the urgency of a case, or push for the fullest possible report. That worker was also in a position to advise the referring agency about the likelihood of obtaining the required information, given any geographical implications and the competency and capacity of the correspondent agency. On the other hand, sending referrals through the GS was a major cause of delays, and as information channels changed over the years, this practice was largely dropped.

Secondly, the ISS Branch or Correspondent in the country receiving the referral will usually have to refer the case on to a welfare agency in the area of the country where the family concerned is located. This means that there is one further link in the chain. Obtaining a service in some countries can take several months, and there are often logistical problems to be overcome. Many people to be interviewed live in remote areas; local welfare services are invariably overstretched and ISS work may not be a priority. Nevertheless, the ISS network offers the best chance of reaching such distant places.

As far as social work standards and skills are concerned, there are huge variations across the network. Part of the training role of the ISS staff with members of the network has always been to make sure that they understand the nature of the various types of referral, in order to explain them to the people being contacted, and that they know something about the laws and social conditions in each country from which they receive a referral. This co-ordinating role is all the more important in countries with weak welfare services.

Approaching the clients

In large countries with many different cultural groups, the Correspondent can try to ensure that each case is handled by someone with experience of the particular culture concerned. This person will know the best ways of locating and approaching people, who may be worried or even frightened by such a contact. When a referral relates to a family member who has left the country under difficult circumstances, it is possible that the very fact of the referral might bring unwelcome attention from the authorities, or cause embarrassment for the family within the community, and so a very careful approach should be made to the family. It has always been difficult to ensure appropriate confidentiality – indeed it cannot be guaranteed. For example, interpreters may have to come from within the same close-knit community. Tracking down people can be complicated by the fact that in many correspondent countries there are not always clear addresses, even in towns. Furthermore, in some cultural groups people do not have family names, or are identified only if the name of the father and father's father are known.

Most cases requiring a full report on a family, for example, with a view to placing a child or planning the return of a sick family member, need some degree of exploration of family issues, which can be sensitive and painful, particularly if the social worker brings bad news about family members overseas. Cultural sensitivities do not always exist easily with the need for exploration of family matters: for example, it might be good practice to interview each person alone, yet in some cultural groups talking to a woman without a male present would be regarded as inappropriate. Sometimes any investigation can be seen as intrusive, and those being interviewed may, for example, not understand how strangers have any right to question their suitability to care for a relative, or to ask questions about their financial status. They might not understand that the visit is an exploratory one, and assume that the fact of the visit means that the relative will be coming. The interviewer has to explain the reason for the visit in unambiguous terms, and make sure that the persons concerned know what the next stages in the process will be. The ISS Correspondent is then responsible for trying to collate all the information that has been obtained in the way that is required by ISS.

THE REPORTS

Thirdly, when the fullest possible report has been obtained, the ISS social worker may need to add explanatory notes to ensure that the child's agency or other decision-making body has enough information about the relevant part of the country, and the culture, to be able to put an assessment report into context. This may include information about laws, migration regulations, and educational, medical and social resources. Once a decision has been made in the referring country, the information is passed back through the ISS channels, so that the people who have been visited in the other country are properly notified of the decision and the reasons for it. If, for example, the decision is that a child will be placed with family members, there will be further work to do concerning arrangements for the actual placement, provision of any resources that are needed, and arrangements for supervision and support of the placement as required. If, for whatever reason, the decision is made not to pursue a placement of a child or the return home of an unaccompanied minor or other relative, it may still be possible to establish or re-establish contact between family members.

It is a crucial part of the role of ISS workers and correspondents in each country to try to sort out any problems that arise. Such problems usually concern delays in obtaining information, or dissatisfaction with the amount or quality of information received. There may be requests for additional information, though this inevitably causes more delays. It may be that the ISS workers have to report failure in finding a family, and yet they can provide important evidence of the searches that have taken place.

It can readily be seen that the potential problems in such complex work are numerous.

In working with other professionals, ISS staff have to show what can be achieved, but also be honest about the limitations of the service. When reports are not as comprehensive as required, or do not come as quickly as expected, then a possible placement may be jeopardised. Not surprisingly, the referring social workers can become frustrated, even when they have been warned about problems in obtaining a service from that country. Often they are under pressure from others to produce a report quickly. It is an unfortunate fact that complaints about any service spread faster than good news of that service. Then the reputation of ISS is put at risk. On the other hand ISSUK social workers may have to take issue with referring agencies when they know that the other agency is acting in ignorance of relevant law, or is behaving in a culturally insensitive way. This issue arises mainly in relation to the practice of sending UK social workers overseas (see also Chapter 8).

Sometimes, Local Authorities or Courts have decided to send social workers overseas to do an investigation themselves. This may seem to be beneficial for that authority, in that they can quickly see the situation for themselves and obtain information for a court report, but these potential benefits have to be weighed against the likely risks of causing severe distress, humiliation or even harm to the people in the other country, through insufficient understanding of their culture and situation. The factors set out above show how any visit to a family overseas has to be set into a much wider framework, with the ISS Correspondent taking responsibility for ensuring that families are given any necessary support. Furthermore, in some countries it is illegal for a social worker who is not registered there to undertake any social work assessment.

All this is conversely true, in relation to the significant number of requests to ISSUK from ISS units overseas for information or reports about families in the UK who are being considered as carers for relatives in another country. The same thoroughness and cultural sensitivity is required by all parties. The staff of ISSUK can often answer these queries themselves, but where an assessment report is required, the referral used to be passed to a voluntary or statutory social work agency, and later to the Children and Families Court Advisory Service (CAFCASS), with the expectation that the work would be done without payment. For workers in those agencies, such referrals from overseas could be of great interest, but once it became usual to charge for services, UK agencies became reluctant to take on this work. ISSUK lacked the staff to do the work itself, and this became a problem, because ISSUK found itself increasingly having to refuse a service to colleagues overseas. Failure to provide reports reflects badly on ISSUK, even when it is powerless to require other agencies to take on such work. It is also interesting to note that there are restrictions in the UK on foreign social workers coming to do assessments in this country without being registered. The management of referrals from overseas poses real dilemmas about how to achieve the best possible outcomes with the minimum of compromise.

3. Special Projects

Over the years ISSUK set up a number of interesting projects, often on behalf of the Government. These are explained in later chapters. Each project was possible because of the special knowledge and links of the organisation. Some of these projects were so successful that they grew beyond the scope of the ISS and moved to separate agencies, notably the British Adoption Project which was the forerunner of the Adoption Resource Exchange.

The economic context

It can be seen throughout this history how the wider economic climate has affected the work of ISS. This has been in two main ways; firstly, that economic deprivation leads people to move to other places to find a better life, and secondly, that the amount of funds available to an organisation limits or enhances the work it is able to do.

Finance and fundraising

The most difficult aspect of running a charitable organisation like ISS is the unpredictability of both the flow of work and the flow of funds. These two are inextricably linked, as each one affects the other. It is always difficult to plan ahead without assurance of sufficient funds to carry out the work, and indeed this has always been a challenge for the organisation.

Throughout the history of ISSGB there have always been two streams of income. Special Funds (Restricted Income), for the various social work projects, usually come from grants from Government or Trust Funds, and this money can only be used for the specified projects. The amount in these funds varies year by year according to the progress of the projects. But money is also needed to run the office, pay the staff who are doing non-project work, provide training and so on. This comes from the Unrestricted or General Funds which are funded through a combination of fees, grants and donations, and money raised from special events. The bulk of these funds traditionally came from two sources – Government Grants and the proceeds of the increasingly important Spring Fair. For many years up to two thirds of the income came from these two sources, and in some years more than half the income was from the Spring Fair alone.

In later years other fundraising events also contributed significantly to the General Funds.

The uniqueness of the work of the ISS presented both opportunities and problems when it came to fundraising, both nationally and internationally. Ruth Larned wrote:

> "The special handicaps in financing this independent international agency are many. Among the more obvious are local-mindedness of potential individual contributors or a nationalistic attitude of governments. Countries differ widely in their ideas of what is worth supporting, thereby threatening the balance in an interdependent service. Moreover, in acting as a link between local agencies in two or more countries, the ISS is inevitably insulated from direct contact with the local public which it serves and should look to for support."[45]

This is certainly true in Britain, where the service users, such as local authorities, pay the costs of the particular cases they refer to ISSUK, and in later years have paid an annual subscription in order to use the service. The question of charging fees comes up regularly through the story, both in relation to fees from local authorities and also from individuals. The individuals who ask for help may pay for the costs of their own case, but are not usually in a position to give more to the organisation. Fees have always constituted a minor part of the income, and repeated efforts have been made to increase this proportion. However, neither individual clients nor institutional service users can be regarded as constituting a supporter base.

By contrast, single issue charities, particularly medical ones, have a core of supporters who have been touched in some way by the condition that is the focus of the charity, and who are committed to fund-raising for that charity.

So, from the start, ISSUK looked to the international diplomatic community to be its supporter base, and it benefitted consistently from the great interest shown by many British and overseas members of that community. A high proportion of Trustees, and most of those involved in fund-raising events had

[45] International Social Service – a History 1921–55 by R Larned 1960 p65.

some connection with the Diplomatic Community, either directly or through friends. The organisation simply would not have survived without the loyalty and commitment of all the supporters and volunteers who have given both time and money, and thus demonstrated their faith in the organisation. They represent one of its greatest assets. If one could count the hours given by the volunteers between 1955 and 2010 it would run into hundreds of thousands.

In addition, individual Trustees have created invaluable links for fundraising in the business community, at the same time spreading knowledge about ISS more widely.

Looking at the history, one can identify periods of satisfactory growth, times of real financial anxiety and occasional times when the finances were in a particularly positive state. The time-scales of planning and of obtaining funds do not always coincide. In addition to the internal state of the finances, the charity has always been subject to the vagaries of the wider economic situation, for example increased inflation. Carefully made long-term plans can be thrown off course by factors that require pragmatic changes to the plans. For example, a cut in a grant can mean the end of a project. Fund-raising is immensely time-consuming, but an essential activity. For every grant received, there are many more applications that are not successful, especially in those times of economic hardship when too many charities are chasing reduced sources of funding. So, when a large grant is made the relief is enormous. The attitude to the financial state of the charity seems to have been generally optimistic – sometimes perhaps too over-optimistic, but then, when the reality hit, there would be a lurch into calls for caution and stringency. When the funds were at their lowest, and the charity faced closure, it was rescued on two occasions by the Trustees who gave or loaned money to cover the deficit.

If there was no alternative, it was sometimes the case that the only way to reduce the expenditure sufficiently was to reduce the number of staff. This was invariably a very painful process, and on occasions the whole staff group, both those made redundant and those left behind, were bruised by the experience. It is not uncommon for small to medium charities to suffer such internal upheavals from time to time, particularly as they grow bigger, but the management of such episodes is crucial. When the focus is too exclusively on the immediate and urgent need to raise money, it is not always easy to give sufficient consideration to the manner in which work is cut back, and any changes in staffing are handled. Yet if the wish to maintain the same level of work is over-riding, which would require the same level of staffing, then a financial crisis can be allowed to go on for too long. Good management finds a way between these two extremes, so that drastic action is very much a last resort when completely unforeseen situations arise. With the benefit of hindsight we can see that there were times when this was not always achieved with ISS, either in Geneva or London.

It takes money to raise money, and for many years there were insufficient funds to put into fund-raising efforts. So fundraising was heavily dependent on volunteers, especially in relation to the Spring Fair. When Fundraisers were appointed they had variable success, particularly in the early stages, because ISS was not well-known, and the numerous applications to trusts and grant-making bodies often produced only a small return.

The records show the wide range of fund-raising ideas that were tried out over the years. The most effective ones depend on making and maintaining connections with potential donors and users. In the following chapters the main ideas for each decade are described.

Publicity

A key element of fund-raising is obtaining good publicity.

The purpose of publicity is to raise awareness of the charity and its aims. There are two aspects to this: firstly, the need to obtain sufficient funding to run the organisation and develop the work, and secondly, to advertise what it does to potential users of the service.

The provision of publicity material, both to potential donors and users of the service, seems to have been somewhat limited during some of the early years, although some excellent documents were produced. But this reflects the pressures of work and lack of resources to take on what might have been seen as secondary activities, and yet were crucial to the promotion of the organisation.

Effectiveness

The effectiveness of the whole ISS body is open to scrutiny from many directions. At any given time there are some parts of the organisation in a more healthy state than others, and it is always easy to focus on the problems, and fail to recognise success. The fact that ISS has developed and survived as an international organisation providing a unique grouping of services, is itself some proof of the effectiveness of the organisation. Holding together such a huge and disparate network is an immense task.

The casework of ISS social workers always was, and still is, necessarily short-term. Whilst it is relatively easy to assess the effectiveness of an information-providing service, it is infinitely more difficult to assess the outcomes of the more complex referrals. There are many different criteria to consider. In relation to the time taken on referrals, simple comparison can be made between countries. But these take no account of the relative difficulties of obtaining reports, or the qualities of those reports, so a more useful comparison might be to look at changes in any one country over time, to monitor improvements or otherwise. In cases where the intervention of ISS led to significant changes in an individual's life, the effects of the work can only be judged over a longer period, and that information is rarely available. A further point relates to the interpretation of results. A response may contain unwelcome information and yet that does not automatically categorise it as a negative one. For example, a person who is trying to trace a missing relative may be consoled by the knowledge that everything possible has been done to find them, even though the search failed. It may help a child to know that investigations were made to see whether they should live with a relative overseas, and that it wasn't found to be the right plan for them, so that they don't grow up wondering why no one bothered to consider that option.

It is from a few of the projects that some of the most interesting feed-back has been obtained, because there can be a longer-term view, and regular evaluation of the work, which enables staff to adapt the work as necessary. But in only one case, that of the adoption of children from Hong Kong, has there been any formal research into the outcome of a project.

The effectiveness of fundraising is seen more directly, but numbers do not necessarily give the whole picture. In periods of economic difficulty, a seemingly low figure for fundraising could in fact be regarded as remarkably successful, given the problems that had to be overcome.

Training

Another theme that occurs throughout the history of the organisation is training: the need for all staff, whether social workers or administrators or fundraisers, to receive appropriate training to keep them up to date with current practice, and the need for them to offer training to others. Well-trained staff are a sign of an effective organisation, but when there are pressures on time and money, training can be one of the first casualties. Yet it seems that there were always efforts made to ensure that staff were given opportunities for some training in appropriate areas of the work. In the early years there is some evidence that ISSGB staff were able to offer training to others – notably to Local Authority workers, or to members of the ISS network. In later years, there was an increasing programme of training events offered by ISSUK to other agencies. The staff were also able to offer training placements to students for much of the period of this history. ISSUK staff were also involved in many international ISS training events. Training, in all its forms, offers great opportunities for those involved, but it also brings challenges of how to manage it with scarce resources.

These themes will be revisited in the following chapters, and it will be seen how, at any given time, some of these factors were more significant than others.

CHAPTER 5

The first five years 1955–59

World events

After the war the movement of people in and out of the UK involved a large number of countries. Many refugees from Europe who had settled in Britain needed continuing help. The Polish Resettlement Act 1947 allowed 200,000 Polish citizens to stay after the war. New waves of migrants arrived in Britain, notably Sikhs from the Punjab, after the partition of India and Pakistan had created huge pressures on land resources, and people from the Caribbean who were offered cheap passages on the ships which had taken returning troops from Britain to the islands. Then there were refugees from Hungary after the Russian invasion there, and others fleeing Egypt after the Suez crisis. By the late 1950s the numbers arriving at airports overtook those arriving at seaports.

Britain was a country of emigration as well as migration. From 1946 onwards and through the 50s there was an extensive assisted migration programme of UK citizens to Australia. Thousands of people left for other commonwealth countries. Extended family groups were split and traditional supports were weakened. Ever since then ISS in Britain has had an interchange of case referrals with Australia and other countries with a substantial population of British origin.

Within Britain there were a lot of problems caused by the breakdown of some marriages between British women and foreign servicemen, especially when there were children involved.

Legislation

There had been many important changes in the law in the few years before the setting up of ISS in Britain. The introduction of the Welfare State, and in particular the Children Act 1948 and the National Assistance Act 1948, ended the restrictions of the Poor Law, with its emphasis on minimum provision for the poor, and instead introduced the concept of attending to the development needs of vulnerable people, especially children. This was in line with the approach of ISS.

The British Nationality Act of 1948 was relevant to the work with immigrants. It introduced a new status of "citizen of the United Kingdom and Colonies" (CUKC) for people born or naturalised in either the United Kingdom or one of its colonies. Provision was also made in certain circumstances for citizenship to be acquired by descent from a CUKC, or by registration. Later Acts redefined the status of some Commonwealth citizens as their countries achieved independence.

In Britain the Adoption Act of 1958 introduced "Provisional Adoptions Orders". These were to be granted by the High Court or county court to couples who were domiciled overseas and wished to adopt a child resident in Great Britain once they had been assessed as suitable to adopt. Conversely, British people adopting a child from a country in which they were based overseas, and provided that the country had an Adoption Law, could obtain some sort of provisional order, giving them permission to take the child out of the country, and could then obtain a Full Adoption Order once they were living back in Britain. ISSGB became involved in obtaining background reports about prospective foreign adopters.

In 1958 ISSGB was asked to submit evidence to the Hague Conference on Private International Law in relation to the guardianship of minors. "For this purpose we in GB reviewed many of the inter-country cases in which the guardianship of children was in dispute, or not established. Among these cases were those of young Hungarians for many of whom no legal guardianship could be established."[46]

In 1959 the United Nations General Assembly proclaimed a Declaration of the Rights of the Child, but it took thirty years before this was converted to the UN Convention on the Rights

[46] AR 1958/9.

of the Child in 1989. This Declaration laid down the rights of every child to a name, a nationality, protection and care and family life. ISS took this up in the International Year for Human Rights in 1968 and stated: "It is part of the task of ISS to do all in its power to bring this about."[47] It is interesting to note that the original Declaration of the Rights of the Child was drafted in 1923 by Eglantyne Jebb, the founder of Save the Children. Her Declaration was adopted by the League of Nations in September 1924.

ISSGB and international headquarters

As has already been seen, the new British Branch was closely connected to the Headquarters in Geneva. "Already, our Chairman has represented us at the ISS Executive Committees held in Paris and Geneva and we have had helpful visits from the international and European Directors. Our secretary attended the Staff Conference in Geneva last April."[48]

A couple of years later, in the Annual Report the advantages of being part of the wider ISS are explained:

"As we become more firmly established as a Branch of ISS we have opportunities for closer working with our HQ in Geneva. In handling the cases from this country we realise the inestimable value of being a truly international service. Even if a case needs enquiry in remote parts of the world we can always call on our HQ for help by their representatives. ISS as a whole has some 35,000 new cases a year, covering 90 countries, and all their accumulated experience is at our disposal. By becoming an integral part of ISS we have benefited not only from their network of social worker correspondents, but also from their considerable knowledge of inter-country casework, international and refugee organisations, and other possibilities for helping our clients. We have been able to give them information about British and Commonwealth social work."[49] In 1959 the two staff attended the ISS Staff meeting in Geneva – these meetings, held almost

[47] AR1968.
[48] AR 1955/6.
[49] AR 1957/8.

every year, were greatly appreciated: "the Staff Meeting is of immense value to the total ISS Service. Here our workers exchange ideas, gain information and discuss cases – but above all they get to know each other and so increase their understanding of the problems of workers in other countries. They come back encouraged and refreshed."[50]

By the time the British Branch was officially launched, Kay Luce and Dani Adzemovic had produced a booklet about the work of the Branch called "Referral technique – imaginative co-operation". It seemed apposite to take part of this title as the title of this book, because the concept of co-operation, which is carried out with imaginative attempts to overcome problems, has always been central to ISS. There is a letter from Dicy Dodds saying how greatly it was appreciated by HQ and other Branches.[51] The casework broadly followed the principles and procedures developed by ISS HQ during the preceding years, but the British readily contributed to moves to improve the service and to adapt it as appropriate to changing circumstances. They were working hard on a whole range of policies: for example, the question of confidentiality when transferring personal information by letter. Kay Luce wrote to Dicy Dodds suggesting that there should be a policy about whether to forward clients' own letters, or put the salient points into a new letter (there is no record of what was decided). In 1959 a paper by Edna Weber was published in the journal International Social Work. It was titled: "The Practice of intercountry social work", and set out the fundamentals of the work.

Governance

The Officials of the Trustees remained as set out in Chapter 3. Frieda Wheeler was Chairman and Olive Hargreaves was Vice-Chairman until the end of 1963. Michael Sadd was Honorary Treasurer until 1959. Louis Blom-Cooper was Honorary Legal Advisor from 1957–1970. Throughout the period of this history both Trustees and staff relied heavily on the advice of the Treasurers and legal advisors.

50 AR 1956/57.

51 Letter from D Dodds to K Luce 7.4.55.

By 1959 there were 16 trustees. It is a notable feature of the ISSGB Trustees, that they always included a number of extremely distinguished and well-connected people. This is not written here as a matter for self-congratulation, but because it says a lot for the persuasive powers of those initially involved, in that they encouraged others to join them in what was then a very small venture. It meant that knowledge of ISSGB spread to influential quarters. For example, Lady (Sylvia) Kilmuir was the wife of the Lord Chancellor, and former Home Secretary, and after his death she married the Earl de la Warr in 1968. For some years she was Vice-President of the Conservative Party. (She was also the sister of the actor Rex Harrison.) She was a Trustee from 1957–76, and President from 1968–72.

Staff

For the first few years there were very few staff to deal with a huge number of cases. Dani Adzemovic left in October 1956 and was replaced by Patty Riddell Blount, who exchanged her role as volunteer for that of social worker. She was regarded as an extremely effective worker, and stayed until the early 60s. It is also recorded that a Mrs Hermann joined the social work staff for 2 years. Each of the social workers spent time at the Headquarters or the French Branch in order to learn more about ISS. Volunteers continued to work with refugees.

Kathleen Luce, always known as Kay to her colleagues, was the middle of five children. Her father was a doctor and MP. She started her social work career in the 1930s by working in a Dr Barnado's home and then for the local authority In Camden and Islington before joining the Charity Organisation Society. When it became the FWA she had her first experience of international social work, and it was a logical move for her to become the first Director of the newly formed ISSGB. She remained in that post until 1967, when she became a Trustee until 1982 and Vice-President from then until her death in 2003 aged 100.

She enjoyed walking holidays with friends, but otherwise her work seems to have been the focus of her life. She lived very modestly on a small income, and then a smaller pension. From the time that she came to London she lived in a couple of rooms in a house providing cheap accommodation for single women. When she was in her 90s and in a Care Home, for the first time in her life she got her own bathroom! (information from her nephew Tom Luce, who was himself a Trustee of ISSUK).

All accounts of Kay Luce show that she was a redoubtable woman who had the strength to drive the organisation in its early days. She was an indefatigable worker, with great skill and a knack for seeing ways out of problems, because she had a great capacity to think laterally. Her nephew spoke of her ability to be both firm and flexible. But he also described her as a tense person, full of nervous energy – as exemplified by her heavy smoking. She had strong personal loyalties to those she worked with, but did occasionally fall out with people who did not see things her way. When she retired the Annual Report of 1967 records: "Kay Luce was held in the highest regard throughout ISS and also amongst many voluntary social service organisations associated with ISS in activities connected with migration… she brought to her work a high sense of vocation and great humanity, and with these she combined a strong will and a determination to get things done. One could not but admire her resolution in the only too frequent presence of frustration, and note the nice sense of humour with which she fortified herself and others in such circumstances."[52] She was awarded the OBE in 1966. An obituary in the Annual Report of 2003 stated: "Kay was an important contributor to the international debate in ISS and participated in important international seminars which led to the development of protocols for the handling of international cases such as inter-country adoption. She was well respected by her peers, nationally and internationally, who delighted in her wit and ironic reflections during meetings."[53]

Finances and Fund-raising

In the early years, much of the income came from donations and subscriptions. "We regard our subscribers as the backbone of the Service, and are particularly glad that during this year so many of them have covenanted their subscriptions. It is they who

52 AR1967.
53 AR2003.

give us such security as we have, though there is an urgent need to increase the number of those giving this regular help."[54]

In the first year ISSGB obtained a grant of £1,000 from the Buttle Trust, nearly £400 from donations and £672 from a radio appeal, plus £850 transferred from FWA. Expenditure was £2,476. In 1958 a legacy of £3,000 was received, which kept ISSGB from running into deficit. As a result, the Annual Accounts of 1958/9 were able to report an excess of income over expenditure of £2,222 and a year later in 1959/60 a surplus of £50. As legacies were, in a sense, an unexpected bonus, it became the practice to invest part of each legacy for future use.

One of the first ways of trying to reach a wider audience was through radio appeals. The first BBC Radio Appeal in aid of ISSGB was made on 2nd October 1955 by Malcolm Muggeridge, then the editor of Punch. It was accompanied by appeals in several newspapers. The next radio appeal was made by Christopher Mayhew MP on 19th January 1958.This raised £1,123.

The Spring Fair

The most important – and well known – fund-raising event since the beginning has been the Spring Fair. It seems appropriate, therefore, to put in this chapter a description of the Fair through the decades.

In 1956 there was one stall at the United Charities May Fair at Caxton Hall, run by Lady (Mavis) Coulson. Kay Luce remembered: The staff had no experience in running bazaars; a few weeks before the Fair one caseworker said: "we've got 30 items – how many do you think we ought to have?"[55] Nonetheless, the stall was filled with knitted objects and stuffed toys and anything they could collect. ISS took the second largest amount of any stall, £213.11s.9d. This was an impressive amount in those days. In 1958 the Fair was held at Londonderry House, and the ISS stall was run jointly by the British and the Americans.

54 AR 1958/9.

55 The Early History of the International Social Service of Great Britain, article by K Luce, 1992.

In 1959 the first independent International Spring Fair was held at the Chenil Galleries. The Fair was opened by the actress Miss Valerie Hobson. Mavis Coulson's team of organisers included Americans and Austrians, and food was provided by a group of Polish exiles. The stalls were typical of Fairs of the time; baby clothes, books, cakes, country produce, nearly new toys, white elephant, bottles and bran tub. In 1961 for the first time there was an International Stall.

The Fair was moved to Chelsea Old Town Hall in 1962, when there were twelve stalls, and then to Caxton Hall from 1964–7. From 1968 it returned to Chelsea Old Town Hall, and was held there until 1981 when it moved to Kensington Town Hall. From then on the Fair was held there for a couple of days in May each year.

Throughout the 1960s a variety of stalls were set up. For example, an advertisement in the Annual Report of 1964, calls for goods for sale – being "Jams, marmalades, pickles for our Food Fair; clothes in good condition for the Fashion Boutique and Children's stall, and anything saleable for the Precious Possessions Stall. There will be the usual delectable Polish buffet."[56]

In 1966 the International Stall featured goods from 25 countries. After this, the annual event steadily grew to include more and more countries, and became a feature of the diplomatic calendar. Each participating country set up a stall selling goods made in that country, and gave the proceeds to ISSGB. Most stalls were manned by the female members of that Embassy, and for many of them it was a great opportunity to get out and meet other people, as well as being a most enjoyable event. It was also a wonderful demonstration of the international co-operation at the heart of ISS work. Each year the organisers also organised a raffle and tombola. Gradually the area supplying food and drink expanded, with numerous stalls from different countries, each selling their own specialities, until a whole floor was given up to the International restaurant. In due course entertainments were introduced, such as dancers and singers from different parts of the world. It is impossible to exaggerate the colourfulness of the

[56] AR 1964.

whole event, and the buzz of activity, heightened by somewhat overcrowded halls!

Such an undertaking requires a great deal of organisation, goodwill and hard work, and each year a Committee was set up to run the Fair. The Fair Committee was always dissolved after the Fair and a new Committee established each year by the Chairman. From 1965 the Chairman of the Fair Committee held a tea party each year for "the ladies of foreign missions in London who by their generosity and good humour, make our Spring Fair the astonishing success it always is – a success, one must underline, not only with regard to vital financial support for the work of ISS, but also in terms of a collective international goodwill rarely experienced elsewhere."[57]

In addition to the Chairman and Committee there was also a President of Honour, who was usually a prominent figure, such as the wife of a government minister, who could add weight to the publicity, and a President, who was more involved in the organisation and offered continuity. For example, Lady Ross was President of the Fair for twelve years 1979–91. The Royal Patron of ISSUK usually visited the Fair. In the early years a well-known person was invited to open the Fair, for example the ballerina Dame Margot Fonteyn opened it in 1960, the Duchess of Kent as Patron in 1965, the actress Susan Hampshire in 1968 and the actor Kenneth Moore in 1972.

Volunteers need logistical backup, and early on a member of staff, Mrs Ruth Eames, was appointed and served in this role for 23 years, from 1957–1980. Her work over these years was greatly appreciated. "No words can convey the debt which ISS owes to Ruth Eames. She runs the Spring Fair, raises funds, controls the information system, corrects our grammar and acts as locum tenens for anyone anywhere who is not immediately available, all with perfect calm."[58] She went on helping with the Fair after retirement. Maggie Durham took over as Fair Secretary from 1980–92, and she was succeeded by Crystal East until 1996. After that the Fair Organiser was also the Events Co-ordinator: Vikki Barrie until 2000, when Nagini Rajendra took on the job

57 M Coulson AR 1982.

58 AR 1975.

for a couple of years, and she was followed by Amanda Stanford in 2003, Lina Saneusanio in 2005, Nicola Power in 2007 and Darren Moses in 2009.

In 1972 the net profit from the Fair reached £10,000 – by 1985 it reached over £57,000, with 96 countries taking part. In 1988 103 countries took part. In 1989 the income from the Fair topped £100,000. By 1993 it raised over £121,380, which was more than 50% of the income of ISSGB. Indeed, it raised half of the income for many years. The peak of income came in 2001, when over £155,000 was raised. (A list of countries with stalls at the Fair in 2001 can be found in the Appendix.)

Particular mention should be made here of Mavis Coulson. Other long-term contributors were Frieda Wheeler and Lady (Françoise) Middleton and Lady (Liz) Emery, who are mentioned elsewhere.

Mavis Coulson became involved with ISSGB at the beginning, when she ran the stall at the first United Services Fair in 1956. In 1959 she launched the first ISS Spring Fair in London to raise funds, manning a stall with a small group of women. During the following years she persuaded an increasing number of London's diplomatic missions to run stalls selling goods from their respective countries. She remained a mainstay of the Fair for many years, serving as Chairman or President in some years, and in 1992 she was named "Founder President" of the Fair. ISSUK would not have survived without the regular input of funds from the Fair, and so she was, arguably, one of the most influential people in its history.

In addition to her work for the Spring Fair she made the following contributions to ISS:

From 1958/9 she was a member of the Executive Committee and Appeals Committee. She then spent three years abroad, and on her return to the UK in 1963 she became a member of Council until 1991. From 1980–85 she was Vice-Chairman of Council. She was elected Vice-President in 1990. She also served on the International Committee for a number of years.

In 1974 she organised an International Symposium for the 50th anniversary of ISS, on the topic "Migration in the 70s". This was the centrepiece of the International Council Meeting.

In 1989 she gave the address at the ISSGB AGM "Thirty years of the Spring Fair and rather longer with ISS".

Her early history gives an insight into why she was so effective.

During the Battle of Britain Mavis Beazley, as she then was, worked as a nurse with Archie McIndoe's burns unit at East Grinstead hospital, where many of the patients were badly burned airmen. Mavis then went to the Foreign Office, where she worked for Gladwyn Jebb, head of the post-war reconstruction department. Shortly afterwards she accompanied Anthony Eden and senior generals on a flight by Liberator bomber to the Cairo conference attended by Roosevelt and Churchill. From there she travelled to Tehran, where Churchill and the American president met Stalin. She left the Foreign Office in 1944, after her marriage to John Coulson. She worked with the Free French in London. Following the war John Coulson was appointed head of chancery at the embassy in Paris. The couple then had postings to the UN in New York, Foreign and Commonwealth Office (FCO) in London and, in 1955 the British Embassy in Washington. From 1960–63 Sir John Coulson was appointed ambassador to Sweden, and was then Chief Clerk at the Foreign Office. Mavis Coulson became Chairman of the Foreign Service Wives' Association, then, in 1965, accompanied her husband to Geneva when he was made Secretary-General of the European Free Trade Association.

Mavis was described as being an open and engaging person, full of good stories. In retirement the Coulsons lived at Selborne, Hampshire. Sir John died in 1997 and she died in 2009, aged 89.

(Information from records and from talking to her nephew, Charles Marshall who, in his turn, served ISSUK for many years, being Honorary Treasurer from 1991–2008.)

The Spring Fair remains a spectacular event, and when some countries dropped out, there were others to take their place, for example, the newer countries that had formerly been part of Russia or Yugoslavia. After the income peaked in the early 2000s it fell slightly. However, it continued to raise a very significant proportion of the income of ISSUK. Some have argued that the enormous amount of planning that is required each year is not justified, in comparison with similar amounts that have been raised from embassy dinners and the Golf Tournament. But such arguments miss the point: that the benefit of the Spring Fair goes well beyond any financial gains. The smaller countries from around the world, who contribute a stall to the Fair, are reminded each year of the value of the ISS to their country, so that links with the Correspondent in that country may be strengthened, and any problems that arise can more easily be ironed out. The Spring Fair is a wonderful advertisement for ISS, not just within the diplomatic community, but more widely through all those who come to it.

The casework

There were three major strands to the work that was taken over from the FWA. Firstly, all the casework with migrants, linking with other ISS Units. Secondly, there were still a lot of cases concerning paternity and maintenance issues for women whose children had been born as a result of liaisons with foreign servicemen, particularly Americans. Lastly, there was ongoing work with refugees in Britain – mainly Poles.

The first Annual Report describes the changes that took place in the new Branch: "During this, the first year of independent working since we became an integral part of ISS, our work has expanded considerably. Not only have there been more cases, but social agencies, Government Departments and foreign embassies have made more frequent use of the service."[59] For example, requests were received from Jamaican welfare services requiring reports on their citizens in the UK who wanted to bring their children over to join them. And a couple of years later: "since ISSGB is becoming something of an international citizen's advice bureau for social workers, a well-kept filing system has become necessary".[60]

The statistics for the first year show the number of countries either sending or receiving referrals from Britain, and the variety of problems being dealt with. In addition to those listed below there were also 135 new cases of Polish refugees in Britain. (Note

[59] AR1955/6.
[60] AR 1958/9.

that the definition of referrals may have included some cases that would later be designated as enquiries.)

Africa		**Australasia**		Cyprus	7
Egypt	1	Australia	35	Denmark	2
Nigeria	3	New Zealand	2	France	22
Rhodesia and Tanganyika	5	**Asia**		Germany	118
Sierra Leone	1	Aden	1	Gibraltar	1
South Africa	16	China	2	Greece	19
Tunisia	1	Hong Kong	1	Iceland	1
Americas		India	10	Ireland	11
Canada	152	Malaya	1	Italy	20
USA	191	Pakistan	1	Malta	6
British Honduras	1	Syria	1	Netherlands	13
British West Indies	23	Turkey	1	Norway	1
Argentina	4	**Europe**		Spain	2
Brazil	1	Austria	17	Switzerland	10
Chile	1	Belgium	8	**TOTAL**	**713**

Categories of problems dealt with 1955–56

Re-union of families	74	Socio-legal problems:		Immigration	68
Desertion or non-support	120	Marriage or divorce	103	Repatriation	18
Adoption or placement	216	Property/ inheritance	16	Health	64
Paternity	29	Compensation	7	Employment/ training	13
Tracing	87	Related to status as foreigner	4	Material assistance	115
Other	133	**TOTAL 1067** (many clients have more than one problem.)			

Numbers alone do not give any sense of the complexity of the cases. Many referrals concerned problems about the legal status of migrant people, with various members of a family sometimes having different nationalities and rights. ISS staff worked hard to keep up to date with the complex laws and rules and regulations in the countries concerned, but could also call on legal advice when necessary. Cases are listed as "socio-legal" because in every instance there were welfare considerations alongside the legal ones. When the official ruling would lead to the splitting of families, or failure to reunite them, then every effort would be made to find a practical and compassionate solution. There was a lot of work helping people settle in a new country – solving practical problems and linking people with local agencies who might help them.

Refugee projects 1987–2004

In 1939 a Polish Relief Fund had been set up to help refugees and it was managed by the FWA and then by ISSGB. The Fund made grants to needy Poles, but also offered a valuable support service. It was wound up in 1958 due to lack of funds. But arrangements were made with a few British pension funds who took on financial responsibility for some elderly and sick Polish refugees, and gave them small regular allowances.

In 1957 a grant was received from the Lord Mayor's Fund for Hungarian Refugees. That year help was given to 43 Hungarians in Britain and the following year to 80.

> Case example
>
> Magda was a young girl of 15 who had fled the fighting in Budapest and arrived in England alone, having spent weeks travelling across Europe. She came to the attention of the Salvation Army as she slept rough. They contacted ISSGB, who were able to arrange for her to join relatives in Canada.

Then in 1959 ISSGB received grants from the British World Refugee Year Committee and the Buttle Trust, and so it was able to set up a longer term project with other refugees, many of whom were professionally trained and skilled people who, nonetheless, were unable to work in Britain, and were living on meagre allowances. ISSGB could give grants for basic items that they could not afford, such as new clothing, and outings for children. In the Annual Report of 1959–60 it is recorded that cases of refugees included a few each of Austrians, Bulgarians, Czechoslovakians, Estonians, Latvians, Russians, Romanians, Ukrainians, Yugoslavs, as well as lots of Poles and Hungarians.

In 1959 the ISS staff had good relations with the British Council for Aid to Refugees which was then a small organisation, working in the same building. In due course it grew into the Refugee Council.

In 1962 the Government allocated £50,000 a year for the benefit of Polish ex-servicemen and women, and ISS was able to use this money to help many of the 2,000 Polish refugees with which it was still dealing. ISS volunteers visited many of the older people in their home. "An important feature of the problem is that the refugees, while grateful for asylum, seek an independent life, and, after years of forced communal life, welcome a little privacy. And so, they cling to a room of their own, no matter how simple, in preference to going into a home. We can make them small allowances, for comforts and necessities, such as getting telephones installed."[61]

Eileen Lawrence and Ruth Black were two volunteers who both gave many years of help to this scheme. The programme only closed finally in 2004, when the remaining monies from the Refugee Benefit Fund were moved into Unrestricted Funds. By this time there were only 2 elderly Poles each receiving £100 a year. They were offered a lump sum of £500 or an annuity of £100 per annum, and chose the lump sum.

Case examples

Jan had been a teacher in Poland before he fled. He had been unable to work in England but had been active in voluntary work with other refugees. Then he became mentally ill and very isolated. The ISS worker visited him regularly and

[61] AR1965.

provided books and records. Slowly he recovered, and said that her kindness had been a major factor in giving him back hope for the future.

A Polish refugee family was referred to ISSGB because Valentin, the father, and only wage earner, had contracted lung cancer and was unable to work. He wanted to return to Poland now that it was safe to do so. ISS in both countries was able to facilitate the family's return to Krakow

Kay Luce was also co-operating with The British Council for Aid to Refugees (BCAR) over 3 schemes to bring displaced people to Britain from Italy. Firstly, up to 100 women to work in the textile mills, then an agricultural scheme in Lincolnshire for families, and finally, a project for single men with agricultural experience to come to Worcestershire.

World Refugee Year

Throughout the 1950s there was growing concern about the sheer number of refugees in the world, so that all systems to help them were chronically overloaded. Other solutions had to be found and the idea for a World Refugee Year came from two British MPs – Chris Chataway and Timothy Raison, together with a couple of journalists, Trevor Philpott and Colin Jones. There were three main aims: to arouse the conscience of the world, to collect funds and to assist in permanent solutions for refugees. Their concern was for 3 groups in particular: Firstly, the estimated 162,000 still in post-war refugee camps in Europe; secondly the 915,000 Palestinian refugees expelled from their homes as the state of Israel was created, and thirdly, the 750,000 refugees pouring into Hong Kong from mainland China as a consequence of Mao Tse Tung's "Great Leap Forward".[62] The UN was persuaded to name World Refugee Year from June 59. In Britain efforts made by charities such as Christian Aid and Oxfam and local churches ensured that there was good publicity, and lots of funds were raised.

[62] A Cause for Our Times – Oxfam, the first 50 years. M Black 1992.

The main contribution of ISSGB to this challenge posed by World Refugee Year was to set up two projects: the first to help elderly refugees (which has already been mentioned), and the second to bring some Chinese orphans to Britain to be adopted by British families.

Intercountry adoption

At this time there was a growing focus on international adoptions. There were large numbers of orphaned and abandoned children, many of whom were the result of liaisons between occupying soldiers and local women. The new ISS Units in Japan and Korea were involved in the transfer of hundreds of children to the United States, where the legislation permitted inter-country adoption on a large scale. Publicity was obtained by the World Adoption International Fund (WAIF), which was funded by Hollywood stars such as Jane Russell. At first there was minimal scrutiny of those seeking to adopt, but over time, procedures were improved in relation to the assessment of prospective adoptive parents and efforts were made to try and ensure that the overseas children really were available to be adopted. When children were brought to the UK for adoption, ISSGB was involved in obtaining the necessary reports from overseas for the Courts. These might be reports on the background of a child or family, or confirmation that the birth parent/s either had given their consent to the adoption, or proof that they could not be found.

ISS staff and those from the International Union for Child Welfare (IUCW) and the UN Europe Office, together organised the first major seminar on inter-country adoption at Leysin, Switzerland in May 1960. The 12 Leysin Principles set out the basic framework for all such adoptions, and remain the basic principles of inter-country adoptions to this day. The first principle stated that adoption was the preferred option for a child who could not live with his or her parents or close relatives, so long as the adoption was based on the best interests of the child. This indicated that there should be rigorous safeguards to ensure that unsuitable people could not adopt. The second important principle was that inter-country adoption should only be considered after all options to keep a child within the country of origin had been explored. The twelfth and last principle stated that any adoption should be legal and valid in both the sending and receiving countries.

In 1961 ISSGB became a Registered Adoption Agency. Kay Luce wrote in a letter to E Weber in Geneva: "you will be glad to learn that ISSGB has been duly registered as an Adoption Society by the appropriate body, the London County Council".[63] This was necessary in order to carry out any placement of children for adoption, although it did not take place until after the first Hong Kong Chinese children had been placed.

The ISS Hong Kong Project 1959–69

In 1958 ISS had opened a Branch in Hong Kong (HK). Its main aim was to work with the Hong Kong Chinese Welfare Authorities to find adoptive homes for hundreds of Chinese refugee children – part of the huge influx of refugees. The population had swelled from just over 1 million to about 3 million in a few years, and several hundred thousand were living on the streets or in flimsy shacks in the expanding shanty towns. The initial plan was to place with Chinese families in HK if possible, but it was soon realised that the only chance of family life for many lay outside HK. ISS USA had been involved for some years in the placement of hundreds of children from Japan and Korea with adoptive families in the States, and so ISS HK could build on this experience to set up a viable adoption system. This was possible because the Government of Hong Kong had passed an Adoption Ordnance in 1956.

ISSUK decided to sponsor a number of Chinese children to come to the UK. The reasons given were:

- Concern for the plight of babies abandoned in the streets of Hong Kong who were herded into overcrowded orphanages with no hope of normal home life.
- To meet the spontaneous demands for these children by couples in GB.
- A strong feeling that Britain should give practical expression to its concern for the conditions prevalent in this British Colony.

[63] Letter from Kay Luce to E Weber 29.9.61.

A trial scheme was launched in June 1959 in conjunction with ISS Hong Kong – whose workers would "select and process" the children, and National Children's Home (NCH) in the UK, who would undertake to find homes for the children. Within a year Dr Barnado's had also agreed to do this work. Both agencies also undertook to take a child back into their care should a placement fail. There is a lot of correspondence about the careful setting up of the project. Much of it relates to the practical issues, including the arrangements for the transport of the children to the UK and the funding of the work. There is interesting correspondence about the legal status of the children – the Supreme Court of Hong Kong appointed the Director of Social Welfare in Hong Kong as Guardian to each child so that he could give consent to the removal of the children for the purpose of adoption in the UK. Then the National Children's Home or Dr Barnado's was given temporary legal guardianship of each child until an Adoption Order could be granted in this country.

The first two children arrived in the UK in May 1960 and the project ended with the arrival of the last two children in 1969. Most came between 1960 and 1963. In all 100 children were brought to the UK through this project – all were girls. The youngest child was 8 months old on arrival in this country and the great majority were under 3 years old. The oldest was 7 years old. There were no sibling groups. As most of the children had been abandoned their birth certificates state: "believed to be born on or about ...." And the certificates note where each child was left – in nearly all cases they were left in a safe place where they would be quickly found. The babies had been placed in one of four orphanages from which they were brought to England. The children had spent an average of 20 months in orphanages.

These babies and toddlers flew from Hong Kong with escorts, who were often British service wives returning home on leave. They were handed to their new parents at Heathrow Airport. ISSGB staff – usually Winifred Klingender or Eileen Lawrence – were present to oversee the handovers. One can only imagine the bewilderment of these tiny children, faced with a strange new family excited to welcome them.

(A small number of other children were brought to the UK from HK for adoption at this time, but not officially through the project. They were either adopted by families who had been working in HK – usually with the military – or came to join relatives.)

The 100 girls were placed with families who had been newly recruited in the UK. 85 children were placed with families through the NCH with 72 families, because 13 families adopted a second child through the project. 14 children were placed with 12 families through Dr Barnado's and one child was placed independently in the States of Guernsey. The average age at placement for adoption was 23 months. Adoption Orders were granted in respect of all the children. After that there was no formal link between the adoptive families and the placing agencies. The only contact that ISSUK had with the adoptees was if and when any of them returned to the agency to find out information about their adoptions. (12 adoptees did come to ISSUK when adult and were given such information as was on their files, and any necessary counselling.)

The project wound down as the numbers of children needing adoption reduced and arrangements for local family placements for those that remained in Hong Kong were put in place. This was consistent with the ISS philosophy of helping people within their own culture whenever possible.

One of the frustrations of the job of social work lies in the impossibility, in most cases, of finding out what happened to people in the long run. So there is particular pleasure in the fact that there has been a follow-up study to see what happened to this group of adopted children.

The BAAF British Chinese Adoption Study (BCAS) 2007–12

It can easily be seen that if ISSGB had not worked as an intermediary in the adoption of these Chinese orphans then the majority of them would certainly have remained in orphanages throughout their childhoods.

There was an earlier study of this group of adopted people – by Bagley and Young in 1979, with a follow-up in 1988. They contacted 51 of the adoptive parents and reported an optimistic view of the general adjustment and progress of these children.

In 2003 the British Agencies for Adoption and Fostering (BAAF) approached ISSUK with a view to undertaking some research with the adopted women themselves, in order to learn from their experiences and to help provide appropriate services for children adopted from overseas in the future. The Secretary of State gave permission for the files to be seen by the researchers and in May 2004 staff from the research team did a feasibility study, which led to the full-scale research project beginning in 2007. Funding was received from the Nuffield Foundation. The ethical dimension to any research with adopted people has to be taken very seriously and this project was thoroughly scrutinised. I was privileged to represent ISSUK on the Advisory Group of this study.

The stated aims of the study were:

"• To document and categorise the early experience, life span development and adult outcomes for these Chinese women, all of whom experienced orphanage care as infants and were subsequently adopted.
• Investigate whether there is excess risk in their psychosocial and physical well-being in relation to matched adopted and non-adopted comparison groups.
• Establish the links between adverse early experience and differential adult outcome and what factors mediate any excess risk
• Explore the variety of responses to the experience of international trans-racial adoption and formation of ethnic identity."[64]

The research team was given information on the 100 girls who had been brought to the UK. Staff and volunteers set out to trace the 100 adopted women and, amazingly, after so long, 99 were traced, either directly or through a relative. Of these, two had died. 72 women agreed to participate in the study, and completed a long questionnaire about their health, views about

64 Briefing Paper for Advisory Group to BCAS research study, March 2009.

their adoption, and past and present family and social situations. That was followed by an in-depth interview by one of a team of specially trained interviewers with 68 of the participants.

This research study was completed after the period with which we are concerned in this history. But it seems incomplete not to give an outline of the results, which were published in January 2013 as "Adversity, adoption and afterwards – a mid-life follow-up study of women adopted from Hong Kong" by Feast, Grant, Rushton and Simmonds, BAAF 2013

By all statistical criteria, this group of women has done as well as a comparable but non-adopted group. But what makes this study so unusual and fascinating, is the picture obtained from the personal stories of the adopted women. The statistics cannot portray the pervasive and often challenging effect of growing up and living in a different ethnic culture. The concluding paragraph of the book sums it up:

> "This study has been a remarkable experience with some very important findings. It clearly identifies the adaptability, resilience and strength of human beings when faced with significant early adversity. It attests to the importance of family life in providing nurture, care, stimulation and opportunity even when children have had a poor start in life. But it does not underestimate the challenge for those adopted and those who adopt. A child born to one family and raised by another will be faced by thoughts and feelings that directly arise from having a family tree with two sets of roots. These vary in significance and change over time. But for the group of women in this study, these thoughts and feelings have become incorporated in time into a picture of achievement, life satisfaction and positive outcomes, even though tinged with feelings of regret, a sense of loss and unanswered questions. It is our fervent wish that this should eventually be found to be so for all those children and adults whose life path is marked by adoption."[65]

A wonderful outcome of the study was that it brought together more than half of those adopted, and they have formed their own

65 "Adversity, adoption and afterwards", Feast, Grant, Rushton and Simmonds, BAAF 2013.

friendship support group. Although a very few of the adoptive families had kept in touch as the children grew up, and there was a reunion of a small group of them when adult, most of the adopted women had had no idea that they were part of a larger group of adopted Chinese, and for them it has brought an extraordinary extra dimension to their lives.

Quite apart from the importance of the lessons learned for all overseas and trans-racial adoption work, this research project recognised the significant part that ISSUK played in the lives of these adopted women. This study also touches on so many of the issues that are found in all ISS casework, when two or more cultures are brought together in a family.

By the end of the decade the fledgling ISSGB had achieved so much that it needed to expand. "The experience of these four years shows clearly that the time has come when we must plan on a long-term basis. During these years we have operated with a small staff and limited resources while experiencing a steadily increasing demand for our services. Even slight publicity brings many additional requests for help, and these serve to underline how small we really are as an agency. We can no longer postpone plans for the extension of our work."[66]

[66] AR 1958/9.

Chapter 6

The 1960s

World events

This decade saw the huge famine in Bihar, the civil war in Nigeria and beginning of the Vietnam War. Across the world, the great increase in air travel enabled those who could afford the fares to reach places that had hitherto been inaccessible. The migrants to Britain still came mainly from the Caribbean, with an increasing number from the Indian sub-continent. There was an increase in young people from African and Asian countries travelling abroad for tertiary education, many of them unaware of the practical and cultural hazards facing them. ISS became involved sometimes if an attachment to someone in the new country conflicted with the expected obligations to their family.

Migration wasn't just one way. Britons continued to migrate to Australia, New Zealand and the United States, or retired to sunnier countries, such as Spain. Some of these Britons experienced problems resulting from family separations and disputes.

Legislation

Some of the main statutes and Conventions in this period relate to the status of immigrants, and ISS staff had to keep up to date with all the changes.

- The UN Convention on Reduction of Statelessness 1961 included a requirement that States should grant citizenship to children born on their territory. This led to the passing of the British Nationality Act 1964, which widened the entitlement to registration to certain stateless groups, especially illegitimate children of a British mother or legitimate children of a stateless father.

- The Commonwealth Immigration Act 1962, together with the Commonwealth Immigrants Act 1968, tightened up the criteria for entry to Britain. The 1968 Act "provided that British subjects would be free from immigration control only if they, or at least one of their parents or grandparents, had been born, adopted, registered or naturalised in the UK. The issue of a passport by a British High Commission thus ceased to be a qualification for entry. For those subject to control a voucher system based on tight quotas was introduced."[67]

There were also two important Conventions leading to a change to adoption law;

- ISSGB made a contribution to the Draft Convention of the Hague Conference on Intercountry adoption in 1964, which later became the Hague Convention on the Jurisdiction and Law Applicable in cases of Adoption 1965.
- The European Convention on the Adoption of Children 1967 was ratified by the UK in 1968. It contained a list of provisions on adoption practice that had to be incorporated into legislation by member states.
- In the UK these two Conventions were incorporated into the Adoption Act 1976, in which Section17 dealt with Convention Adoption Orders.

ISSGB within the wider ISS

In Geneva the American William Kirk was the International Director until 1962. He had also been Director of the American Branch, but from now on the International Director was not connected to any unit of ISS. Kirk was succeeded by a Canadian, Stewart Sutton, who remained until 1966. In 1961, Edna Weber had replaced Dicy Dodds as Assistant Director, and then became Director for a couple of years from 1966–8, when she was succeeded by a Briton, Robert Menzies. Audrey Moser, a British social worker, joined ISS as Programme Co-ordinator in 1963, and stayed until 1968. An Australian, Peter Fry, joined in 1967.

[67] UK Immigration Service — Wikipedia.

Another reason why this was a time of close co-operation between ISS in Geneva and ISSGB was that there was also good British representation on the International Council. From 1969 to 1970 Frieda Wheeler was International President.

There was an International Council meeting in 1969 when representatives of 20 countries met in Geneva. "Before the Council Meeting, Directors of Branches and Delegations together with the professional staff from Headquarters met to discuss their common problems and to re-affirm the principles on which ISS work is based. These meetings and exchanges of views between people of widely differing national backgrounds who are, nevertheless, working together for the same ends along almost incredibly extended lines of communication, are always inspiring experiences and are essential if ISS standards of service are to be maintained and improved."[68]

In 1961 Trustees of ISSGB were asked to represent ISS on UN Committees on Refugees, Human Rights and Status of Women. Also in 1961 ISS HQ was given Consultative Status to the Council of Europe.

In September 1968 ISS was one of 8 NGOs with consultative Status B with the Economic and Social Council of the UN to be invited to send an observer to the Conference of Ministers Responsible for Social Welfare. ISS submitted a statement urging more co-operation between governmental and voluntary agencies in the field of social welfare, and for special training in inter-country matters for social workers.

ISSGB: Governance

In December 1963 a new Council was formed, consisting mainly of members of the old Executive Committee. Sir Robert Black became the first Chairman of the new Council and remained in that post until 1973. The Council was also referred to as the Board of Trustees, but this term was not used widely until 2004. The Council, as the governing body, derived its powers from Sections 22–28 of the Constitution. Its task was to set policies and strategy, delegate the day-to-day running to the Director and approve long-term plans and initiatives.

68 AR1969.

From 1965 the Council met four times a year, though in later years the number of meetings increased. Although in due course a time limit was set for membership of the Council, at this time there clearly was no such arrangement. Long-serving members offered stability and the knowledge of the issues of the past, but there was also a need to refresh the membership and outlook of the Council regularly with new members. The members of the Council were never paid for their services.

A General Purposes Committee was set up to handle the more detailed work. Provision was made for "a Finance Committee and such other sub-committees as from time to time are found to be necessary".[69] At that time this meant having a Refugee Sub-Committee, an Adoption Sub-committee, and an Appeals Sub-Committee. Some members of Sub-Committees came from the Council, but others were appointed because they brought additional expertise in important areas. In particular, the Adoption Committee in its time included luminaries of the adoption world such as Kate Lewis, Margaret Kornitzer and Jane Rowe. The Committees attracted people who made a long-term commitment to the ISS. For example, the Chairman of the Refugee Committee for many years was William Lidbury, the London Regional Controller for the National Assistance Board. He was a member of Council from 1962–1987.

Also in 1963, it was felt to be appropriate to have a Patron, and Princess Marina, Duchess of Kent took on this role until she died in 1968, when her daughter-in-law, the new Duchess of Kent became Patron. In turn, when she retired from public life in 2000, her sister-in-law Princess Alexandra of Kent took on the role. All these Patrons have taken a real interest in the ISS and have often attended the Spring Fair and other fund-raising events.

All these changes entailed revision of the Constitution, and the new Constitution was adopted at the AGM in November 1964. The objectives of the organisation were now stated to be:

> "1. to promote all or any purposes for the benefit of the community which now are or hereafter may be deemed by law to be charitable, and in particular the advancement of social education, the furtherance of health and the relief of poverty,

[69] AR 1963/4.

distress and sickness in the contest of the family or the individual with personal or family problems, in particular, but not exclusively, where such problems transcend national boundaries.

2. to promote and organise co-operation in the achievement of the above purpose and to that end to bring together in ISSGB internationally, nationally and locally representatives of both voluntary social agencies and statutory authorities engaged in the furtherance of the above purposes

3. to study and report upon the conditions of inter-country demographic problems and their effects upon the individual, family and community life.

4. to engage in social action to alleviate conditions of inter-country movement of people which produce discord or disharmony to family life and human welfare.

5. to engage in the work of arranging the fostering and adoption of children both internationally and nationally."[70]

There were several minor alterations to the Constitution thereafter: in 1967, 1970 and 1991, introducing changes, for example, to the length of terms of office, subscriptions and membership.

Lady (Frieda) Wheeler was the first Chairman of ISSGB, and held this post until the end of 1963, after which she remained as a Trustee until her death in 1972. She steered the organisation through its early years, and when she died the Chairman wrote: "We have lost an outstanding colleague in Lady Wheeler… She was an inspiration to us all in her selflessness and devotion to ISS."

In 1963 she was joined on the Council by her son **John Wheeler**, who remained as a Trustee for an astonishing 41 years, and for almost half of them was Vice-Chairman. After retiring from the Board in 2004 he was made a Vice-President and he continued to support fundraising efforts until his death in 2007.

[70] AR 1964.

Staff

The most notable staff change in the 1960s was the retirement of Kay Luce in 1967 – after 20 years with FWA and ISSGB. She did not disappear but joined the Council, and remained on it until 1982. She was then appointed as Vice-President until her death in 2003 aged almost 101.

Miss Winifred Rouse succeeded her, and served as Director from 1967–90.

By the mid-60s there were 4 social workers in the London office; Miss Janet Moss, Lady (Jean) Martin, who was known as Mrs Martin, Mrs J Horbaczewska and Mrs (Winifred) Klingender. There are no surviving records of the numbers of administrative staff at this time, but of course these included shorthand typists, and one of them, Winifred Hatfield, worked in the office for 11 years. When she left it was said about her: "She was, and indeed is, a unique personality, and the office is not the same without her."[71] During the second half of the decade four new social work staff joined the team to run the two new projects that will be described later in this chapter.

Winifred Klingender holds the record for the longest continuous service as a social worker with ISS in the UK. Winifred joined ISSGB in 1960 and remained until 1985. She specialised in adoptions and was the main worker with the Hong Kong adoption project. She became a well-known authority on adoption generally, but especially on intercountry adoptions, and was often consulted by social workers in that field. Indeed, that is how I first came into contact with ISS. When she retired it was said of her: "She had made herself a national and international expert on adoption law and practice, was constantly consulted by organisations of all kinds as well as would-be adopters, and dealt with all these enquiries and her numerous clients with patience and meticulous attention to detail."[72]

Eileen Lawrence was a volunteer who helped ISS in many different ways. She started as a voluntary worker in 1956, spending five years with ISS Italy, working in refugee camps.

71 AR 1973.

72 AR 1985.

When she came back to England she joined the Executive Committee in 1960 and served until 1972 on the Council, Refugee Committee, Finance and General Purposes Committee and Appeals Committee (which she chaired for some years). From 1963 she was the ISSGB representative to the International Council. At the same time she worked as caseworker with refugees as part of the Elderly Refugee Programme. She also seems to have volunteered by going into the office on a regular basis for two days a week, to help with whatever needed doing. She gave up her work with refugees and her committee work when she moved to Somerset in 1972. In 1973 she became a Vice-President of ISS. She died in 1981. The Annual Report of that year says: "She was the ideal volunteer, attending with perfect regularity, carrying out her duties without supervision, but reporting meticulously on what she had done. She was a real friend and her death is a great sadness to us all."[73]

Finances and Fundraising

In order to conform with ISS HQ and other Branches, the Council decided in 1964 to start the financial year on 1st January instead of 1st April.

This decade exemplifies the up-and-down nature of the finances of ISSGB. There are some difficulties in interpreting the figures. For example, the Annual Report of 1963/64 records that at the end of the year there was a deficit of over £1,669. This is explained by the fact that the Spring Fair was not held within that financial year. The report of 1966 shows an excess of £65 of income over expenditure, partly due to a legacy of £600. The Annual Report says that it was "a strictly hand-to-mouth existence",[74] dependent on grants coming in – an uncertain situation that led to concerns about staff cuts. The fee to Local Authorities for case referrals was increased from 5 guineas to £8.

The actress Dame Flora Robson made a broadcast appeal in July 1960, the actor Rupert Davies (Maigret) in 1962 and the broadcaster Jack de Manio in 1966.

73 AR1981.
74 AR1966.

For the first time a membership scheme was started – members to pay "not less than 2 guineas a year". This continued for many years, but never attracted many members; however it did keep the members informed about the organisation.

From 1967 there was an annual collection in London every June on Alexandra Rose Day. This seems to have been held in the Strand, near the Law Courts, or in the Inner Temple. This continued until about 2004, and several hundred pounds were raised each year, and members of the legal profession were nudged to remember ISS.

There is no record of what publicity material was produced at this time, except for advertisements for the Spring Fair.

Links with other agencies

All the time, the staff of ISSGB were establishing and developing relationships with the key agencies with whom they worked – notably, Government Departments like the Foreign Office and Department of Health, Local Authorities, and others who were relevant to the various projects. By the 1960s ISSGB had also established links with many national bodies, of which the following are a few examples:

- British Caribbean Association
- British Council for Aid to Refugees
- British Government Grant Aid Committee for Polish Ex-servicemen
- Consultative Committee on Overseas Students and their Families
- Family Welfare Association
- Joint Council for the Welfare of Migrants
- National Council for the Unmarried mother and her Child
- National Council of Social Work
- Standing Conference on the Economic and Social Work of the UN
- Standing Conference of Societies Registered for Adoption – (later to become BAAF).

- Standing Conference of Voluntary Organisations and Service
- Women's Council.[75]

The level of involvement with the various organisations would have varied – ISS staff were closely involved with some, and only nominally connected to others.

Casework in 1960s

Although the majority of cases are concerned with children, there have always been a number of cases related to health issues – people enquiring about a sick relative in another country, or wanting information about facilities for a sick or disabled person in the country to which they were going. 1960 was designated World Mental Health Year, and so this is the place to mention the prevalence of mental health issues in the cases referred to and from the Branch. Many mental problems are exacerbated by living in a new and strange environment, and ISS has always had to liaise with other organisations to obtain support for sufferers or to negotiate for people to move to a more suitable country.

Case example

Lyn was an English woman, living in the United States with her husband and two young children. The case was referred to ISSGB when she was due to be discharged from hospital following a mental illness. Her marriage was in difficulties and she was encouraged by her parents to return to Britain with her children. However, this meant that she would be refused re-entry to the USA for mental health reasons. The implications of such a move were fully discussed with family members by ISS workers in both countries. In the end she decided to remain in the States, and appropriate counselling help was offered to the family.

An analysis of where referrals came from in one year may demonstrate the wide-reaching nature of the work. For example, in 1965 the figures are as follows:

75 AR 1965.

Referrals from GB		**Referrals from abroad:**	
Clients personally	258	from ISS Branches	249
Children's Departments	261	ISS HQ	20
Family Casework agencies	123	Statutory Services	51
Refugee Societies	46	Voluntary Services	56
Press	33	Embassies	3
Other voluntary organisations	151	Private Individuals	4
Citizen's Advice Bureaux	57	Total:	383
Other Statutory organisations	52		
Private Individuals and Firms	66		
Hospitals	18		
Central Govt Departments	26		
Embassies	4		
Commonwealth Departments	14		
		Total:	1109
		Total of all referrals	1492

Number of Local Authorities in the UK who referred cases or were the agency to which overseas referrals were passed: 63

Number of Countries involved in cases:

Africa	16 countries	87 cases
Europe	23 countries	424 cases
Asia	11 countries	167 cases
USA		276 cases
Rest of the Americas	7 countries	284 cases
Australia and New Zealand		86 cases

Total of 60 countries with 1324 cases.

The discrepancy in the totals is explained by the number of refugees and other foreign nationals in Britain, where no other country is involved in the referral.

Apart from the regular supply of cases, there were four major projects taking place during the 1960s. The first one, bringing Chinese orphans from Hong Kong, began in 1959 and is covered in the previous chapter. The other ones were concerned with adoption, immigrants and cross-cultural marriages.

British Adoption Project 1965–68 – Adoption Resource Exchange (ARE) 1967

During the first years of this decade there was a noticeable increase in the number of cases with the West Indies, as the influx of workers from the Caribbean arrived in Britain, often leaving children behind with relatives. Later, when they had settled, they might send for these children, but there were often problems for the children in adjusting to a very different life, and for both them and their parents difficulties in forming relationships with virtual strangers. Some children were rejected by their families and were received into the care of the Local Authorities. Added to these were children of mixed racial identity, usually born to white mothers and African or West Indian fathers. Although some mixed race children were being adopted, many of them by their long-term foster parents, there were substantial numbers for whom no family placements were found.

Planning for this innovatory project started in 1962, at the instigation of Kay Luce, who set up an Action Committee at ISSGB. A draft project was discussed with representatives from the Home Office and voluntary and statutory child care organisations. Funds were raised for a three-year project, but it did not get off the ground until April 1965, when a Canadian social worker, Mary King was appointed to set up the project. Two other social workers were recruited and a year later Lois Raynor took over and led the project, and wrote the book telling the story – "Adoption of non-white children: the experience of a British Adoption Project, 1970". The ISS collaborated with the Social Research Unit of Bedford College, University of London, and the workers were based in the College.

The main aims of the Project were:

> "First, to provide an adoption service for babies born in England who are either whole or part Asian, African or West Indian; second, to study through research methods those factors which emerge during the process of placing the babies, and to publish a report at the end of a 3 or 4-year period; and third, to offer a liaison service between relevant agencies to facilitate the adoption of such children."[76]

[76] AR65.

Lois Raynor explained that the purpose of the project was not primarily to find homes for as many children as possible, "but rather to learn from a small number what was involved in placing non-European and racially mixed children in Britain, during the years 1965–69".[77]

Although enquiries were made about more than 300 children, most did not proceed to placement. The project only accepted those cases where the mother had received a casework service from the referring agency, and when she had made a firm commitment to place her baby for adoption. 40% of the mothers were students. In two thirds of the cases the father of the baby had acknowledged paternity. By the end of 3 years 53 children had been placed with adoptive parents and legally adopted. 25 of these were of full Asian, African, or West Indian origin and 28 were of mixed racial background. Two-thirds of the babies were placed with adopters before six months of age, and all but 5 of the rest were under a year old, while the oldest child was 24 months old when placed. Some of the applicants to adopt had originally enquired about a child through the Hong Kong Adoption Project.

The project's chief conclusion was that: "children who are of minority race in Britain today can find adoptive parents who will love and cherish them."[78] The most significant innovation was to enable the placement of a child in the care of one authority with prospective adopters recruited by another agency. Lois Raynor wrote: "The Project found that people interested in adopting non-white children often lived in a different county or city from the children needing homes, so in 1967 the staff organised the first Adoption Resource Exchange (ARE) in Britain in order to help agencies to work co-operatively in bringing adopters and children together. Since the Exchange began to operate a year ago, member agencies from most parts of the UK are learning to work together and children are finding homes."[79] The Gulbenkian Foundation made a grant to fund the ARE for three years.

77 Raynor in AR1968.
78 Adoption of Non-white Children by L Raynor, BAAF 1970.
79 Raynor in AR 1968.

The first leader of the ARE was Madeline Carriline and in 1970 she was joined by Phillida Sawbridge, who subsequently ran the ARE for many years. By 1975, 79 agencies, both voluntary and statutory, had joined the Exchange.

The 1975 Children Act required all local authorities to offer a comprehensive adoption service and so ARE was set to expand rapidly. In 1975 the Exchange moved out from ISSGB and became an independent agency, but the Director of ISSGB continued to serve on the Board of the ARE, so the link was maintained. During the seven years since it was founded over 550 children had been placed in adoptive homes, and over 250 were currently listed as needing placement. As well as the non-white babies and toddlers, there were children of school age or over, those in sibling groups, and those with some form of disability. The staff of the British Adoption Project and the ARE had demonstrated emphatically that it was possible to find adoptive families for all sorts of children previously regarded as "unadoptable".

Lois Raynor had predicted that: "organised by ISS through the British Adoption Project, the ARE has aroused much enthusiasm and is expected to grow into a truly national Exchange".[80] These words are an understatement! – from these very small beginnings of the Adoption Resource Exchange a mighty programme emerged – Be My Parent – now under the auspices of BAAF. Through it permanent families have been found for thousands of children. This is certainly the most far-reaching of all the projects that ISSUK was ever involved in.

The London Airport Project 1966–67

In October 1966, after some preliminary discussions between ISS and the Home Office (HO), Maurice Foley, the Minister at the HO responsible for immigration, asked the Council of ISSGB if it would set up a pilot scheme to explore the welfare and social needs of immigrants arriving at Heathrow. The Council felt that such a study would fall within the competence of ISSGB and would follow the pattern of previous studies carried out by ISS

80 Ibid.

internationally. They agreed to operate the scheme for six months, provided that costs could be covered. The HO paid for accommodation at London Airport and the Noel Buxton Trust gave a grant of £4,000 for the research. The primary objectives were:

- "To study the welfare and social needs of immigrants following arrival
- To explore the community resources that can be utilised to give services at the point of settlement
- To provide casework services at the airport, to those travellers referred by Immigration Officers".[81]

Bette Sprung-Miller, an American who had extensive experience of ISS internationally, was appointed to run the project, and a second social worker, Heloise Tindal was soon appointed. The project continued until June of the following year.

The report of the project begins by setting the scene:

> "The activities of the Project at the airport began in the first week of December 1966. Our office was situated adjacent to the Buffer Lounge in No 3 Building, and here we were referred to as "The Welfare Unit". It had been agreed with the HO and HM Inspectors at the airport that the following working principles would be observed:
>
> a) the service would be available to all travellers whatever their origin,
> b) the social workers would not participate in the operation of the immigration control, but would assist with matters referred by the Immigration service, and
> c) the social workers would be in attendance 40 hours a week and relate this to the arrival of the main immigrant flights from India and Pakistan."[82]

From their office the workers could observe all travellers as they passed through Immigration Controls. They noted that many of the travellers were dependants – wives, children or parents –

[81] Report on "Immigrants at London Airport and their settlement in the community" ISS 1967.

[82] Ibid.

coming to join a male relative in Britain. Others were returning residents or students, and, occasionally, a man with an employment voucher. The report says that many had "almost no awareness of the complexities of their new environment, nor of the adjustments that they would have to make."[83]

In the first month there were 17 referrals, the majority from the Indian Sub-Continent. As expected, the majority of problems concerned unaccompanied minors and stranded dependent relatives of people already in Britain. The main role of the ISSGB workers turned out to be to support new arrivals when there was a delay in them being met. It quickly became apparent that very few people needed welfare help at the stage at which they had passed through Immigration, but there was seen to be a need for services to be available to those who were detained for further questioning before being allowed to enter the country, or denied entry. The workers were also asked to help three people in transit who had health problems that prevented them from continuing their journeys.

The identified need for many immigrants was to have appropriate services available in the community where they were going to live. A system was required to identify those who were most vulnerable, and to get them the help they needed. The social workers found that local authorities were only being notified of the arrival of immigrants with Entry Certificates, and the majority of dependants from the Sub-Continent did not have this documentation. So they arranged with the Immigration Service that basic information would be collected for two months on all arrivals from India and Pakistan, and that Medical Officers of Health and Children's Officers would be asked for the dependants in this sample to be visited. There was enough information on about half of the new arrivals, and so almost 700 requests for visits were made: "The comments of the workers who had interviewed the immigrants overwhelmingly demonstrated how important their early contacts were for the welfare of dependants. They showed that they had given attention to immediate health needs and had provided the families with relevant information

83 Ibid.

on matters concerning education, employment and recreation."[84] The social workers visited several Local Authorities and Health Departments in towns which were receiving a high proportion of these immigrants, especially Birmingham, Bradford, Leeds, High Wycombe and various London Boroughs.

The survey also provided information on 387 unaccompanied minors, of whom only 4 were girls. The youngest was 8 years old, but most were about 15. 80% were Muslims from Pakistan and the rest were mainly Sikhs from India. Few had had more than a rudimentary education. Most had left their mother and siblings and come to join their father, in order to work and earn money to be sent back to the home country. In addition, the workers considered the cases of children arriving from Caribbean countries, most of whom were coming to join their mothers in the UK. In both groups there was evidence of problems that arose when insufficient arrangements had been made for the care of these youngsters. The survey "revealed cases where it seemed that it would have been in the child's best interest that he should not have been permitted to come to this country."[85]

Case example

Ravi did not know his age, but looked barely 15. He had come to join his father, but his father then returned to Pakistan, leaving the boy living in a hostel with a number of men. He was working in a factory, but could not tell the worker what it was called or what he was earning. He showed signs of extreme insecurity, and the worker stated that he needed a lot of guidance and help.

In the light of these findings, the final report made three firm recommendations to the Home Office:

1. that a social welfare service should be available at all main points of entry to the UK to offer advice and help with social aspects of migrants' problems. "This service should be given by social workers with an international orientation, and

84 Ibid.
85 Ibid.

should be available to any traveller, before and after he has passed through Immigration controls".[86]

2. there should be a comprehensive system of notification of the arrival of immigrants to the appropriate local authority. There should be one department with responsibility for receiving the information about each new arrival and of seeing that the appropriate social services were alerted to that arrival.
3. in the case of unaccompanied minors under the age of 16, it was proposed that an assessment of the home situation in the UK should be made before the child left the country of origin. It was suggested that Entry Certificates should be mandatory for this age group, and should only be issued after receipt of a satisfactory report on the home.

In addition the report recommended supplementary training for "professional workers who encounter the needs and problems of migrants".[87]

In spite of such clear recommendations, the HO instead tightened immigration regulations (Commonwealth Immigrants Act 1968 and subsequent Rules) so that a Commonwealth child wishing to join one parent in the UK had to prove "compassionate circumstances" – ie to prove some compelling reason why the child could not remain with the parent or relative in the overseas country, and also prove that the parent in the UK had sole responsibility for the child's upbringing. Although this new legislation served to protect Pakistani and Indian youths from being brought here to work under-age in factories and living in all-male households, it also prevented many Caribbean children from joining their single mothers here, which was certainly not the intention of the ISS recommendation. Some workers in the race relations field blamed ISS for providing information to the HO which resulted in this restrictive legislation.

ISSGB was then invited to join a working group at the HO on immigration. This met regularly throughout the early months of 1968 under the Chairmanship of the Immigration Minister, Hon Merlyn Rees MP and presented its report to the HO in July 1968.

86 Ibid.

87 Ibid.

Heloise Tindal described it as a "very lively committee"[88] with some radical voluntary organisations deeply opposed to the proposed legislation. Out of it came the UK Immigration Advisory Service – a voluntary organisation funded by the HO.

Later ISSGB was involved in obtaining reports from overseas for Immigration Tribunals in cases where children were refused entry certificates. Carol Page (ISS social worker from 1995 to 2003) became expert in immigration legislation and developed this part of the ISS service to good effect.

Heloise Tindal joined the staff of ISSGB as worker on the London Airport Project in 1967. When it finished she joined the general social work staff and after her marriage was known as Heloise Kareem. She left in 1974 to have her first child. She returned in 1984 as Co-ordinator of Professional Information, and left in 1988, only to rejoin in 1990 and she then remained at ISS until she retired in 2003. She was responsible for supervision of some of the staff. For the final year she was Deputy Director. However, her links with ISSUK remained and she went to Libya with the group in 2004.

Although she took her fair share of the international cases, it seems that Heloise's outstanding contribution was in the setting up and taking part in various projects, especially the Travel Assistance Scheme, the Foreign Marriage Advisory Service and the Libyan Project. She was very much a focal member of the social work team. "She has been an assiduous supervisor and a contributor internationally to identification of appropriate standards as well as methods of supervision."[89]

Heloise trained as a social worker at the LSE and then worked in voluntary agencies in London and Edinburgh, and went to the United States on an exchange programme, before joining ISSGB. She married the eminent psychotherapist Jafar Kareem.

Foreign Marriage Advisory Service 1964–2003

One part of the work of ISSGB from its foundation was work with British women who had married servicemen from overseas

88 Interview with H Kareem.

89 AR2003.

during or after the war, and who had experienced difficulties or breakdowns of their marriages. Therefore, because of its experience in this work, in August 1964 ISSGB was asked by the FCO to provide "a service of advice to British women considering marriage with men of another nationality, race, religion or culture".[90] The women were referred to them by Registrars, the FCO, foreign embassies and social work agencies. This service differed from the more usual ISS casework in that it was not designed primarily to solve problems, but to offer advice and information, and it did this through direct personal contact, and the provision of information leaflets in a number of different languages, which were provided to Registrars of Marriages.

Heloise Tindal set up this service and in due course Essie Grives ran it. During the first few months 40 young women sought help regarding marriages to men from 22 different countries; most of them were considering marriage but a few were already married. Each woman had an interview with a trained social worker, who would find out how much the woman already knew about her fiancé's country, and how much she had considered the various issues, such as the role of women, her position in the husband's family and the various customs and laws that she would have to observe. Heloise Tindal wrote: "bald information about polygamy, about the lack of a mother's rights, about easy divorce for the husband can be misleading when stated in black and white, but in an interview one can learn something of the girl's expectations of marriage, of her family background, of her ability to adapt to different patterns of living, and of the fiancé's own background and attitudes, and in this context one can discuss together how much importance to attach to the different laws relating to marriage in the fiancé's country".[91] The social workers were horrified by the ignorance and naivety shown by many of the women, but had to go carefully: "There is a fine line to tread between dispelling doubts and injecting realism."[92] If appropriate, a woman could be put in touch with someone from the other country in question.

90 AR 1964.
91 Tindal AR 1970.
92 E Grives AR1990.

By 1966 they had already dealt with requests from about 200 young women, and in the early 70s it is recorded that there was a significant increase in the number of referrals. In 1975 146 clients sought advice regarding marriage with citizens of 42 different countries, but most were with Egypt, Iran and the USA. Finance for the project was a problem, because the Government grant was not sufficient. In 1971 plans for engaging a separate worker to deal full-time with the work was abandoned. This was very disappointing when the need was so obvious. Nevertheless, the project continued for many years, until 2003, though with lower numbers, and ISSGB became a point of contact for workers in other ISS Branches who were dealing with similar cases

Because of the legal complexity of many situations, it was important to have access to good legal help. This was obtained from the Legal Department of the School of Oriental and African Studies (SOAS). The lawyers could give advice if, for example, laws conflicted so that it was not possible for a marriage to be regarded as legal in both countries. In many instances there were questions about the nationality and guardianship of children of mixed marriages.

It is impossible to evaluate the success of such a project, and the workers expressed concerns that in many cases their intervention was too late to prevent unsuitable marriages, but, nevertheless, there must have been many married couples who were helped to a better understanding of each other's cultures.

The experience gained from this gave rise in the 1990s to a project in Libya, which will be described in Chapter 9.

ISS was involved in another aspect of inter-racial marriages by advising those who were affected by a measure announced by the Home Secretary in 1969. This was designed to prevent immigrants from Commonwealth countries from using marriage as a means of living in the country without an employment voucher. It applied both to men seeking to enter the country and also to Commonwealth students who wished to remain after finishing their studies, and who might have a wife and children in Britain. Bizarrely, this meant that it could be easier for a non-Commonwealth immigrant to stay in Britain than one from a Commonwealth country. For some years ISSGB provided assessments for the United Kingdom Immigrant's Advisory Service (UKIAS) in cases where a social assessment was likely to help those lodging an appeal.

Chapter 7

The 1970s

World events

This decade saw more huge mass movements of people, which inevitably highlighted all the familiar problems of migration.

In the chaotic aftermath of the huge cyclone in the Bay of Bengal in November 1970 there were over 4 million displaced people, and then tensions led to civil conflict and the break-up of Pakistan and founding of Bangladesh in December 1971. Over nine million people fled to West Bengal and elsewhere. Many came to Britain. Those who were already in Britain were anxious for news of relatives, but it was extremely difficult for all organisations, including ISS to establish any reliable contact with Bangladesh.

In 1972 thousands of Asians were expelled from Uganda with 90 days warning, and the majority – 27,000 – went to Britain. Most of them had UK passports, but there were problems for some families in which the wives and children had UK passports but the head of the family did not. About one hundred such stateless men were put in a camps, such as one at Greenham Common. UNHCR asked ISSGB to help by providing social histories of each family, on the basis of which UNHCR could press for admission to the UK on compassionate grounds. Heloise Kareem remembers the treks to Greenham Common, where they interviewed families with the help of interpreters. As part of their reports they had to show whether they had any existing connection with the UK, which was a condition of being allowed to stay in Britain. Otherwise they were moved on to Canada, South America or elsewhere. She told me: "it was a very difficult intervention, working among desperate uprooted people."[93] ISSGB also co-

93 Interview with H Kareem.

operated with Branches overseas who were dealing with displaced Asian families.

The Vietnamese war had led to an exodus of refugees including the "boat people". "The German Branch took the lead, with the General Secretariat, in getting together social workers from the concerned ISS Branches and other organisations and exchanging knowledge and experience with colleagues."[94] ISSGB worked with the British Council for Aid to Refugees, particularly to help those who wished to move on to a third country, but also to visit and support those staying in Britain.

By the 1970s the main immigration of workers from Commonwealth countries had slowed down, but there were still many dependants arriving. The strains of adapting to a new country, together with increasing unemployment, led to a lot of family breakdowns.

One of the most significant events for Britain was joining the European Community in 1973. The expansion of the community led to increased movements of people within it, as people had new and better opportunities for jobs and an improved life-style.

Legislation

In this decade the major impacts on the work of ISS were caused by the following:

- Local Authority Social Services Act 1970, which changed the whole structure of Social Services in Britain.
- Immigration Act 1971: this introduced the concept of "patriality" – that only those with strong links to the UK would have the right of abode. Work permits only gave temporary residence. Apart from the five-year residence qualification, the right to live in the UK and enter free from immigration control was determined by birth or parentage, not by nationality.

94 Young People in Migration: Keynote Speech by A Moser at International Council of ISS in 2000.

- Children Act 1975 – This Act required all Local Authorities to provide an adoption service. The most significant clause for ISS was Section 26, which enabled adopted persons to obtain a copy of their original birth certificate. The Act did not, as was widely believed, automatically give adopted people the right to access other information about their adoption, but they could be referred to an adoption agency. This Act led to an increase in the tracing work of ISSGB.
- Adoption Act 1976 – This Act set down a requirement for all Local Authorities to establish and maintain an adoption service. It also had clauses relating to the approval of Adoption Societies, the setting up of an Adopted Children's Register.

ISS Headquarters and the network

1974 was the 50th anniversary of the founding of ISS and a Symposium was held in Geneva on "Migration in the 70s". By now there were 12 Branches and a further 4 Affiliated Bureaux and Delegations.

The Executive Council of the International Council set up an investigation into the structural framework of the ISS. New International Statutes were adopted in 1972, and the Headquarters became the General Secretariat, and the International Director became the Secretary General. Ingrid Gelinek, former Director of the Austrian Delegation, became Secretary General after Robert Menzies stood down in 1971, and remained until the end of 1978 when Audrey Moser succeeded her.

The new Statutes did not alter the original Constitution fundamentally (see also Chapter 2), but it clarified the structure of the ISS as follows:

"• The International Council acts as the General Assembly of ISS and comprises a representative from each Branch and Affiliated Bureau, plus a few elected individuals (Statute 9). This council meets at least once every three years.

- It elects the Executive Committee which is the governing body of ISS and is responsible for the overall policy, programmes and the budget of the General Secretariat

(Statute 10). The Executive Committee is answerable to the International Council. It meets once or twice a year and appoints the Secretary General.

- The General Secretariat (GS) is the operational structure of ISS and co- ordinates its activities. It comprises an administrative department, an inter-country casework department and a Reference Centre for the protection of children in relation to adoption (IRC) (Statute11).
- A national Branch is a body which, having legal status according to its national law, adheres to the Statutes and general principle of ISS, undertakes to promote all the aims of ISS, is organised accordingly, and has been admitted as a member by the International Council (Statute 4.1).
- An Affiliated Bureau is a body linked to the ISS by a special agreement, which may or may not cover the entire activity of the associated body, and has, in this capacity, been admitted as a member by the International Council (Statute 4.2).
- A Correspondent is an organisation or an individual having an agreement with ISS with the purpose of an exchange of services (Statute 9). A Correspondent may attend the International Council meetings as an observer, stand for election as an individual member to the International Council and may use the name of ISS with the agreement of the General Secretariat."[95]

At an international level, co-operation is carried out according to the three following different patterns;

i) Directly between Branches and Affiliated Bureaux (AB).

ii) between Branches/AB and selected Correspondents; ie those deemed by the GS to have a good level of integration into the ISS, adhering to the principles and practices of the organisation.

iii) via the GS for referrals between Branches/AB and all other Correspondents, and inter-country casework between Correspondents.

[95] ISS Manual 2000.

"It is remarkable that in many ways the great strength of ISS at the moment lies not in its independent Branches, but in the network of correspondents in less developed countries. There is no doubt that many of these correspondents, working in very difficult conditions locally, draw strength from their association with ISS, but there is no doubt either that they contribute to the general work of the organisation more than they can ever hope to receive from it. The British social workers know that many of the cases in which they have managed to reunite families, secure the best possible placement for a child, or arrange the return of an elderly person to his native country could not have been successfully completed without the help of a social worker overseas whom neither they nor the client will ever see."[96]

In 1973 there was an ISS Asia-Oceania Conference in Japan to discuss the protection of children across national boundaries, migration and nationality problems, and inter-cultural marriage. ISS became involved in projects to demonstrate feasibility of local adoption and foster care. Unlike the response to the Hong Kong Refugees a decade earlier, ISS now had serious reservations about the practice of removing children for adoption overseas, unless there was really no adequate care available locally. In 1975 there was an ISS seminar on Asian perspectives of inter-country adoption.

"In the ISS caseload during the 1970s and onwards, we observed the growing number of social and legal conflicts connected with adult problems in the form of trans-cultural marriages, separations and divorce – and the consequences for children; questions of care, custody, visiting rights and maintenance."[97] ISS was asked to present cases of child abduction by a parent to the Hague Conference on Private International Law and from its records gave information on 110 cases. This information was used in the preparation of the Convention of 1980 on the Civil Aspects of International Child Abduction.

The Geneva Office sent staff to Vietnam to explore what could be done there, and this led to the setting up of a fostering

96 Young People in Migration: Keynote Speech by A Moser at International Council of ISS 2000.

97 Ibid.

programme for orphans. It also carried out a survey for the UNHCR of unaccompanied minor and handicapped refugees in the camps in Hong Kong. These are mentioned as examples of the many projects set up by the Headquarters and other Branches. These are not directly relevant to the story of ISSUK, except in as much as the staff learned from the experiences of colleagues at the international meetings.

1978 was designated International Year of the Child, and ISS published a book by Peter Fry "The effects of Migration on Families and Children."

The GS staff produce Guidelines for aspects of the work and a Manual for Inter-country casework. Over the years the GS and some of the Branches have produced publications for use by the network and other agencies. The British Branch often contributed to these publications.

ISSGB within the wider ISS

The end of the 1970s and the 1980s was a time of close links between ISSGB and the General Secretariat because the British Audrey Moser went back to Geneva in 1978 as Secretary General, and the Australian Peter Fry left the GS and joined the Council of ISSGB In 1977.

Audrey Moser's connection with ISS was both from working in Geneva, and later as a Trustee of ISSUK. She had been a Civil Servant before qualifying as a child care social worker. She spent some years with the Children's Departments of Berkshire and Oxfordshire before joining the International Union of Child Welfare (IUCW) in Geneva in 1955. She was a field worker in both Asia and Africa, and supervised the care of child victims after the mass displacement of children after the war in Biafra. She was Assistant Editor of the International Child Welfare Review and became Deputy Director of the IUCW. She had worked closely with ISS when at IUCW, particularly in relation to inter-country adoption, as she was instrumental in getting the UN interested in the subject and helped to set up the Leysin Seminar. She joined ISS as Programme Co-ordinator in 1963, and was then Associate International Director until 1970, when she returned to work for IUCW because of disagreements within ISS. Yet eight years later she was invited back to ISS as International Director and served in that role from 1978–1986. "I think that we as a team in Geneva, developed a much closer relationship with the British Branch, because we knew more about the problems they encountered."[98]

Audrey never lost her Civil Service understanding of the need for precision and an attention to detail. She was responsible for seeing that the highest professional standards were set, as shown in her writings and speeches. She expected the best from her staff, but in return was supportive and encouraging.

From 1998–2003 she was a valued member of the Board of ISSUK. The breadth of her knowledge about social work nationally and internationally was tremendous. Therefore, for much of the period covered by this history, Audrey played a central role in developing and maintaining the links between the British Branch and the General Secretariat of ISS. (Interview with AM and comments from colleagues.)

ISSGB office

For the British Branch a major event in 1972 was the move to new premises at Cranmer House, 39 Brixton Road, SW9, where there was more space for the expanding staff team.

Governance

At the end of the decade, ISSGB was no longer eligible for approval as an Adoption Agency (under Section 9 of the Adoption Act 1976), because it was an "unincorporated body". The Adoption Resource Exchange had become an independent body, and so ISSGB was no longer involved in the placement of children for adoption, although it could undertake other aspects of adoption work. Debates about whether to become an incorporated body went on for some time, but then the matter was put to one side, and ISSUK finally became an incorporated body only in 2000. So the charity did not reapply for approval as an Adoption Agency, and in 1977 the Adoption Sub-Committee was dissolved.

98 Interview with A Moser.

Council

When Sir Robert Black retired as Chairman in 1973 he became President, and Sir Stanley Tomlinson was Chairman from 1973–8. He was succeeded by Sir Peter Scott in 1979.

Over the years, there were several married couples, a brother and sister and indeed families, who contributed hugely to ISS. The Wheelers, Luces and Coulsons have already been mentioned. Others were:

The Calvert-Smiths: Stella was one of the earliest Trustees and served on the Council from 1959–1992 and was Vice-Chairman from 1974–79. During this time she served on various Committees, and was Chairman of the Shop Committee from 1976–1980.

Her Husband **Arthur** was a lawyer who was Honorary Legal Advisor to ISSGB from 1968–1989.

Much later, in 2005, their son **David Calvert-Smith**, a High Court Judge and former Director of Public Prosecutions, was elected to the Council of ISSUK. His work did not enable him to attend many meetings, but he proved most helpful in making links between ISSUK and some other institutions.

Sir Geoffrey and Lady (Helen) de Freitas were both very active supporters. **Helen** was a Trustee from 1968–89 and Vice-Chairman from 1970–75. "With her vast international experience, and her deep knowledge of East African countries in which her husband had been UK High Commissioner, she had a strong commitment to international responsibility and co-operation in policy and in meeting the particular needs of individual people. Her contributions to the debates in the UK about the development of the organisation were always helpful and well received."[99] From 1973–9 **Sir Geoffrey** was a British delegate to the European Parliament, and then became International President of ISS from 1979–81.

Sir Robert Black (1906–99) was Chairman 1965–73, President 1974–81 and Honorary Vice-President until his death. "He was deeply respected by members of the Council and the staff. The developments which he helped to initiate remain a living

[99] AR 1998/9.

memorial to him."[100] This refers to the help he gave to the setting up of several projects.

Robert Black was a Colonial administrator who served overseas from the 1930s, starting in Trinidad before moving to the Far East for the rest of his career. He was interned in a Japanese camp during the war and later served as Governor of Singapore from 1955–57 and Governor of Hong Kong from 1958–64.

His sister **Ruth Black** worked for many years for the World Council of Churches, including work with Hungarian refugees in Austria in 1956, and as WCC representative in the Middle East in the late 60s. She spoke fluent Arabic. On her return to Britain she came to work as a volunteer for ISSGB in 1975. She is listed as Refugee worker until 1977 and then from then until 1992 she was Refugee Consultant. She worked with recipients of pensions from the British Council for Aid to Refugees (BCAR), visiting them regularly. She died in 1998.

Annual general meetings

It was the custom to invite a distinguished figure from a relevant field to talk at the AGM each year. For example, during the 70s the speakers included: in 1972 Sir Geoffrey de Freitas on the Council of Europe, in 1975 Mr van Hoogstraten, Secretary General of the Hague Conference, and in 1976 Mrs Sarah Curtis on UNICEF.

Staff and volunteers

Winifred Rouse remained Director throughout the 1970s – indeed up to 1990.

Winfred Rouse – known as Win – was a hospital almoner (medical social worker) before joining ISSGB in 1966, and becoming Director in 1967. She was described as a formidable woman, of whom some members of staff were a bit scared, but she did show empathy to clients and was regarded as a good social worker. She was a hard worker, but was not always good at delegating. She had a somewhat conservative approach to new work, but this may have been caused by a determination to keep within the budget as far as possible. In spite of this,

[100] AR 1999/2000.

during her 23 years as Director the organisation continued to expand.

She had served at Bletchley Park in the war, and then married Victor Serebriakoff, a fellow member and promoter of MENSA, who later became President of that organisation. She died in 1995.

In the early days of the organisation there seems to have been a feeling that staff who worked for charities should accept low salaries for philanthropic reasons. So there was an over-reliance on middle-aged married women who were not dependent on their salary as their only source of income.

In 1970 there were just three caseworkers, Winifred Klingender, Jean Martin and Heloise Tindal, plus the two workers of the Adoption Resource Exchange. However, during the following years, a number of other staff joined, and the team took on an international flavour. Each brought a different experience and expertise to the job. In 1971 came Otilia Charlton, a Chilean, who stayed for two years, a Canadian James Weber, and Frances Killick. The following year Judy Clark joined the staff, and then Carol Page came in 1972. These last three were British. An Australian, Essie Grives came in 1974 and in 1976 Jacqueline Lee, a Jamaican became responsible for the Travel Assistance Scheme until she retired due to ill health in 1981. In 1977 a Zambian, Nkathazo Ngubo, joined ISSGB.

At the end of the decade, Ruth Ellis and Ruth Furnival joined the team. Ruth Ellis worked for ISSGB for 11 years, from 1977–88. She had trained as a psychiatric social worker and brought that perspective to the work, which was very useful, given the number of cases with a mental health component. Ruth Furnival had worked in the social work department of the DOH and provided a useful link with that Department from 1978–89. Another Ruth – Ruth Eames – who spent 23 years with ISS, as Fair organiser and for some years as Director's Secretary and then Appeals Secretary, retired in 1980. Add to them Ruth Black, the volunteer with refugees, and there must have been some confusion in the office!

Jean Martin was another of the very long-serving members of staff, joining the Branch in 1963 and retiring in 1987. The following warm tribute was paid to her when she left: "We are conscious every day of the gap she has left and it is not an exaggeration to say that her place can never quite be filled.This is not only because of the length of her ISS experience, intelligence, international knowledge and exceptional personality: Jean did much more than her excellent work on the intercountry cases. She was a very good ambassador for ISS in many circles and always willing to speak at meetings on our behalf. She helped at the Spring Fair and supported any other efforts we undertook. Officially a part-time social worker, she put in more hours than most of us."[101]

Judy Clark worked as a social worker at ISSUK from 1972–78 and 1981–2001. No other member of staff has equalled her total of almost 28 years with the organisation. Before joining ISS Judy worked in the London Boroughs of Islington and Brent. She wrote: "I did general ISS casework in my first period at ISS (including Travel Assistance – we all did a bit of that). When I came back in 1981 Win specifically asked me to do tracing. This, due to demand, led to more work in the direction of adoption."[102] In 1994 she agreed to take the lead role in relation to the intercountry adoption work. She was a most assiduous and effective social worker. Her development of the tracing work undoubtedly enhanced the reputation of ISSUK.

In 1978 a socio-legal assistant called Mark Pilgrim was appointed, and stayed for two years. He had a law degree and had studied foreign legal systems. He was able to advise on individual cases, to research into issues relevant to the work and build up a resource base for the social workers.

The organisation continued to rely heavily on volunteers – who visited refugees and helped with the accounts, administration and fundraising.

Finances and fundraising

In 1971 the first government grant, of £10,000 a year for three years, was received for the core work, rather than for projects.

In spite of this, the financial situation fluctuated throughout the 1970s. At the end of 1970 the reserves, which should have been enough to cover the running costs for three months, had

101 AR1987.

102 Comment from J Clark.

dropped to £5,500. In 1977 notes in Council Minutes expressed concern because there was no money for a member of staff to travel to an important international conference, and deplored the lack of any overall plan for fundraising.[103] In 1979 the deficit was worse than it had ever been – over £5,000. Heavy inflation caused costs to rise, especially costs of communication which, of course, was central to the work. Fortunately, by the following year a number of legacies improved the financial position of the charity.

The fundraisers were always thinking of new ways of obtaining funds. One new venture was to open a charity shop in Churton Street, Pimlico, London in 1975. It moved a year later to 1 Ranelagh Road, SW1. A Shop Committee was formed to oversee the running of it. Although it enjoyed a modest success, the shop closed in early 1984 when the lease ended and the rent was considered to be too high.

There were four radio appeals during the 1970s.

Links with other agencies

During the 70s ISSGB was listed as being represented on, or remaining affiliated to, the same social work agencies, refugee agencies and relevant government departments, as was noted in the previous chapter. However, I have found no records of how closely involved the ISSGB workers were with most of these other organisations, apart from the good links with Government Departments in relation to the various projects, and with Local Authority workers in relation to the casework.

But this was not true of adoption agencies, with whom there is plenty of evidence that Winifred Klingender had good links. For example, in 1970 ISSGB gave evidence to the Houghton Committee on the Adoption of Children, and in the late 70s Winifred contributed significantly to the BAAF publication "Intercountry Adoption – some basic guidelines for social workers" 1979.

103 Council Minutes 21.4.77.

Casework

1971 was a year of great change in social work in Britain, with the formation of new Social Service Departments. Social workers who had previously specialised in child care, mental health or welfare of the elderly and disabled, found themselves required to deal with all these groups. In the short-term there was a lot of confusion, but in the longer term work was streamlined – one social worker could tackle work that would formerly have been the responsibility of staff of three departments. This was beneficial in that all cases regarding work overseas could be referred to and from the same department, and ISSGB took the opportunity to make fresh contacts in the new departments, and also issued new guidelines for the referral of cases.

Although the presentation of figures varies over the years, making comparisons difficult, it happens that for each year of this decade there was a similar statistical summary in the Annual Report, except that the Adoption Resource Exchange became independent after 1975. These figures give an idea of the different groups of cases dealt with, but no figures can show how much time was spent on each case.

Cases referred:		**1970**	**1975**	**1979**
Inter-country cases:	new –	1,010	1,424	1,427
	re-opened	139	92	123
Foreign Marriage Advisory service		77	146	221
Elderly Refugees cases		157	86	103
Adoption Resource Exchange babies placed:		46	123	–
		1,429	1,871	1,874
Enquiries:				
Adoption Resource Exchange		919	1,621	-
Intercountry adoption		121	406	332
General		301	842	2,082
		1,342	2,869	2,414
Numbers of countries involved in the work:		83	98	110

"The categories which specifically concern children make up forty per cent of the year's total. In addition, of course, children are also involved in a large number of other cases. Most often, these figures represent efforts to try to ensure that children caught up in international problems of one sort of another are enabled to grow up with the people best able to care for them in the countries which seem to offer them most hope for the future. This is an awesome responsibility which makes immense demands on the casework skills of ISSS social workers and their co-operating agencies everywhere."[104]

Consultation Service – Duty System

From the start of ISSGB social workers had been available to answer telephone enquiries, but as these increased there was need for a more systematic approach. In the Annual Report of 1973 there is the first mention of the Consultation Service, which in due course became known as the Duty System and then the Advice Line. One of the social workers was on duty each day to receive and deal with telephone enquiries and personal callers. Some enquiries could be dealt with quickly, while others might require some investigation before resolving the issue or taking the case on as a referral; ie a case that required ongoing work and negotiation with an overseas correspondent. Calls came from individuals, local authorities, Citizens Advice Bureaux, Foreign and Commonwealth Office (FCO), embassies, press and a number of other agencies. The calls covered a very wide range of topics, and social workers became skilled at knowing where to find out the more obscure pieces of information.

Tracing and Contact Service

The work of ISS had always included the tracing of missing relatives, but this work was developed into a distinct specialism within ISSUK in the 1970s by Judy Clark. It operated both in relation to requests from people in Britain seeking relatives abroad, and also referrals from ISS colleagues in other countries about people seeking their relatives in the UK. ISS tracing was restricted to searches where there was a social work component to the case, as well as an international one. The aim of the work

[104] AR 1975.

was to facilitate direct or indirect contact between family members, if appropriate, as long as both parties consented to it. "It was the usual practice for ISSUK to act as intermediary, particularly in socially sensitive cases such as children separated from parents by divorce or adoption."[105]

Judy Clark, who was later assisted by Lesley Austen from 1995, established the most efficient ways of working, including co-operation with the two other major tracing agencies, the Red Cross and Salvation Army. They knew how to access all possible information in the public domain, from a number of government departments. Similarly, their colleagues in other ISS units were often able to access information in their countries. This area of work differed from the bulk of the casework, most of which ISS undertook on behalf of other agencies, as the Tracing Officers dealt directly with the clients. Sometimes this would be by letter or phone, but often there would be a number of meetings between the worker and client. Enquiries could take many months, and clients were kept up to date with the progress of the searches. In an effort to make this part of the work self-supporting each person requesting the service was asked to make a donation, and to pay for all documents that were obtained.

> "So often the requests are from elderly parents who have not heard from their children for years, and now feel they may never see them again before they die. These cases present great difficulties and need very tactful handling, but when they are successful they are extremely rewarding in a very immediate way."[106]

The work increased substantially after the Children Act 1975 gave adopted people the right to see their original birth certificates, and thus have an increased chance of tracing their birth families.

This work demanded great sensitivity on the part of the staff members. Although many enquiries led to happy outcomes, in some cases the circumstances of the relatives, once traced, might

[105] Comment from J Clark.
[106] J Clark in AR 1976.

come as a shock to the enquirer. Hopes of meeting would be dashed by news that the relative was dead or did not wish to re-establish contact. Some people turned out to have had tragic or difficult lives, or just very different lives from those seeking them.

Occasionally it turned out that the relatives had no common language. Therefore, there was much to be done in the way of preparation and counselling.

The total number of people who were helped by this service is not known, as the statistics are no longer available for every year. But, taking 1991 as a sample year – there were about 200 enquiries and the missing relatives were traced and contact renewed in 35% of the cases; a similar number were traced but did not want contact and the rest could not be found. There were many more enquiries which could not be followed up for lack of adequate information.

There has been no research into this work, and any evaluations are difficult, because what may be seen as success; eg renewing contact, may not be a good experience for everyone, while for others whose relatives cannot be traced, the fact of knowing that every avenue has been explored may be a satisfactory outcome. However, the volume of messages of gratitude to the staff demonstrate that the service was highly valued by many.

This tracing work also had an impact on other areas of work: "we have been made very much aware, from our programmes for adults seeing to reconnect with their birth families, of the importance of providing an ongoing service to keep contacts going when families have split up."[107]

Lesley Austen joined ISSUK in 1995 as assistant to Judy Clark. She took over as the Tracing and Contact Officer when Judy left in 2001. She carried out her task with thoroughness and empathy for those involved. She took immense trouble with every case, and offered a first class service. However, by 2007 it had become clear that other agencies were doing similar work and enquirers could be referred to them. Also, the growth of the internet enabled people to do a lot of searching themselves, although they might still need access to counselling and support while doing so. At the same time, the CSCI review of ISSUK as

[107] AR2001–2.

an Adoption Support Agency highlighted the fact that only qualified social workers could do post-adoption counselling, and Lesley, in spite of her immense experience and skill, was not a qualified social worker. Furthermore, the financial situation of ISSUK required cutbacks to the service, and so in 2008 the Tracing and Contact Service was terminated, and Lesley just stayed on for a few months to finish outstanding work. This was the end of service that had been widely used and highly regarded, and was a blow to many in the organisation.

Case examples

Sarah had been born in Ceylon and adopted there by a British couple. She was brought up by them in the UK. When she became adult she had the support of her adoptive parents to search for her birth parents. Enquiries showed that they had emigrated to Australia. A discreet approach was made to them and they were happy to renew contact and a successful reunion eventually took place.

Michael was living in Portugal when he contacted the Tracing Officer because he wanted to know why he had spent part of his young childhood in an orphanage in the south of England, before going to live with his paternal uncle. He had not asked about his past while with his uncle, but was now curious. His mother had an unusual name and so it was possible to trace her. She had died but the records gave details of the problems she had had with mental illness, which had led to her son going into care.

The correspondent in Cyprus contacted ISSUK on behalf of a grandmother who was worried about her daughter and granddaughter Julie, aged 3. She had lost contact with them, as they were living at a secret address in the north of England following a divorce from an abusive husband. ISSUK contacted the local authority, who traced the family, and contact was resumed with the grandmother.

Paul in New Zealand wanted to trace his daughter in the UK who would now be adult. He understood that she had been adopted and he wanted to pass on to her his family history, including medical information. As his name was not on her original birth certificate, the General Records Office would not give him any information. He was advised to put his name on the Adoption Contact Register, to show that he would be willing to be contacted by her should she wish this.

At the end of the decade a referral came from a hospital which was treating a mentally ill Cambodian man, Sam. He was very anxious to find out what had happened to his family in Cambodia with whom he had lost contact since he fled the country. The doctors said that it would help his recovery to have some information. The Correspondent in Cambodia made enquiries and found out that his parents and brother had disappeared during the Pol Pot regime and were assumed to have died, along with everyone in their village. Although this was bad news, it enabled the man to give up his false hopes of reuniting with his family and to start facing up to what had happened in Cambodia.

Repatriation

There was an increase in the number of "elderly British in all parts of the world who, as they become infirm and find themselves in financial difficulties, decide to return to Britain."[108] Those without close family members to help, might turn to the ISS for assistance in making connections with the necessary agencies and services.

ISSGB had also been dealing with cases of those in Britain wishing to be repatriated overseas, and this led to the start of the longest running of all ISSUK projects.

The Travel Assistance Scheme 1971–2012

In 1971 ISSGB was asked by the Home Office to operate a voluntary Repatriation Scheme under the provisions of Section 29 of the Immigration Act 1971. (Later, the Scheme came under Section 58 of the Nationality, Immigration and Asylum Act 2002.) This dealt with repatriation for immigrants who had "settled status" in the UK, and who had been in the UK for at least three

108 AR75.

years, and who voluntarily wished to return permanently to their country of origin, or some third country. This was a difficult and somewhat controversial project for ISSGB to undertake – the word repatriation had developed emotive overtones with a flavour of compulsion, far removed from the philosophy of ISS, and so the name was changed to the Travel Assistance Scheme. It caused the resignation of the Legal Advisor to the Council, Louis Blom-Cooper, who objected to it on the grounds that he considered it to be racist. Some workers in the fields of race relations and welfare rights were critical of the project, but then useful support for it came from the politician Bernie Grant, and gradually, over the years the sensitive work by the ISS social workers led to a change of attitude among other workers.

Most of the applicants gave one or more of the following reasons: retirement, old age, poor health or unemployment, or just inability to settle. ISSGB had the duty of seeing that repatriation was in a person's or family's interests, and so this could involve them in making enquiries overseas, as well as interviewing all members of the family in Britain. The role of the ISS worker was to ascertain the feasibility of every application, by discussing with all applicants their economic circumstances, accommodation prospects in the home country and the nature of the relationships to people they expected to help them on their return. The workers tried to help them all to understand the implications of repatriation, and the difficulties that might face them. Sometimes the applicants had an unrealistically rosy picture of life "back home", when the reality was widespread unemployment and lack of resources. In a few cases the family was divided, with some members wanting to return while others preferred to remain in Britain.

Case examples

Jacob, applied to the scheme for him and his wife to return to the West Indies because his wife was developing dementia and was now only able to talk about her early life in Barbados. Enquiries to Barbados confirmed that there were resources there to help them, and some cousins were keen to help them too. It took some months to arrange everything, but eventually they were safely settled back in her home town.

Mona had come from Trinidad in 1966 to train as a nurse and had worked for many years in Britain. But she suffered a stroke and could not work, and so applied to return to her home country. ISSUK helped her to obtain a Trinidadian passport and made arrangements for her belongings to be shipped to Trinidad. They provided an escort to take her there, where she was greeted by relatives.

Travel Assistance was not available to people who had assets or income that enabled them to pay for their passages themselves, and so those applying were a poor and vulnerable group. Once accepted, they received help with their fares and the cost of shipping a small amount of baggage. No resettlement grant was paid, and there were no programmes set up to help people reintegrate, and rarely any social benefits. So the returnees were usually dependent on help from family or friends. It is not surprising that a large number of those making initial enquiries decided to go no further. On a brighter note, some applicants had acquired skills that enabled them to obtain work on their return home. The ISSGB social workers spent a considerable amount of time on these cases, not only those being repatriated, but also those of the unsuccessful applicants, for whom other solutions to their problems had to be sought.

In the first year of operation 1972 there were 301 applications of which 39 were approved for repatriation; 85 were found to be ineligible, 160 withdrew and 17 were still being investigated at the end of the year. The 39 families repatriated varied from 9 single people to a mother with 8 children.

In the year 1976–7 110 persons went to 12 different countries. "34 East African Asians went to Canada, 31 persons to Jamaica, 21 to Nigeria and the remaining 24 to Grenada, Mauritius, Somalia, Pakistan, Malaysia, Barbados, Ghana, Trinidad and Bangladesh ... the ages in this group ranged from 7 months to 71 years, with 9 applicants being over 60. The applicant who had stayed longest had resided in the UK for 49 years. There were 37 children of whom 29 were born in Britain. Eighteen heads of household were unemployed."[109]

109 AR1977.

The figures increased slightly in the following years. The peak was reached in 1981 when a total of 218 people from 92 families left Britain. In 1998 there were 209 enquiries about the service. "After talking the issues through and discussing the eligibility requirements with the enquirers 42 applications were received. Of these, 33 cases, involving 50 individuals, returned to their original countries, which were: Australia, Barbados, Congo, Dominica, Ghana, Jamaica, Mauritius, Seychelles, St Lucia and St Maarten. A few cases followed family breakdown, but the majority were elderly people wishing to return home, because of illness or loneliness following the death of a spouse."[110] By 2009 only 12 people were repatriated. The cases had become more complex, and larger proportion of applications was from those who had been unable to settle in the UK, and were unemployed, homeless, or with mental health problems. Marek Ganther wrote: "it is important to work alongside the other professionals involved. We must be satisfied that someone is able to understand all the implications of the scheme, and be able to make an informed decision."[111] Many were found to be unsuitable for the scheme, so the low figures do not reflect the numbers who were helped.

Heloise Tindal started this project, then Ann Preston and Frances Killick worked on it for a couple of years until Jacqueline Lee, who was herself from the West Indies, took on the responsibility for it from 1976–1981. Nkathazo Ngubo also worked on the programme from 1978–83. Phyllis Jackson, also from the West Indies, joined ISSGB in 1982, and ran this scheme until she retired in June 1999, when Marek Ganther took over the role.

The project was funded by a Home Office grant, which had to be re-applied for every 3 years. It came to an end in 2012, when the Government stopped funding for it, in spite of evidence that it saved the Government a significant amount of money. However, the result of the project was that, by the end of 2009, over 2,800 people from 1,460 families had been repatriated. There was no systematic follow-up to evaluate the success of

110 AR1999.

111 Travel Assistance Annual Report 2007–8 by M Ganther.

these returns, and the many messages of appreciation only show that the initial effects of repatriation were positive in many cases. However, the fact that the project was able to continue for so long can be taken as some proof of its value.

Work with foreign prisoners

From time to time ISSGB was asked by Prison Welfare Officers to handle the overseas end of family problems of foreign prisoners. This might be to let the family know what had happened to the prisoner, or to get news of the family for the prisoner. As early as 1962 it is noted that such cases involved Nigeria, Pakistan, Hong Kong and Cyprus.[112]

In 1978 there was a request from the Government for ISSGB to set up a programme to help foreign prisoners in British jails, but this was not followed up due to pressures of work. However, ISS staff were able to deal with occasional requests for help.

Case example

A referral was received from Holloway Prison about Tunde, a woman from West Africa imprisoned for drug trafficking. Her two children remained in the home country with relatives. During a recent phone call, one daughter hinted that she was being abused by an uncle, and the mother was very worried and causing disruptions in the prison. The ISS correspondent was able to locate the family and ascertain that the children were all right, and that the daughter admitted that she had told her mother that story to get her attention (or perhaps to punish her for leaving them?)

[112] AR1962–3.

Chapter 8

The 1980s

World events

Some of the most searing pictures of the mid-80s were of the famine in Ethiopia, which followed earlier famines and years of conflict in that country. In subsequent years many people found any means they could to escape from the conditions there. Often they did not have any documentation and arrived in Britain or elsewhere as asylum seekers. Other migrants continued to arrive from all over the world.

Legislation

- The British Nationality Act of 1981 introduced several categories of British nationality, each with different rights, and removed the automatic right of Commonwealth citizens to be British subjects. It also tightened the citizenship criteria on foreign spouses.
- In 1983 the Hague Convention on Civil Aspects of Child Abduction 1980 came into force. It had two goals: to secure the prompt return of children wrongfully removed or retained, and to guarantee access rights of children and parents
- UN Convention on the Rights of the Child 1989: ratified by the UK in 1991. It contains 54 articles, including those concerning the rights to protection from various forms of harm, and rights to family life or appropriate alternative care. Article 3 of the Convention states: "In all actions concerning children ... the best interests of the child shall be a primary consideration."[113] These principles the ISS had always held,

113 UN Convention on the Rights of the Child.

but the organisation was now enabled to refer to the Convention to back up its actions.

- Children Act 1989 – confirmed the principle that the best interests of children should always be paramount, and that undue delay should be avoided in reaching decisions about children's futures. It also provided guidance on private fostering.

ISS General Secretariat

In October 1980 the ISS headquarters in Geneva moved to new premises at 32 Quai du Seujet, and it is still there at the time of writing.

Audrey Moser was Secretary General until 1986, and her deputy was Damien Ngabonziza, a Rwandan who had joined the ISS as a social worker with the ISS in 1980. From 1986 to 1989 the SG was a Canadian, Marcelle Brisson, and then in 1989 Damien Ngabonziza took over as Secretary General.

ISSGB within the wider ISS

The close links between ISSGB and Geneva continued, with Sir Clive Bossom as International President for 5 years from 1984 to 1988 inclusive. Both he and Sir Geoffrey de Freitas went on tours with Audrey Moser to visit a variety of ISS units.

This was a decade of continuing financial problems, not just for the General Secretariat but also for Branches, especially the American Branch. However, in the 1980s ISS Regional Representatives were established in Latin America and East Asia.

In 1980 ISS was granted Observer Status to the Committee of Experts at the Conference of European Law in relation to adoption. In 1982, ISS co-operated with ICSW and UN Centre for Social Development and Humanitarian Affairs, to draft a UN Declaration on Social and Legal Principles relating to the Protection and Welfare of Children, with special reference to Foster Placement and Adoption.

In 1987 ISS published a "Field Guide for the Care and Protection of Unaccompanied Children in Emergencies" – by

Audrey Moser and Jan Williamson. The purpose of this Guide was to help prevent hasty action in emergency situations, whether natural disasters or man-made conflicts, where families were separated. It stressed the importance of obtaining maximum information about each child and the circumstances of separation, in the hope of reuniting children with their families quickly, but also to provide information for future tracing should children be removed to another country.

Council

In 1982 Sir Michael Palliser took over from Sir Robert Black as President.

Sir Peter Scott was Chairman from 1979–1984, but remained as Vice-Chairman until 1990. He was also a member of the International Council. He was succeeded as Chairman by Peter Foster, who was ex-army. Peter Foster resigned in 1989 following a stroke.

The Trustees always came from a number of influential backgrounds – the majority from the diplomatic community, and many from the business world. Others had specialist financial, legal, governmental, charitable or social work expertise. But, after Kay Luce retired as a Trustee in 1982, Peter Fry was the only social worker member of Council for much of the 1980s.

Staff

There was a small increase in staff numbers during the 80s, from a total of 16 in 1980 to 19 ten years later. Winifred Rouse continued as Director. From 1980, and throughout the decade, Jenny Jessup was her Personal Assistant.

Chris Platt joined in 1980 as clerical officer for a couple of years, and was also administrator of the Travel Assistance Scheme. An addition to the administrative team was Ian West, who kept the accounts from 1979 to 2000. He was self-employed and worked part-time on a consultancy basis, and his contribution over the years was invaluable.

On the social work side, Dawn Temple came to ISSGB in 1985 and worked there until 1997. She was originally from

Canada and had lived in Hong Kong, giving her a particular understanding of Chinese culture. She was also responsible for helping to set up the Unaccompanied Children Scheme in the 1990s. "During her for 12 years she contributed much to the Branch, among other contributions she set up a series of lunch time meetings for social workers from statutory and voluntary organisations, to exchange experience and ideas about working with unaccompanied young people from abroad."[114]

There continued to be a variety of nationalities in the staff team. Jacqueline Lee left in 1981 due to ill health, but that year Violah Makewa from Zimbabwe joined the staff for a couple of years, followed by the Jamaican Phyllis Jackson in 1982. Isabel Aragoneses, a Spaniard, came in 1989 and was particularly useful in checking documents about adoption from South America. Judy Clark commented: "I particularly remember our delight at appointing Isabel because of her European background and experience, and also her relative youth".[115]

Essie Grives was an Australian, who had worked in the ISS Australian Branch and then came to work for ISSGB in 1974 and retired twenty years later, in 1994. She took over the running of the Foreign Marriage Advice Service. For many years she supervised staff, and she had particular expertise on legal issues in relation to child abduction. "Her contribution to the professional work of the organisation was of national and international significance. She gave a social work perspective to meeting at The Hague Conference of Private International Law. This was particularly important in regard to the revision of the 1961 Convention on the Protection of Minors."[116] From 1991 she was Deputy Director. She was described as being very conscientious and good at ferreting out details. Judy Clark said:

> "Her real strengths, apart from those already mentioned, lay in supporting the social work staff – both in professional and personal matters."[117] Heloise Kareem told me that Essie held the social work staff group together during changes of Director.

114 AR1997.
115 J Clark comment.
116 AR 1994.
117 Comment from J Clark.

Technology

There had been improvements in the office too. It was reported that David Todd and Christopher Platt "had enormously improved our registration and filing system".[118] By 1985 most ISS Branch offices had Telex machines and some were installing Fax machines. One report refers to the wonders of being able to receive an answer by Fax within 40 minutes. But of course this was dependent on the recipient having a fax machine, and in many Correspondent countries the technology lagged far behind that in the Branches. By the end of the decade ISSGB was falling behind other organisations with regard to new technologies, especially computers.

Publicity

There was a trickle of articles in the press, usually in relation to a specific area of work. But it was always difficult to maintain the momentum, given all the other calls on staff time. H Kareem wrote: "As well as informing the public it is also important that we communicate with our policy makers. ISS offices are packed full of information about the specific problems of people in migration, and in a very real sense we are experts. However, it has not always been easy to extract this information and make it known to the relevant Government bodies. We are trying to find appropriate ways to do this."[119]

Finances and fundraising

This was a period of galloping inflation and unprecedented unemployment in Britain. The budget was in deficit at the beginning of the decade but a series of government grants throughout the decade gave a degree of stability. Nevertheless, the staff had to manage the available resources very carefully.

Staff salaries had always been lower than equivalent salaries in local authorities or major voluntary agencies, but were now falling even further behind. In 1980 an Internal Review was set

118 AR1980.

119 International Social Service of Great Britain 1974–84. A Report by H Kareem 1984.

up to look at comparative salaries. The new recommended salary scale started at £5,000.

In 1983 the South London Action Group was formed, which became the Thames Area Support Committee – it raised £900 in its first year. David Todd was the organiser and Chris Platt was a volunteer. In 1987 the Christmas Bazaar in Battersea Town Hall raised £2,000. The Group was finally disbanded in 1990 having raised over £11,000 for ISSGB. But the money raised isn't the only important thing – all fund-raising events introduce ISS to a new group of people, many of whom continue to give valuable support.

Links with other agencies

Throughout the 1980s the only available documents are the Annual Reports and some Council Minutes. There are few mentions of links with other agencies, but it is recorded that the Director was on the Executive Board of the UK Immigrant Advisory Service, and a member of the Joint Co-ordinating Committee for refugees from South East Asia, set up by the Home Office.[120]

Casework

In 1984 Heloise Kareem returned to ISSGB to look at trends in inter-country cases. She wrote:

> "The one thing that has not changed is the vast range of seemingly insoluble problems which are presented daily in the office. I am continually impressed with all the careful thought and imagination that goes into the correspondence. No one case is exactly like another. Although the annual number of cases handled by ISSGB has remained fairly constant over the last ten years, the nature of our intervention has changed and ISSGB is increasingly seen to play a more direct and positive role in a number of its inter-country cases. There has been a dramatic increase in the number of self-referrals (from 264 in 1974 to

[120] Council Minutes 10.9.80.

511 in 1983) often involving ISS social workers in numerous office interviews. Formerly, interviews with clients usually occurred only in Foreign Marriage Advisory and Repatriation cases, but social workers now find it valuable to handle other cases directly too, particularly where the case is internationally complex."[121]

"Another development has been that ISS workers often have more involvement with the decision-making process within local Social Service Departments, for example by participating in a case conference to decide on future plans for a child, and in general there has been more face-to-face discussion with social workers in the field."[122] Such decisions usually related to the placement of children.

Assessments of families overseas for return or placement of a child

There are several reasons why requests are made for the assessment of a family overseas. These concern the reuniting of families, or the placement of children with relatives in another country. This topic was introduced in Chapter 4, but will be developed here. There are also many cases that are concerned with re-establishing contact between children and their parents or other family members, but these are considered in the next chapter.

i) The largest group of children includes those in the UK for whom there is a possibility of placement with relatives overseas. When children cannot live with their birth parents, it has always been good practice to investigate the possibility of placing them with other relatives in preference to placement with strangers, as long as such a placement would be in their best interests, and this has been a requirement of British law since 1989. There are difficult questions to be considered about placements overseas, particularly when children have never known the family members with whom they might be placed. For example, what priority should be given to the blood tie and cultural identity? Would it be in a child's interests to be brought up by his closest relatives,

121 Ibid.

122 Ibid.

who want to care for him, if they live in a country with fewer facilities and more limited life chances than those in the country in which he is currently living? Would the child's developmental needs be met? What effect would it have on a child to leave all familiar people and relationships? In other words, what should be the dominant criteria in making a decision?

So this immediately shows the need for as thorough an assessment of the child's history, current situation, social, educational and emotional development, language, attachments and any special needs, as would be done when considering a placement in this country. This will then be considered alongside a good assessment of the family and their social and economic situation; information about how well the relatives know the child in question, and their likely capacity to understand and respond to his or her present situation and cultural and psychological needs. It is necessary also to know about the level of supervision and support that would be available should the child be placed with the family overseas.

Two further factors come into play here: on the one hand, the alternatives for placement available to the authorities in the UK, and on the other hand both the short and long-term prospects for each child. If there are relatives overseas who already have a good relationship with a child then that may influence a decision towards placement with them. Alternatively, if there is a good placement available for a child in the UK then any decision may be weighted in favour of leaving the child where his or her needs can be met, often in an already familiar environment. In some cases the fact that major cultural adjustments would be required might be a valid reason for questioning a placement overseas, if a child has lived in a westernised country for many years and knows nothing of life in the country of origin, or of the family offering him or her a home. But, although this may seem right at the moment – and almost invariably it will be easier than moving a child overseas – it may be that the longer-term benefits of being placed within the family and culture of origin override the drawbacks of any possible dislocation from a present placement. This is a particularly important consideration with regard to children and young people without British citizenship, who may face deportation at the age of 18.

Furthermore, the views of the children have to be taken into consideration, if they are of an age to understand the implications of the options being discussed. That means that every effort has to be made to help them understand what life would be like with relatives in another country.

Case examples

Ronan was 3 years old when ISSUK received a request to investigate an application by his grandparents in the Canary Islands to look after him, because he had been taken into care following neglect by his drug-abusing parents. A positive report was obtained, and the grandparents came to be near Ronan for a few weeks before taking him back to live with them.

Mehreen – born of Pakistani parents, who had come to the UK when the mother was 6 months pregnant. At 3-month-old the baby was admitted to hospital with non-accidental injuries, and, after careful assessment, it was decided that the baby should not be left in his parents' care. Meanwhile, ISSUK was asked to find out whether the family in Pakistan could take the child, although the couple had been very against this idea. A report came back, saying that the couple had no contact with their families in Pakistan because theirs was a "love marriage", made without the consent of either family. There would be no support, and even a risk to their lives if they returned to Pakistan. ISSUK relayed this information to the local authority, and later they heard that Mehreen had been adopted by an Anglo-Pakistani family in the UK.

Patrick was 9 when his mother died and he came into the care of the Local Authority. He was placed in a foster home. Nothing was known of his father, but he had an aunt and uncle in Ireland whom he had visited twice on holiday. They offered him a home and so ISSUK was asked to arrange for an assessment on the family. The report was satisfactory, and the aunt and uncle were keen to have him, but it turned out that Patrick did not want to move to Ireland and wanted to stay with his foster parents. There were pros and cons to both placements, but eventually it was decided that the foster parents would adopt Patrick, and that he would visit his relatives in Ireland regularly.

ii) There are different issues to consider with the second group of children – those who have come to the UK, having been separated from the relatives in the country from which they have come, so that the question is whether or not they can and should return to that country. The task is usually to find out where their relatives are and decide whether the children can return to them, or at least have contact with them. It is not just a matter of establishing facts, but also of finding out whether the children would be safe and adequately cared for if they were to return. An understanding of the reasons for the separation is crucial, because, whilst some parents or other relatives will be thrilled at the prospect of being reunited with a missing child, others may not want this at all. This may be the case with unaccompanied minors coming to the UK. Some parents have encouraged their children to migrate, in the hope that the child can get a foothold, for example in Europe, so that they can follow in due course. They may be hostile to any suggestion that their child be returned to them, although there have been examples of families who have regretted the sending away of their children and are relieved to have them back.

Case example

Tadesse had come from Ethiopia when he was 15. He was picked up at the airport, and as he had nowhere to go he was taken into care and placed with a family of West Indian origin. Enquiries were made about his family in Ethiopia. It turned out that the story he had given was true – his parents were dead and he had been living with an aunt who had encouraged him to go to Britain, but on hearing about his situation offered to have him back. By this time Tadesse was 16 and was settling in London and did not want to go back to Ethiopia. However, he had not been granted leave to remain in the UK and was liable to be deported when he was 18. Finally, he agreed to go back to Ethiopia and reports were received to say that he seemed to be glad to be back in his homeland.

Sometimes it seems as though there is no point in finding out about family overseas because there are such strong arguments for a child to stay in Britain. But, not only does the law require it, but it is important for all children in care to grow up knowing why decisions were made about their placements, and what other options were considered. However, care needs to be taken not to raise false hopes in relatives overseas. The following case illustrates a real dilemma for all the people concerned.

Case example

Kiran was abandoned by his prostitute mother at a few weeks old. His father was an African student who had overstayed his visa and had to leave the country. The local authority asked ISSUK to find out about his family in Zambia. By the time a report was obtained from Zambia, saying that the paternal grandparents were keen to take the child, and could offer him a loving home, it had been decided that it would be better if he were adopted in the UK, and a mixed race family was found for him. It was not clear whether the local authority had ever seriously intended to send this baby overseas, or whether they were going through the motions as required by law, but had concluded that a mixed race family was the best option. The effect on the family in Zambia was profoundly unsettling,

iii) A third group of children includes those living overseas for whom placement with relatives in the UK is a possibility. These may be children coming to join a parent who has already come to the UK, or children who might be placed with a relative here.

Case examples

Eva and her family fled from a country in central Africa in fear of their lives. In the chaos she was separated from her 3 children. They were scooped up by another family and landed up in France. Eva came to Britain. It took several months for Eva to find out what had happened to them, but when she knew where they were, ISSUK was able to liaise with the French Branch, and the children came to join their mother.

After her parents died in the DRC, neighbours took Rachel to South Africa with them when they fled. Rachel was taken into care by the SA authorities. She spoke of an uncle in the UK and ISSUK was asked to investigate. After a satisfactory assessment of the uncle's family, Rachel was able to come to the UK to live with them.

ISS Spain referred the case of two small British children, Jack and Melanie who were in residential care, having been removed from their mother and her partner because of neglect. The mother was still in Spain and the father was believed to be in Manchester. The Spanish social workers wanted to find their father and grandparents. A great deal of information emerged from Manchester Social Services about contact with the family over many years. Older children had been removed and were with relatives in the UK. The father had left the area and was not found. The maternal grandparents went to Spain to meet the children, but felt unable to offer them a home. It was decided that the children should remain in care in Spain, with regular contact with their mother, but that they should also build up links with their grandparents in England.

Problems in obtaining reports

However, a major problem for all concerned has always been the great variations in the responses from the members of the network to requests for reports, both in relation to the time taken and to the quality of the response. At this time the countries causing most concern were Nigeria, Ghana, the USA, Middle East and Pakistan and Bangladesh.[123] Heloise Kareem had visited

[123] Council Minutes 29.1.87.

Bangladesh on behalf of ISSGB and her report sets out succinctly the problems of obtaining reports from overseas. "It was – and still is – an ongoing problem for ISS social workers when those referring cases are impatient about the time that it can take to get replies to requests for information. It is tempting for local authorities to try to speed things up by sending their own social workers overseas to assess for themselves the situation, for example, of a relative offering a home to a child in Britain".[124]

From the point of view of the child's social worker there are two over-riding concerns; firstly, the need to comply with the time scales set by courts, which have become tighter in recent years. And secondly, good social workers feel a huge commitment to the children for whom they are responsible, and want to see for themselves that the suggested placement will meet the identified needs of a particular child. But can they do a "good enough" assessment in the time available to them?

At the very least, British social workers should not do any social work overseas themselves unless 1) the local welfare services cannot undertake the work, and 2) the social worker has obtained permission from the appropriate authority in the country concerned. One might add two further conditions: that the worker has sufficient time to do a proper investigation, and not just an information-gathering exercise, and that there is adequate support from a local welfare agency. Having said this, there remain grave concerns about the ability of social workers to undertake sufficiently good assessments in another country if they do not have good knowledge of that country, including local customs and sensibilities.

Heloise explained her reservations about sending UK social workers overseas:

> "I realised that as a foreign Social Worker trying to understand and assess families in a completely unfamiliar situation, I was trying to do something quite impossible. I could not speak the language or understand what was going on around me. I could

[124] International Social Service of Great Britain 1974–84. A Report by H Kareem 1984.

only observe and try to pick up some of the signals. Without help from a representative of the local Social Welfare Department my judgement would have been quite unreliable. How do you judge poverty, housing standards, employment unless you know the norms of the area? How do you assess personality and capacity which are culturally tied? Questions have to be asked in the right way. Answers have to be interpreted with an understanding of local pattern of behaviours. ISS has to help the local worker to become aware of the whole background, and so be able to work well with the family in relation to it."[125]

When British social workers go out independently to obtain reports for their local authorities or courts, they usually obtain local help with interpreters and so on, but do not necessarily have the benefit of the backup of the local ISS Branch or Correspondent to guide them, and to offer appropriate follow-up support to those being interviewed. There is also a danger that social workers who are unused to being in a very different environment can suffer from culture shock that affects their perceptions, and can cause them to question a particular life-style, not from the point of view of the child, but from the perspective that they themselves would find it difficult.

For these reasons the ISS has always urged that all cases should be referred through its offices, on the grounds that its involvement helps ensure that a thorough job is done and that cultural misunderstandings are avoided. Unfortunately, this position has meant that ISSUK has not usually been consulted by social workers intending to go overseas, even when such consultation would have been very useful.

So the issue is still not straightforward – even if the criteria set out above are met, and a visit would be the only way to obtain any sort of information, is that better than nothing? Or is the need for understanding of the cultural context so fundamental that no outsider should attempt to assess a family living in an unfamiliar environment? If so, does that not deprive some children of the chance of growing up in their own family circle?

125 AR1985.

This is one of the most fundamental dilemmas for all social workers involved in intercountry work.

Private fostering

Private Fostering is defined as: "the care of a child who is below the upper limit of the compulsory school age (or 18 if disabled or with special needs), for 28 days or more, by a person who is not the child's parent, relative or guardian."[126] The Children Act 1989 placed a duty on both the foster carer and parents to notify the local authority of the intention to place a child in private foster care, and limited to three the number of children whom a carer could foster. But there were no accurate figures of the numbers of children with private foster parents. The Department of Health stopped trying to collect statistics in 1991 because of the inaccuracy caused by the low number of notifications. The Utting Report of 1997 estimated that there were 11,000 such children.[127] The ISS staff in Britain have always been concerned about those children of foreign nationals who have been placed with private foster parents in the UK, often while their parents undertake training. In many cases the parents returned to the country of origin, leaving the children "to get a good education". Of course, there are many privately fostered children who are well looked after, but even some of them lost contact with their birth families. But sadly there are many children who were in unsuitable placements and have been received into local authority care. Some cases of great cruelty to children have hit the headlines, and a lot of children have been removed from private foster homes, but perhaps the greatest concern is the belief that there is almost certainly a large number of children placed with unregistered carers, who are not known to the authorities because they are not going to school or getting health care.

A large proportion of privately fostered children come from Africa. In 1984 Ruth Furnival wrote: "ISS finds itself in the roles of fact finder about the family's circumstances in West Africa,

126 Foster Children Act 1980.

127 Quoted in: A Very Private Practice – an investigation into Private Fostering by T Philpot BAAF 2001..

and interpreter of the different attitudes to the family and rearing of children, which is a two way process both to social workers here and our colleagues in West Africa. The third role is being a negotiator for a child's reunion with its family circle in the home country. Our role requires the assistance of our colleagues in the various Ministries responsible for Social Welfare in West African countries and we are very grateful for the help they give by seeing members of the children's families and providing reports. In our role as interpreter, much has been learned from our West African friends, and in particular the High Commissions, the African Children's Advisory Service and the African Women's Association, who have given us valuable aid." "We are happy to report that a number of children who have been in the care of Social Services for some years have recently been restored to their families in West Africa. We are hoping to follow their progress in order to provide evidence of the wisdom of these decisions."[128] (There is no evidence that such a follow-up took place.)

Case example

Alice, aged 10 had been brought to the UK from Cameroon a couple of years earlier by "an aunt". She came to the notice of Social Services when she was admitted to hospital with injuries. She was removed from this woman and put in a local authority foster home. It turned out that she had travelled on false papers. She remembered the name of the town she had come from, and her family was traced. The ISS correspondent confirmed that they wanted Alice back and that they could care for her, and so after a few months she returned to her family.

Some years later, in 1992 one member of staff travelled to Nigeria with other professionals "to learn more about the country and reinforce our co-operation and working relationships with overseas colleagues".[129]

128 R Furnival AR 1984.
129 AR1992.

In 2009 ISSUK became part of a National Private Fostering Campaign, called "Somebody Else's Child", initiated by BAAF. The aim of the campaign was to increase awareness of the needs of overseas children in private foster homes, and to increase the level of notification and supervision of such placements. "The types of children who are privately fostered can vary greatly – they include teenagers who have had a row with their mum and dad and have left home to live with friend's family, children whose parents are in prison, children sent to the UK from overseas for educational reasons, and trafficked young people who could be used as domestic slaves, or sold into prostitution".[130]

The experience of staff in working with African countries led to another initiative:

Return of talent to Africa 1983–93

The Intergovernmental Committee for Migration in Geneva (ICM) set up a scheme in 4 European countries and the United States, to help African nationals who had acquired technical or scientific skills abroad to return to their home country to work in its development. From the end of 1983 this scheme was operated in the UK by ISSGB as the UK was not a member of ICM at that time. For two years Nkathazo Ngubo was the Operations Officer for this project, and then in 1985 Jessie Oladele, as Organising Secretary was responsible for the rest of the first phase. In 1987 Ken Jessop was appointed as Operations Officer. In 1989 the ICM became the IOM – International Organisation for Migration. By this time ISSGB was working jointly with IOM, who had offices in the same building from 1985.

In the first phase, which was a pilot project, concerned the return of people to Kenya, Somalia, Sudan and Zimbabwe. The countries were encouraged to identify key posts in industry or services that they were unable to fill with suitable or adequately trained people from within their own borders. These vacancies were notified to ICM and by them to ISSGB.

130 BAAF website and ISSUK Newsletter 2009.

After four years the scheme entered its second phase, and was extended to include Ghana, Uganda and Zambia.

By the end of the first eight years, 460 nationals had returned from the UK to these target countries. They included doctors, engineers, accountants, nurse, teachers, physicists, agriculturalists and computer scientists. Help was given with fares, job finding, migration and resettlement.

In 1992 South Africa was also included in the Return of Talent Programme. But, separately from this scheme, in the previous year 1991, ISSUK was asked by UNHCR to co-operate in the repatriation of professional South African refugees who wished to return voluntarily to South Africa. By the end of 1993 600 exiles had been helped to return to South Africa.

The collaboration with IOM continued until the end of 1992, when IOM moved into its own office near Victoria. In addition to the Return of Talent to Africa scheme, the ISSUK staff worked closely with the IOM staff in relation to many other cases concerning migrants.

CHAPTER 9

The 1990s

World events

This decade found people trying to cope with the daunting economic, political and social consequences of the break-up of the Soviet Union and the collapse of communism in Eastern Europe, and the conflict in former Yugoslavia. Suddenly millions of people had a new freedom to move abroad, although of course most of them did not want to go or could not afford to do so.

More refugees fled from Africa due to famine and conflict, especially from Rwanda. The steady flow of asylum seekers from all across the globe increased, including many children and young people. Separate statistics were not kept for asylum seekers to Britain until 1979, when 1,563 applications were recorded; by 1991 this figure reached 44,840. The authorities lacked the resources to deal with these numbers and a backlog increased. Only a minority of cases were accepted; in 1994 510 people were granted full refugee status and others were given "exceptional leave to remain". It is well known that many of those refused this leave disappeared into the wider population. ISS sometimes became involved when, for example, family problems brought such people to the attention of the authorities, who wanted to find out the family background.

Legislation

- Hague Convention on Protection of Children and Co-operation in Respect of Intercountry Adoption 1993 – ratified by UK in 2003.
- The Hague Convention on Jurisdiction, Applicable Law, Recognition, Enforcement and Co-operation in Respect of

Parental Responsibility and Measures for the Protection of Children 1996 (known as the HC of 1996 on the International Protection of Children). "The Convention takes account of the wide variety of legal institutions and systems of protection that exist around the world. It does not attempt to create a uniform international law of child protection; the basic elements of such a law are already to be found in the 1989 UNCRC. The function of the 1996 HC is to avoid legal and administrative conflicts and to build the structure for effective international co-operation in child protection matters between the different systems. In this respect, the Convention provides a remarkable opportunity for the building of bridges between legal systems having diverse cultural and religious backgrounds."[131] It provides a wide range of measures of protection of children, a structure for the resolution of issues of custody and contact, a reinforcement of measures to deal with child abduction, procedures for dealing with unaccompanied minors and cross-frontier placements of children. This Convention was not ratified by the UK until 2008.

- Human Rights Act 1998 – finally enshrining in British law the European Convention on Human Rights 1950.
- Data Protection Act 1998 – regarding protection of information about individuals.
- Adoption (Intercountry Aspects) Act 1999 – enabled the ratification of the HC Convention 1993. One purpose of this was to establish a system of co-operation among contracting states.

In 1997 the UNHCR produced "Guidelines on Policies and Procedures in dealing with Unaccompanied Children Seeking Asylum". This is just one example of the number of documents giving guidance on every possible subject by international bodies and government departments that accompanied new legislation.

There were also some new relevant laws introduced for England and Wales: "in the UK we have felt the changes and emphasis in social work brought about by the 1989 Children

[131] Ibid.

Act, the Criminal Justice Act, the Adoption Law Review and the changes in the Health Service and Education."[132]

General Secretariat and the network

A major innovation of the 1990s was the setting up of The International Reference Centre for the Protection of Children in Adoption (ISS/IRC) as a division of the General Secretariat in 1994. "Its principal goal consists of sharing, distributing and promoting good practices in the realm of inter-country adoption and more broadly the protection of children deprived of their family or at risk of being so, or in need of adoption or already adopted. It aims at supporting professionals across the globe."[133] To this end it produces regular bulletins and reviews of adoption practice and research around the world. Within a short time this centre "was attracting support from workers in many countries eager to ensure that best practice is followed in such complex work."[134] In 1999 the Centre produced an important document to mark the 10th anniversary of the UNCRC: "The Rights of the Child in Internal and International Adoption – Ethics and Principles – Guidelines for Practice". In 2006 the name of the Centre changed to "The Reference Centre for the Rights of Children deprived of their Family" (still ISS/IRC).

A second major step by the GS was the production of a new and updated ISS Manual – a reference and training document for all members of the network. It re-stated basic principles about objectivity and confidentiality, and the need to work at all times in the best interests of the child, the individual and the family. It updated existing guidelines for good practice, and provided a thorough, clear and usable guide to every aspect of inter-country casework. Specific guidelines were provided for inter-country adoption, international family conflict, separated and unaccompanied minors, family reunification and search for roots. These helped all members of the network to understand the issues in each case and to produce coherent responses. The Manual

132 HC of 1996 on the International Protection of Children.

133 AR1996.

134 Ibid.

was prepared by the end of the decade and published in 2000. Efforts were made to encourage all units to use it, and it led to improved standards throughout the network. However, only four years later ISSUK was involved in redrafting parts of the Manual to bring it up to date with legislation and practice.

A third change was to the Statutes; in 1992 the Council set up a Professional Advisory Committee (PAC), consisting of the Directors of all the national Units, which meets annually. "The PAC brings expert knowledge and makes recommendations to the International Council, the Executive Committee and other Committees. It works in close co-operation with the GS" (Statute 12).[135] The British Branch Director was the first Chairman of the PAC.

By 1990 ISS had a network of 15 national Branches and a network of correspondents in more than a hundred countries, and there was a lot of work on network development. In 1993 a Solidarity Fund was set up to help Correspondents who faced financial problems in dealing with ISS cases. The Fund was managed through the GS and offered either yearly lump sum grants, or reimbursement on a case-by-case basis. From 1996 the GS sought payment from those requesting Home Studies of adoption applicants which were undertaken by Correspondents. The GS still depended for its funding on contributions from the Branches, and if a Branch was in financial difficulties, this money did not always come, and so the work of the GS was constantly hampered by lack of funding. The German, French and Hong Kong branches, which were largely subvented by their governments, carried a disproportionate share of the funding of the Geneva office. It seems that not enough effort was put into trying to attract funding from the many organisations and institutions in Geneva, and one of the problems was the reduction in the involvement with many of them.

Staff in ISS Branches all over Europe found themselves dealing with lots of unaccompanied minor refugees, and had to learn about less familiar countries like Albania and Romania, with whom there had hitherto been little work.

135 Statutes of ISS: Geneva 1992.

ISS staff took part in a mission to Albania in 1991 to help draft a law regulating adoption, particularly inter-country adoption. ISSUK obtained a grant from the Department of International Development (DfID) to develop the ISS service in Albania, and to set up an ISS Delegation in Kosovo. ISS also held a regional seminar in Bulgaria to collect and exchange information about child abandonment.

ISS staff worked with the UN Centre for Social Development and Humanitarian Affairs and the International Council on Social Work (ICSW) on the preparation of the 1993 Hague Convention on the Protection of children and co-operation in respect of inter-country adoption, which came into force in 1995. This led to the Brighton Guidelines for inter-country adoption – finally endorsed by the ICSW conference in Hong Kong in 1996.

In 1999 ISS published "The Rights of the Child in International and Intercountry Adoption – Ethics and Principles."

Damien Ngabonziza was General Secretary throughout the decade (1989–2003), and as a Rwandan he was able to set up an ISS Delegation in Rwanda in 1995 following the war and genocide, to run a programme called "A Child… A Family". The aim was to integrate orphaned children into local foster families, without financial compensation because there were no funds for this. By the end of 1999 over 650 children had been placed. By 2001 this programme moved to local leadership and began to focus on children affected by HIV Aids.

ISSUK within the wider ISS

From its foundation, the Council and staff of the British Branch have played a prominent part in the international deliberations of the agency. The staff have contributed their experience to ISS papers and studies about inter-country adoption, abduction of children abroad, and the protection of children who are not nationals in the country in which they may be living. They also assisted the organisation in its submission to the UN relating to the Convention on the Rights of the Child.

Over the years ISSUK social workers took part in international seminars and shared in their leadership. They provided training experience for ISS colleagues from abroad as well as local students. In 1996 social worker Dawn Temple went to Ethiopia with General Secretary Damien Ngabonziza to discuss the problems of unaccompanied minors from that land, especially those who were being refused leave to remain in the UK after reaching the age of 18.

In 1997 ISSUK hosted the triennial International Council Meeting in London and an ISS International Training Seminar for 36 social workers from 26 different countries. Participants were half from countries with an ISS Branch office or an Affiliated Bureau and half from Correspondent countries. There were 3 themes: Rights of Access, Separation and Search for Roots". The resulting seminar report: "Keeping families together across frontiers: Principles and Methods of Inter-country Casework," 1997 is a valuable document in bringing together some fundamental elements of ISS work. It says "The seminar was also an important step in redefining the common working principles and methods to be applied among ISS caseworkers. Because ISS is an agencies' agency, and therefore does not always have direct access to the clients, there is a need to agree on what basic information – social, legal, cultural and other – we need to collect and transmit in order to ensure rapid and efficient responses. The very fact that we depend on written communication implies clear, concise and accurate formulation in describing the circumstances of a presenting problem."[136] Another aim was to "define principles of co-operation with local partners (administration, judges, lawyers, social welfare agencies), consulates and embassies and international organisations."[137]

ISSUK

The organisation changed its name from ISS of Great Britain (ISSGB) to ISS of the United Kingdom (ISSUK) in May 1991.

136 "Keeping families together across frontiers: Principles and Methods of Inter-country Casework", 1997.

137 AR1992.

Council

Sir Terence Streeton was Chairman from 1990 to the end of 1993. He had been Head of Administration in Brussels. Lady (Liz) Emery became Chairman from 1994 to 2003. Lady (Dora) Pink was re-elected as Vice-Chairman. Charles Marshall became Honorary Treasurer in 1991 and carried out that role until 2008.

In 1998 Sir Clive Bossom retired from the Council – he had been President of the International ISS Council in Geneva from 1984–88, and was then elected to the Council of ISSUK for the next ten years. He was briefly appointed as Interim International President in 1997. He was described as "such a supporter, friend and mentor to ISSUK and the GS".[138]

In 1990 Council met 5 times, and Finance and General Purposes Committee met 10 times.

From the mid 90s the Professional Advisory Group provided a link between trustees and staff, and Sheila Poupard was particularly appreciated by staff for her Chairing of this group. For a while she was the only Trustee with a real knowledge of local authority social work, because she had been head of Children's Services, and then Assistant Director in the London Borough of Wandsworth for many years.

Lady (Liz) Emery was the wife of an MP, and so was unusual in not having a diplomatic background. She had been closely involved in the Spring Fair since the mid-1980s, serving as Vice President and then President of the Fair. She became a Trustee in 1991 and was Chairman of the Council from 1994–2003. She was elected to the International Bureau in 1999. She played a prominent part in many fundraising events in addition to the Fair, such as the first Mansion House dinner. She was someone who wanted to get things done, and had a reputation for being able to take difficult decisions. As Chairman of the Council she worked hard to hold the organisation together through difficult times, but when the financial situation became critical in 2003 she resigned. It was a painful conclusion to a long commitment to ISSUK and ISS internationally.

[138] AR1998/9.

Review of the governance and functioning of ISSUK

The 1992 Charities Act put increased emphasis on the responsibilities and obligations of Trustees, and in 1994 the Trustees set up a thorough review of the organisation by CAFcert Consultancy Services. The reasons for this were the continuing financial difficulties, with an increasing gap between income and expenditure, a recognition of the pressures on the Director and low staff morale. The Terms of Reference for the consultants were:

> "to examine all aspects of the Charity's scope, organisation and functions; to consult fully with the staff and members of the management bodies, and to design a model which would enable ISSUK to work as effectively and efficiently as possible within the constraints of expected income."[139]

The reviewers were also asked to look at external perception of ISSUK and its services, and opportunities for charging for the work.

The consultants concluded that the charity had a good future, but stated that substantial changes were required. There was a "need to inject new meaning and purpose into the ISS management".[140] As a result of the Review the following changes were recommended, and subsequently implemented:

- That the leadership be strengthened.
- That the Council change its composition, size and procedures.
- That the Finance and General Purposes Committee should end, as it duplicated the work of the Council. The review recognised the "certain decisions have been taken by a select group of members within the FGPC and the Council."[141]
- That a Professional Advisory Group be established to provide a forum for staff to reflect on difficult practice matters. The policy implications of these discussions would then be presented to Council.

139 Terms of reference for review by CAFcert Consultancy Services, 1994.

140 Report by CAFcert Consultancy Services, 1994.

141 Ibid.

- That the arrangements for staff supervision and development be more structured.
- That the profile of the organisation needed raising, and that there should be a broader donor base and a coherent marketing plan.
- That an improved system of charging for services be introduced.

As a result of this review, the Director was removed from his post, the membership of the Council was widened and the social work representation was improved. In 1998 Audrey Moser was elected, together with two social workers, Sheila Poupard and Julia Miles, and a retired senior official from the Home Office, Bob Morris. The schedule of meetings was increased from 4 to 8 per year – a decade later these were reduced to 6 per year. In between meetings the Chairman and Treasurer were to meet regularly with the Director to formulate policy in more detail.

Staff

David Harrison had been brought in as Director in October 1990. He had been a career Civil Servant in the Foreign and Commonwealth Office (FCO), and had been Consul in Pakistan. However, he had no experience of the voluntary sector or social work and, although he introduced improvements to the day-to-day running of ISSUK, he was not able to drive the organisation forward. When his contract was terminated in 1994, Peter Fry was persuaded to take over as Interim Director before being appointed as Director for the rest of the decade.

Peter Fry – an Australian social worker, first worked for ISS in Australia, and then went to Geneva in 1967. He was in charge of casework for five years, and Audrey Moser remembers that they worked well together, and it was a productive time for the organisation. Peter started by reviewing ISS casework services, and the method of collecting statistics. Audrey said that Peter was exceptionally good at working with the network, as he was "international in thinking and got the role of ISS very clearly. He had a great ability to understand different communities and cultures, and then explain them to other members of the network. The network improved greatly due to his input." Audrey also described Peter as a "reliable colleague and friend and a marvellous cook!"[142]

After leaving ISS in Geneva he worked for The Central Council for Education and Training in Social Work in London (CCETSW). For the next fifteen years he spent a few weeks a year volunteering for ISS. In the mid 1970s he was instrumental in getting a research study undertaken by CCETSW to which ISSUK, the GS and other units of ISS contributed. The purpose of the study was to look at "legal and social issues arising when individuals and families are caught between different countries."[143]

Peter brought both his knowledge of social work training and his experience of working for the ISS General Secretariat to his roles with ISSUK during the following 26 years. He was on the Committee of the Spring Fair by 1977, and was elected to the Council in 1977 and remained a Trustee until 1994, when he became Director of ISSUK. He was described as hardworking and deeply committed to the organisation. He was essentially a committee man, who liked to work co-operatively. He also addressed the immediate concerns in the London office, which was still somewhat old fashioned in some ways. His relaxed Australian manner eased relationships between Trustees and staff. He played a central role in obtaining the contract for ISSUK to run the Child Migrant Fund. Peter retained the respect of those in the network, and was especially good at seeing ISSUK in its wider context. Perhaps he was less effective at engaging with local authorities and building up the position of ISS in the UK.

He retired from ISSUK in 2003 due to serious illness. He died in January 2005.

The 90s saw the highest number of staff in the charity's history. By late summer 1992, there were 21 staff in total. In addition to the Director, there were 8 social workers plus the Refugee Consultant, the Operations Officer for Return of Talent to Africa, the Spring Fair Organiser, Appeals Organiser and 8 Administrative staff. Christopher Platt, who had returned in 1990, was appointed Administrative Officer in 1992, when David Todd left after 13 years. Mark Hunt was appointed in May 1995.

142 Interview with A Moser.

143 AR1976.

Elizabeth Sweeney had joined as secretary in 1988 and stayed until 2008. Among the social workers who joined the staff in this decade were Carol Page, Christina Birch, an experienced manager from a Social Services Department, Alison Pickles and Marek Ganther, also with good local authority experience and Ariane Carouge. In 1995 Lesley Austen joined as Tracing Officer. Staff who left included Essie Grives, who resigned as Deputy Director at the end of 1994, and Dawn Temple and Phyllis Jackson.

Administration

"The primary function of the administrative team is to support the professional social work service in delivering effective and efficient services to vulnerable people. It provides the immediate 'public window' to the organisation through its reception responsibilities. It is responsible for supporting the key activities of the professional staff and Boards, managing most of the finance, IT and HR functions and looking after the premises."[144] This sets out the complex and vital role of the team.

Chris Platt described the organisation in the early 1990s as "professional but not organised",[145] saying that although he had inherited very good filing systems, there was a need for more systematic keeping of information, but added that systems, procedures and policies were steadily sorted out. It seems that there were really significant changes – staff were better paid and in 1995 they finally got proper contracts and terms and conditions of service. The Honorary Treasurer Charles Marshall chaired an Operations Committee, of Trustees and staff, whose brief was to revise and compile all necessary policies and procedures. Peter Fry championed the practice of producing materials "in house" rather than paying outsiders. A contributory pension scheme was introduced in 1995, but no-one signed up to it!

At last there were some innovations on the technical front. A paragraph in the Annual Report of 1991 makes quaint reading

144 S Dixon: Review of Administrative Support 2007.
145 Interview with C Platt.

now, but indicates just how quickly equipment had changed in a short time: "On the mechanical side we acquired a much-needed new photocopier, and replaced our archaic Grundig stenorettes by modern, if modest, dictating equipment. The ancient plug-and-socket switchboard has gone, replaced by a telephone system which gives access to cheaper tariffs."[146] In 1992 the Director wrote: "That our one full-time and one part-time typists cope with the output of all the social workers is a matter of amazement."[147] The first computer was donated to the office in 1992. It may seem odd, looking back, that the organisation was so slow to embrace the new technologies, but this can be explained by the fact that the staff group consisted predominantly of older members, many of whom could not even type. It was the member of staff working on the Spring Fair, who taught other staff how to use the new computer. Later in 1992 funds were obtained from the DOH to install a computer network, and the Minutes of September 1997 record that ISSUK was now on the internet. The number of administrative staff was reduced as a result of these technological changes.

Publicity

There was a recognised need to target accurate information at Local Authorities, Guardians ad Litem, Courts and the Law Society, especially because of the negative view of ISSUK by some Local Authorities and other agencies due to the slowness of the service with many countries. Newsletters were introduced in 1994 to be sent to users of the service and potential donors twice a year.

In 1995 a Publicity and Promotions Committee was set up and produced much needed new-look brochures. By the end of the 1990s the arrival of the internet changed the way in which information could be obtained and transmitted.

ISSUK now needed a strapline, and the chosen one was "Resolving Family Problems across the World".

146 AR1991.
147 AR 1992.

Finances and fundraising

The challenge of the 90s remained fundraising. These were years of continuous deficit. In 1992, the Treasurer, Charles Marshall, said: "ISSUK walks a tightrope between larger deficits, which will be unsustainable, and reduced services, which will be detrimental both to the interests of the families we help and to the whole international network of ISS."[148] In 1999 the Accounting Year changed once again – back to what it had been in the early years – 1st April – 31st March. This was to bring it into line with the UK Treasury and other government departments.

At the beginning of the decade, the core grant from Government continued at the same level, and was approximately one-sixth of the income. This was in addition to continued funding for projects such as the Travel Assistance Scheme. However, from March 1996 Core Grants from the DOH were phased out. From then on all funding to voluntary agencies had to be for projects. A Fund-raising Committee started in 1997.

As a result of the CAF (Cert) Review in 1994 the standard fee for cases referred from local authorities was increased. The figures for 1998 record that charges to statutory agencies produced over £56,000.

The Friends of ISS was launched in 1991 and by the next year had 76 members. They supported the charity financially and in return were kept informed about the work. This group of continued until 2005, when the remaining members were offered Life Membership.

In 1994 the broadcaster Sue Lawley spoke about ISSUK for the Week's Good Cause and raised over £5,600.

From the late 90s the President, Sir James Weatherall and the Chairman Lady Emery, organised a reception at St James' Palace for newly appointed heads of diplomatic missions from abroad. The aim was to inform them about the work of ISS and involve them in the Spring Fair. The organisation remained hugely dependent on the Spring Fair.

[148] Ibid.

An increasing number of other major events, in addition to the Spring Fair took place – including a 70th Anniversary Dinner at the Hilton Hotel in January 1995. In March 1998 there was a Buffet Dinner and Fashion Show at the Embassy of Kuwait, organised by Françoise Middleton, and later a lunch at the Egyptian Embassy and dinner at the French Embassy.

Lady (Françoise) Middleton was a most energetic and committed volunteer. She had been the wife of an Ambassador and closely linked to the Diplomatic Community for many years. She was closely involved with the Spring Fair from 1980, serving both as Chairman for 12 years and then President. She was a member of Council from 1986 to 2007, then a Vice-President until 2008, when she was elected Patron. She also served on some International ISS Committees.

Perhaps her greatest contribution was as a central figure in the organising of events. She used her diplomatic connections, her charm and her great energy to find venues and persuade others to join her organising committees, which arranged at least one major fund-raising dinner or other event every year for over 30 years. "Over the years Lady Middleton had been largely responsible for raising over £2million for ISSUK."[149] This was almost certainly more than anyone else in the history of the organisation.

There were also a number of special fund-raising cultural events; for example in 1991 a cello concert at the French Ambassador's Residence; in 1992 a Royal Gala evening at the Chichester Festival Theatre, a piano recital at the French Ambassador's residence in 1994, an Evening of Christmas Music at Lancaster House in 1996, an opera soirée at Harrow School in 1997, a concert at the Bulgarian Embassy, also in 1997.

A Fun Run was organised in Hyde Park in 1996 and was repeated for the following four years. In 1997 there were 386 runners including representatives of 33 diplomatic missions, and over £13,000 was raised. In 1998 "Over 300 people, including 3 Ambassadors took part on the day and the flags of many nations were carried by the runners. Push chairs, dogs on leads, fathers

[149] Minutes of AGM 2007.

with children on their shoulders, serious runners and an enormous Paddington Bear were in evidence."[150] In 1999 the weather was atrocious and only 150 people took part and £4,245 was raised, and in 2000 £6,500 was raised. Although this run was stopped because it did not raise large amounts of money, its value lay in the participation of members of a lot of diplomatic missions.

Links with other agencies in Britain

ISSUK's involvement in international law gave the organisation a voice in discussions with government departments and other agencies about changes to legislation. In 1997 ISSUK made representation to the Department of Health in regard to the Adoption Bill, and to the Lord Chancellors Department and the General Secretariat with regard to the Revision of the 1961 Hague Convention on the Protection of Children, and the Convention on the Abduction of Children abroad by a Parent.

In 1998 ISSUK was a member of a working group of lawyers and judges set up by the Centre for Advanced Legal Studies, to examine the law with regard to cross-border movement of children.

It was necessary to keep good links with government departments, especially when there were changes of personnel in the ministries, so that new staff had to be reminded of the work of ISSUK. ISSUK continued to maintain relationships with other social work agencies, both statutory and voluntary. During this decade efforts were made to make links with judges and CAFCASS. Dame Elizabeth Butler-Sloss was particularly helpful.

Staff contributed to working groups on private fostering and children affected by deportation, and unaccompanied minors. In 1996 staff participated in the European Social Services Conference in London on "children caught between countries – the welfare response".

150 AR 1999.

Training

Social workers need to keep up to date with current policies and practice and there has always been a regular provision of training seminars and courses within the ISS network as well as with other international agencies. Staff of ISSUK continued both to give and receive this training. For example, in 1991 a social worker from ISSUK gave a talk at a seminar in The Netherlands on inter-cultural marriage. In 1996 the Branch organised a seminar on adoption for the network.

And ISSUK has provided training for British social workers on many aspects of working across national borders. In 1993 a seminar on intercountry work highlighted a gap in training provision for British social workers. In 1995 staff gave seminars on the subject of unaccompanied children in the UK to social work students. All training gives people valuable tools for their own work, and important insights into the context in which colleagues elsewhere are working. ISS training courses and seminars helped to strengthen and develop the ISS philosophy and built common high standards of service.

Monitoring

Monitoring is only possible in a formal way when the objectives have been clearly stated, so that progress can be measured. Yet there is also constant monitoring by all staff of all aspects of the work they do. During this time there was more focus on measuring the outcomes of the work, with predictions set for what should be achieved in each case, so that it could be seen how far the outcomes matched the predictions.

The Annual Report of 1996 includes a section called "Objectives of ISS and how we tried to realise them in 1996". For example, one stated objective in that year was to make recommendations as a result of studying the consequences of migration, and the evidence given was that ISSUK had presented its findings to the discussions about the Hague Convention for the Protection of Children.

From then on, most of the Annual Reviews included a section on the Objectives and how far they had been achieved. For example, one report showed the staff had run workshops, attended all-Party Parliamentary Committees and established a data-base – all these proving that objectives had been met (see also the next chapter).

Casework

The Children Act 1989 placed an emphasis on the wider family when making decisions about children, and so ISSUK was increasingly asked by Local Authority Social Services Departments to obtain assessment reports on relatives overseas. There was an overall increase in such referrals concerning children deemed to be in need of care and protection, including cases concerned with actual or alleged child abuse. This posed extra demands on the social workers to make sure that the potential carers in another country understood the implications of abuse and could cope with the possible consequences.

In 1992 a total of 1,584 cases were handled by four full-time and four part-time social workers. Of these, 619 were newly referred cases from the UK, and 240 were new cases from overseas countries, while the rest were ongoing cases. The rest were ongoing cases that had not been completed by the end of the year. "The cases are if anything becoming more complex and often involve more than two countries. This increases the difficulties in reconciling different legal and social system. ISS social workers are spending increased time directly with clients, join interviews with local social workers and attending case reviews, etc. All the staff are working to full capacity, which leaves little room for manoeuvre."[151] So the Duty system was once more re-organised so that enquiries and urgent cases could be better dealt with. That year there were 800 enquiries. By 1997 the total caseload for the year was 1,799, which was a slight increase, but the number of enquiries had increased significantly to 1,678.

The referrals continued to come from a range of agencies and individuals. For example, in 1994 cases were referred from a

[151] AR92.

total of 90 different local authorities, plus 7 Probation Services, 14 Court Welfare Services, and several Guardians ad Litem.

Some staff built up expertise in specific areas of the work, but this had to be balanced with the need for all social workers to be able to respond appropriately to all requests. In the late 90s the number of cases referred from abroad increased, while referrals from within the UK decreased slightly.

Vulnerable adults

Although the preponderance of the workload was cases related to children, there was always a substantial number of cases concerning vulnerable adults. These included people suffering from physical or mental illnesses, and lonely and isolated elderly who wanted to re-connect with their family or homeland.

Case example

Dorothy was an elderly British woman who was suffering from increasing deafness, so that she could no longer talk on the phone. She felt cut off from her only daughter who lived in Canada. Her social worker referred her to ISSUK, who were able to liaise with colleagues in Canada and make sure that adequate resources were available so that she could move to Canada.

Unaccompanied minors

There was also growing concern about the number of children being brought by charitable organisations from areas of conflict in Eastern Europe, who were becoming alienated from their families. Added to them were the growing number of unaccompanied minors reaching the country from many different countries.

Local authority social workers turned to ISSUK to try to find out where these youngsters came from and whether they had families to whom they could return. Attempts to get this information had to be made, but it was frequently impossible because of the conflict situations in the countries of origin, and a reluctance on the part of the asylum seekers to give any information that might lead to their compulsory return. Moser explained: "These young people, escaping conflict and war have not, in general, been met with understanding and sympathy in Western European countries, and have encountered greater social, legal and cultural problems."[152] One of the most difficult problems was proof of age, because of the likelihood of deportation of any illegal immigrant over the age of 18.

Case example

Victor was 16 when he came to the notice of the authorities. He had arrived in a lorry, and had no idea of the route they had taken. He was put in a residential unit and ISSUK was asked to verify his story. He gave information about his family in Russia, but a report came back saying that he was not known. He was distressed by this and gave more details, including maps, names of teachers and so on. The Russian authorities reported that the information was accurate but everyone denied knowledge of him. By now Victor was pleading to go back to Russia. It turned out that his family had paid for him to go ahead and establish himself in the UK so that they could follow him. His wish to come home was, therefore, unacceptable to them. When he heard this, Victor disappeared and it is not known what happened to him.

Unaccompanied Children Scheme 1995–99

In 1995 a grant from the Department of Health provided for 2 full-time workers, Igor Tojcic and Caroline Blake, to set up a programme with young asylum seekers from former Yugoslavia. Dawn Temple, an ISSUK social worker, acted as advisor to this programme. The programme was subsequently funded by Comic Relief. Initially the clients came mainly from Bosnia and Croatia, but were soon joined by young people from Kosovo. During the next three years 300 unaccompanied young people were referred

[152] Young People in Migration: Keynote Speech to the International Council of ISS 2000 by AMoser.

to the project. They were helped to use housing and education services, given guidance about their immigration status, and assisted to develop the skills to live away from home. English language classes, after school group and a wide range of weekend sporting activities were provided. "The programme has established that their seeming ability to cope in the initial stages has masked quite deep-seated anxieties about their future and strong feelings of isolation. There is a clear argument, particularly with a group of adolescent young people separated from their families, which themselves are under stress, to have a focused programme which, through ISS, has the capacity to contact other members of the families in other countries."[153] In March 1999, when the crisis in Kosovo deepened, many of these young people lost touch with their families. So an international delegation from ISS, including the Chairman of ISSUK, went to Kosovo to address the plight of separated families. As a result, a grant was obtained from the Department for International Development for 3 years, and an ISS office was set up in Pristina.

Because of the rapidly increasing demand for this service, in March 1999 the programme was established as a separate organisation – Albanian Youth Action – run by Caroline Blake, and situated in the ISS office until 2000.

Using the experience gained from this work, ISSUK ran regular seminars for social workers from local authorities who were working with unaccompanied young people.

Former UK Child Migrant Support Fund 1999–2000

In 1998 the UK government asked ISSUK to administer a travel support fund set up for former UK Child Migrants who had been sent to Australia, Canada and New Zealand before and after the Second World War. Most of them had been in care. The fund was the outcome of a belated recognition by the British Government of the suffering endured by many of these migrants as a result of a very ill-conceived policy. It came into operation in April 1999, and lasted for 3 years, and made it possible for those without reasonable resources to visit close relatives in the

[153] AR1996.

UK for the first time. Some had medical conditions so that they required an escort to travel, and this was covered by the fund. ISSUK carried out this work in close co-operation with ISS Branches in the three other countries, and with the original sending agencies and the Child Migrant Trust in the UK. As an Australian, Peter Fry was well-positioned to oversee this programme.

By the end of the second year the Fund had approved 220 applications. Most of these related to Australian migrants. "Our Branch, and our co-operating colleagues in Australia, Canada and New Zealand, are now receiving letters and calls in which those who have travelled tell us about how the visit has affected their lives and their perceptions of themselves."[154]

In total, ISSUK assisted 324 migrants to be reunited with family members.

> "In summing up the results of a survey of the scheme, the colleague in ISS Australia wrote:
>
> > The vast majority of the users of the Support Fund scheme have reported post travel that the reunion was an event that has changed their lives forever. They now have somewhere to belong. They know who they are. They feel more 'whole'."[155]

Case example

Julie, was one of three sisters who had been separated when young. As the eldest child, Julie had been sent to Australia, while her next sister was placed with foster parents and the youngest was brought up by an aunt. They had had no contact with each other until they were reunited through this scheme.

Intercountry adoption

As far as adoption was concerned, ISSUK was no longer a Registered Adoption Society and so could not take part in the

154 AR2001.

155 ISSUK Information leaflet 2002.

placement of children for adoption, but it was very much involved in advising those interested in adopting a child from overseas and also with post-adoption issues. In a worrying number of cases it transpired that adoptions that had taken place overseas were of doubtful legality, for example as regards obtaining parental consent to the adoption. News spread of mothers in some places being paid to give up their children. ISS passed on any information of malpractice to the Central Authority in the UK. It also contributed to the discussion about changes to Adoption Law.

ISSUK performed the following roles in any adoption case concerning either British citizens wanting to adopt a child from overseas, or the adoptive placement of a British child with a family overseas:

- Advising on Adoption Proceedings in other countries
- Advising would-be adopters about obtaining Home Study reports from Adoption Agencies
- Arranging for the assessment of biological parents and/or the child in connection with an adoption plan
- Obtaining birth parents' consent to adoption
- Obtaining information on a child's background to be part of his or her adoption record.
- Obtaining Police and Social Service checks on prospective adoptive parents when they have lived or originate from an overseas country.
- Liaising with Central Authorities overseas
- Arranging for the provision of supervision reports before an adoption..
- Facilitating and assisting in post-adoption contact
- Helping adoptees to search for their roots.
- Helping biological parents to search for their now-adult child.

Case examples

Pedro was brought to the UK from Peru by prospective adopters. During the adoption proceedings, ISSUK was asked to obtain proof that the birth parents had freely agreed to the adoption of their child and understood the implication of this. The ISS Correspondent was able to trace the parents, obtain proof through DNA testing that they were indeed the parents, and confirm that they were willing for their child to be adopted.

Clara was placed in care voluntarily by her mother. Her Malaysian parents had both come to Britain as students, but their relationship ended before Clara was born and the mother requested adoption as she thought it was more important that she finish her studies. The baby was placed for adoption, but the mother and father had both disappeared before the adoption process was complete. ISSUK was asked to try to find the mother to obtain her consent to the adoption, and she was traced to her home town in Malaysia and gave her consent. She was relieved to know about the family who were adopting her daughter.

In his book "International and Trans-racial Adoptions" Christopher Bagley wrote in 1990:

> "It can be said that ISS will continue its involvement and its quiet, careful advocacy and practice in inter-country adoption, supervising certain cases, discouraging many potential adopters, and try to encourage high standards and the development of indigenous services wherever possible. One is continually impressed by the high professional standards maintained by ISS, despite an extremely limited budget; it will continue to have a major voice in the development of practice and policy in this area. Its most potent influence is in the receiving countries, where it can advise governments on ways of controlling the practice of ICA so as to ensure that only properly selected and motivated adoptive parents are involved, and that visas are not given for the entry of a child unless the fullest safeguards and enquiries have been applied in the country of origin."[156]

[156] Quoted in AR 1992.

Custody disputes

Throughout the years there were many examples of custody disputes, where a parent in one country was seeking contact or to resume care of children in another country.

Case examples

Two German girls, Greta and Hilda, aged 4 and 6 came to Britain with their mother and new stepfather. Mother was awarded sole custody of the girls, but 7 years later she died. The girls had had sporadic contact with their father in Germany, and he applied to have the girls with him in Germany. But the stepfather, who had brought up the girls for years, also applied for custody of the children.

ISSUK was asked to obtain reports on the home situation in England, while ISS Germany was in touch with the father. It transpired that the elder girl wanted to return to father and the younger one wanted to stay with stepfather There was conflict between the jurisdictions of Britain and Germany – the Germans claiming the right to decide because the girls were German nationality, but the Court in Britain was involved because the girls lived within their jurisdiction. It was finally agreed that the girls should remain in Britain, and the case was closed. But a year later the elder girl went to visit her father and said she wanted to stay there. So the case was re-opened. This time the father was given custody of the girl. The role of ISS in both countries included making sure that the welfare of the children was kept in the forefront of discussions, in spite of the legal wrangling.

A man contacted ISSUK asking for help in regaining contact with his son Thomas, who was living with his mother in Vienna. He had applied to a court in Austria, who had granted him a contact visit of 2 hours a month, but this was impractical, given the distance involved. The ISS worker counselled the father about further action he could take, and he was able to negotiate longer visits less often.

The Adolescent Mental Health Services in one London Borough referred the case of a 15-year-old boy Manuel, whose father had left the family when he was 6 years old and returned to Venezuela. Manuel had developed behavioural problems and it was felt that it was important for him to re-establish contact with his father. The whereabouts of the father was known, and, although he was reluctant to have anything to do with his ex-partner, he did show some interest in his son. The local welfare agency agreed to work with him to try to find a way forward.

This experience of working with families separated not only by national borders, but also by legal disputes, led to the following project.

The Libyan Family Reunion Project 1997–2010

The FCO knew that ISSUK staff had an understanding of the difficulties that could arise in marriages between British women and men from an Islamic culture. So in 1996 it asked ISSUK to help resolve the problems arising from the abduction of children from Britain to Libya, and the subsequent loss of contact between parents and children. The children were the offspring of marriages between Libyan fathers and British mothers.

Maintaining contact between a child and non-custodial parent following the separation of parents is especially complicated if the parents are living in different countries. Laws concerning custody and contact in the two countries may be incompatible. Libya is not a signatory to the Hague Convention on International Child Abduction, so there is no legal way of compelling a father to return a child to the mother, whether or not she has legal custody under British law. Libya did however accede to the UN Convention on the Rights of the Child in 1993. Article 9 of the Convention states that: "State Parties shall respect the right of the child who is separated from one or both parents to maintain personal relations and direct contact with both parents on a regular basis, except if it is contrary to the child's best interests".[157]

[157] UN Convention on the Rights of the Child 1989.

The FCO initiative was prompted by a small group of British mothers who had been taken to Libya in 1994 by two journalists, who made a film for Channel 4. Whilst some mothers were able to see their children, others were refused access by the father. In Libya the visit was co-ordinated by the Higher Committee for Children (HCC) – the agency with responsibility for child welfare. These mothers wanted to repeat the visit but the Libyan Government indicated that they would first like to see a reciprocal visit by Libyan fathers to the UK. As there were no full diplomatic relations between the UK and Libyan governments, the Libyan authorities could deny visas to the mothers until this request was granted, and so the mothers turned to the FCO for help.

In early 1997 Naima Saghir, the Secretary of the HCC came to London to meet staff from ISSUK and the FCO. They were able to clarify a lot of issues that had arisen, in relation to selection of group members, payment and the practicalities of visits. Perhaps the most important outcome was the establishment of good relationships between the agencies, which made it easier to deal with the inevitable moments of friction over the years.

There were problems in getting visas for the UK for the Libyan men, in spite of FCO backing for the trip, so that the visit had to be delayed; but in the end a group of 8 fathers came to Britain in September 1997, to see their children who had remained with the mothers here. This visit went well for some, but not all of the families, and fathers and children who had not met for years were able to re-establish contact. Identified problems were around accommodation, activities, use of interpreters and payments. The emotional impact of the visit for everyone caused added tensions. The organisation Reunite was also involved, in order to offer support to some of the families after the visit. The ISSUK staff had opposed any press coverage, on grounds of confidentiality, and also because the Channel 4 film of the 1994 visit had caused great offence to some of the fathers, and threatened their future co-operation with the project. However, the HCC persuaded Reunite to arrange for an article in the Daily Telegraph, and this gave them useful publicity for use back in Libya.

From this time, the important role of ISSUK as intermediary between the fathers, the mothers and children, the HCC, local

Social Services Departments and the FCO was firmly established. A brief description of each visit will give the best flavour of how the project proceeded.

It was extremely difficult for individuals to get visas to visit Libya, and sanctions meant that there were no direct flights between the UK and Tripoli – travel was via Tunisia. So it was with some trepidation, and excitement, that a group of 8 mothers, 4 grandmothers, 1 friend, 1 sibling and 2 social workers set off to Libya in 1998. The preparation had taken months, and Heloise Kareem had gone out to Libya to sort out the details. The group stayed for 2 weeks at a holiday complex near the beach a few miles from Tripoli, with good facilities. 20 children joined their families. Only one father insisted on being present, though others visited to check their children were all right. Problems arose over language difficulties, conflict of loyalties, and misunderstandings about culture, but on the whole, the visits were successful. Heloise Kareem and Christina Birch, staff from ISSUK, and Naima Saghir from HCC were on hand to advise on legal matters, or just offer support. A Libyan volunteer acted as interpreter when necessary.

Diplomatic relations between the UK and Libya were resumed in 1999, and so direct travel became possible. The next visit was arranged in 2000. Final confirmation that the visit could take place was only achieved two weeks before departure. This time there were 7 mothers plus 4 relatives, accompanied by Heloise Kareem. 15 children joined their mothers. But this time there were quite a lot of problems and contact was only straightforward in 2 cases. The reactions of the children differed: "Some seem overly conformist, others untypically rebellious, some seem withdrawn or over-anxious to please. Some are manipulative and unable to relate. Some seem aggressive and confused and yet many seem remarkably normal, happy children."[158] Nonetheless, there was evidence of gradual building up of trust between the various family members.

It is unlikely that the visits could ever have taken place without the input from staff of ISS and HCC. It may seem that a

[158] H Kareem – paper for European Seminar 2001.

disproportionate amount of time, effort and cost went into the organisation of a trip for a small group of people, but this is consistent with the ISS philosophy and policy of helping individuals, and it was hoped that the Libyan experience would pave the way for similar projects in other countries. In 2002 Heloise Kareem and Judy Baba made a trip to Cairo to explore the possibility of setting up a similar project there, but in spite of an initially positive response, the idea was not pursued, mainly because the personnel at the British Embassy had changed.

In 2002 a group of 17 people went to Libya, including 7 mothers, 2 siblings, 2 grandmothers, an aunt, niece, 2 friends and 2 staff members, Heloise Kareem and Judy Baba. The time that the families could spend together was often dictated by the father. Some would not leave the children alone with their mother at all, while others were prepared to let their children to stay with their mother throughout the two-week visit. Workers also negotiated between parents to try and ensure some ongoing contact between the children and their mothers during the year. The staff from the Libyan agency had a chance to meet the families and could work with the fathers and children after the visit to try and resolve any outstanding issues. Indeed the success of each visit depended greatly on the work done in each country to prepare the various individuals for contact.

After the visit in August 2002 it was felt that a two-year gap was too long for the children and so efforts were made to raise funds for a visit in 2003. This time the visas only came through two days before departure day! In August 2003 a group of ten relatives and two staff, Heloise Kareem and Judy Baba, travelled to Libya. Two went to stay with their families, while the others went to the holiday village. For those family members who had been in previous years, there was evidence of improved relationships with their children. Some of the families in the group now knew each other from previous visits and could enjoy activities together. However, there were difficulties, such as those between one mother and her teenage daughter, who had been taken to Libya by her father at the age of 3, and she spoke very little English. Conversation with her mother through an interpreter was hard, and they had had no communication in the year since the mother's first visit to her.

"Although not impossible, it is far from easy for a British woman to make her own arrangements to visit her child in Libya. To be granted an entry visa, she needs approval for it from her ex-husband. Many fathers, especially in the early years of separation, fear that the mother may attempt to take the child back to the UK, so are unwilling to give their consent. The Higher Committee, through their volunteer, Mr Muftah El Fagi, makes contact with the fathers prior to the group visit to secure their approval. Where this is withheld unreasonably, the Higher Committee itself has the power to sanction the visit. The group visit helps to ease the fears of both parties: the Libyan father trusts that the semi-official nature of the visit safeguards to a degree against the likelihood of children being removed; the British mother appreciates the safety of group travel, the support of accompanying ISS staff and other members and the greater freedom to enjoy their precious time with their children in a relaxed holiday setting."[159]

Case examples

5 children, aged between 2 and 12, had been abducted by their father two years earlier. The father insisted on a very strict Muslim upbringing, with the two eldest daughters having to be totally covered except for their faces. The father insisted on staying at the complex, and so the children found it difficult to relate to their mother, because of conflicts of loyalty. Some ongoing work was undertaken with both parents before the mother's next visit.

Mona and Kassim, aged 10 and 8 had not seen their mother for 3 years, and were very shy at first, but after a few days they became more confident in speaking English and showed that they had some good memories of their life in England. By the end of the visit Mona, in particular, was able to be affectionate with her mother. They both showed some distress when she had to leave them, but the father agreed that they

159 Report of British Mothers' Family Reunion Visit to Libya 2003.

could keep in contact by phone during the coming year. During the visit he had significantly softened his attitude to the mother, mainly because of the work done by the Libyan staff.

Funding had always been a problem – the group members paid their own costs, but some needed subsidies from ISSUK. Then administration costs and staff travel expenses had to be covered. ISSUK raised some funds from companies with Libyan connections, and the FCO had made a contribution each year, but finally in 2004 they agreed to cover all the ISSUK costs.

In 2004 Heloise Kareem and Marek Ganther led a group of 7 mothers to Libya. One mother, who was on her first visit, had not seen her children for 9 years. The report describes their reunion as a "roller-coaster" during the two weeks.

In 2005 there was a group of 20. Once again the visit achieved the primary object of contact between the mothers and children. However, this year there was need for more intervention by the staff, particularly in the case of fathers interfering with the children's contact with their mother. The children's reactions were very varied, depending on their ages at separation from their mother, what they had been told about her, and the attitude of the father and other family members to her.

In 2006 there were huge problems in arranging the visit because of the closure of the Higher Committee for Children. Visas were only obtained through the intervention of the Libyan Ambassador to London. By 2007 there were changes. Marek Ganther of ISSUK was now working with the General People's Committee of Social Affairs and the Wa'atasimo Charitable Organisation, with whom a co-operation agreement was signed. They offered complete funding of flights, accommodation and meals for all family members, thus enabling other families to join the group. Changes in the Libyan Government held things up for a while, but at the last minute Marek Ganther was able to take a group there. The holiday complex had been refurbished and was much pleasanter, and a good neutral venue for the visit.

In 2008 the group of 22 included members from France, Czech Republic and Bulgaria as well as the UK. There were three British mothers making their first visit to their children.

As usual, the control exercised by some of the fathers, by arriving late with the children, or insisting on watching the mothers with the children, caused real tensions which tended to affect the whole group. But on the positive side the bonds between mothers and children were very strong. "It is amazing to see how the mothers re-establish and strengthen their rapport with their children, and the fondness with which the children gravitate towards their mothers. This connection lays the groundwork for a positive and loving relationship throughout the child's life, where this is allowed, as in some families, despite regular visits, contact outside of them remains difficult."[160] In a few cases, the mothers were able to visit their children in between group visits.

In 2009 the volunteer Muftah El Fagi was awarded an Honorary MBE for his services.

Unfortunately the visit was cancelled in 2009, but one in 2010 was successful, and resulted in a film being made by Sky TV. The fall of the regime in Libya in 2011 stopped the scheme, and, at the time of writing, it is not clear when, or if, it might start again.

It is hard to evaluate the success of such a project – while the numbers involved were small, the visits had a profound impact on those mothers, children and other relatives who were able to re-establish and maintain contact with each other. It was always hoped that this project could be repeated with other countries, and while this has not happened, it may be that the lessons learned will be of use when dealing with cases of abduction, and the maintenance of contact between children and absent parents.

160 Report "Family Reunion visit to Libya 2008 ".

Chapter 10

The 2000s

World events

The major global recession in the middle of the decade led to large movements of economic migrants. Families were often split while one member went away to find work, hoping that others would join him or her. Conflict in many countries, especially in Afghanistan, the Middle East and Africa, caused huge numbers of people to flee their homes. The majority were internally displaced, or in camps just inside neighbouring countries – the burden of caring for the displaced often falling on governments who had little or no resources to do so. Most of these migrants had no possibility of going further. But the ingenuity and determination of desperate people to reach safety and better opportunities in Europe, led to an increase in people-smuggling, by middle-men who had little regard for the wellbeing of their clients. Most of these migrants went elsewhere in Europe, but many of those that reached Britain disappeared into the unofficial labour market, as virtual slaves until they could repay their passage. These people only came to the notice of ISSUK if they were rescued by officials and there was a need to reconnect with family members overseas. Some of these were unaccompanied children and young people under the age of 18.

Other minors came in by themselves or were brought by adults who claimed to be relatives or friends. All these migrants who were picked up at ports of entry, and who were, or claimed to be, under the age of 18, became the responsibility of the local authority. The numbers coming to the attention of ISS in the UK and in other European countries continued to rise.

By contrast, the official number of adult asylum seekers reaching the UK fell in this decade, partly due to more rigorous immigration procedures.

The definition of "family" had changed over the decades, to include a wide range of family structures, both formal and informal. In cases where parents were not married, for example, finding the best outcome for a child could involve complications of nationality, parental responsibility and different legal understandings. For most families coming to the attention of ISSUK, the aim was to find a long-term solution to a problem. But ISSUK was also becoming aware of another group of families, some of whose members were not migrating but moving regularly or frequently between countries, usually for work reasons. These were defined as "transnational families". The members of one family might come from more than one nationality or ethnic group. Most of these families managed complicated lifestyles and kept the links between themselves without extra help, but ISSUK's involvement could become necessary when families were not coping, especially when there were breakdowns of relationships and communication. "Transnational families have to develop new strategies to cope with the dispersed family network and to interact within and beyond borders, and intervention is necessitated by the complex social and welfare needs of many such families."[161] "The greatly increased mobility of peoples across the world, in response to globalisation and economic factors, or as a result of conflict and persecution, may significantly improve the life chances of many, but others become victims of this phenomenon, the most vulnerable being children."[162]

Legislation

Several laws and regulations in this decade were of immediate application to the work of ISSUK on issues of child protection and placement, unaccompanied minors seeking asylum, adoption, contact and tracing. Topics like access to information, or trafficking of children come up in more than one statute.

Some related to the organisation and inspection of charities and to access to information:

161 ISS Newsletter Spring 2009.

162 ISSUK Core Document 2005.

- Care Standards Act 2000 – set the regulatory and inspectoral regime and established National Minimum Standards. Inspections of ISSUK took place under this Act.
- Freedom of Information Act 2000 – gave individuals the right of access to all public records, subject to exclusions of some confidential material.
- Charities Act 2006 set out new standards and regulations for the reports, accounts and fundraising of charities.

There were several pieces of legislation relating to adoption:

- Adoption and Children Act 2002 – this law modernised the whole framework of domestic and intercountry adoption and introduced a new status of legal Guardianship. In accordance with the Hague Convention 1993, the Act required that safeguards be put in place to ensure that inter-country adoptions take place in the best interests of the child. It established a system of co-operation between countries who have signed the Convention to prevent the abduction, sale or traffic in children. It also introduced new mechanisms for adopted persons to obtain information about their adoption, and set up the Adopted Children Register and the Adoption Contact Register. This is significant in all tracing work.
- Children and Adoption Act 2006 – this included provision for suspensions of adoption where there are concerns about practices in connection with adoption of children in another country.

Some laws relating to immigration and trafficking:

- The National Immigration and Asylum Act 2002 – this controversial Act cut off support to asylum seekers who did not seek asylum on entry to the country, but the policy had later to be dropped in 2004, when the European Court held that it breached the European Convention on Human Rights. It was amended by the Immigration, Asylum and Nationality Act of 2006.
- UK Borders Act 2007 – abolished the Immigration Service and set up the Borders Agency. The Act also requires the Secretary of State "to publish a Code of Practice for keeping

children safe from harm, and ensure that acts of trafficking aimed at the UK are liable to prosecution.

In addition there were a whole range of Regulations issued for England and Wales, including:

- The Children (Private Arrangements for Fostering) Regulations 2005 – this included a requirement to check whether the contact between fostered children and their parents were satisfactory.
- Working Together to Safeguard Children 2006 set out a framework for co-operation by all agencies concerned with the welfare of children, and required the setting up of Local Safeguarding Children Boards in all local authorities. It also laid down a Framework for the Assessment of Children in Need and their Families. Relevant sections for ISS deal with children who go missing, migrant children, victims of trafficking and unaccompanied minors.
- Guidance issued jointly by the Department of Education and Home Office on safeguarding children who may have been trafficked.

The general secretariat and the network

In the year 2000 ISS celebrated the 75th anniversary of its founding – actually a year late! The Headquarters in Geneva held an Open Day for all relevant organisations, and Audrey Moser gave the keynote address "Young People in Migration – in historical context."

At the International Meeting of the Council of ISS in 2000 some changes were made to the Executive Committee of ISS, which was now made up of all the Directors of the Branches and Affiliated Bureaux (instead of just representatives of this group), seven individual members, the International president and the International Treasurer. The members of the Council of ISSUK opposed this change on the grounds that the Executive should include officers of the governing bodies of the Branches, who were, in their own countries, responsible for the policies of the organisation, and for implementing any international decisions. Nevertheless, the changes went through and Liz Emery and John

Wheeler from the ISSUK Council were elected as two of the seven individual members in 2000. Liz Emery was also elected to the Bureau which met every six months to oversee the work of the GS. Later, in 2008 Doug Lewis became an independent member of the International Board.

By 2009 it had become apparent that this model of governance was not working well, to the benefit of the network, and so the Statutes were revised in 2010, after the period covered by this book.

Staff of GS

Damien Ngabonziza was SG until the summer of 2003. Vincent Faber became SG in January 2004, and after he left in December 2006, for a short while the General Secretariat had neither a Secretary General nor an International President. The Director and Chairman of the Swiss Branch were assisting the staff. Jean Ayoub became SG in July 2007.

In 2001 there were only the equivalent of 6 full-time staff in the GS. "They provide the organisation and servicing of meetings, ongoing Secretariat duties, organisation of training, casework, staffing of the Resource Centre, maintenance of standards throughout the network and development of new correspondents. The Secretary General personally supervises two external programmes, in Rwanda and Kosovo, and represents ISS in Geneva and internationally. What the SG and his small staff have achieved is to be remarked" (AR2000/1).

The Casework Division of the General Secretariat in Geneva was seriously under-staffed, with one full-time caseworker, and so it was dependent on volunteers to undertake most of the casework. The volunteers spoke a number of languages and were able to translate a lot of referrals. While Branches could pass cases between themselves, it had always been the procedure that, when a case involved a country with a correspondent, it went through the General Secretariat. In 2000 they handled 636 open cases, and many more enquiries. With effect from January 2003 Branches were handed the responsibility for direct referrals to most of the correspondents. Referrals only continued to go through the Casework Division to 38 countries which were particularly problematic due to financial or political reasons. This certainly speeded things up, but left a lot of Correspondents without the support they needed.

The ISS network

Several of the Branches hit hard times and the French Branch had to close. The Director of the Greek Branch kept it going by working without pay. Canada was in serious difficulties for much of this period. The impact on the GS was serious as the branches were not able to pay their contributions.

But in other parts of the world ISS was growing. In 2000 the Department of Welfare in South Africa was granted Affiliated Bureau status. The Delegation in the Philippines became a Branch in 2006. A Delegation was established in Albania, originally as a satellite of the Italian Branch.

The Branches at the end of 2009 were in Australia, Belgium, Canada, Germany, Greece, Hong Kong, Japan, Netherlands, Philippines, Switzerland, UK, USA, and Venezuela.

Affiliated Bureaux were Israel, New Zealand, Portugal and South Africa, and there were 120 Correspondents.

In Athens in 2003 there was a seminar on "Unaccompanied and Separated Minors", which was attended by 78 ISS workers from 35 different countries, including Sue Gilbert.

In 2007 the General Secretariat published "The activities of International Social Service and their legal bases". This sets out the International Laws and Conventions under which ISS operates.

ISSUK within the wider ISS

ISSUK was the only Branch that was totally self-funding, as all other branches were linked to other organisations, or totally reliant on their governments for funding. The British Branch had always recognised its responsibility to contribute to the running of the GS, but even they were not able to do so when funds were low. For example, in 2004 they only paid £3,000 instead of the expected annual sum of £15,000.

At the International Council Meeting in 2000 the representatives of the UK Branch were able to show a video of the work of ISSUK: "it was considered by colleagues from around the world that it conveyed, in an imaginative way, information about ISS, its values and its working methods which would be appreciated in their countries."[163]

The ISS Director usually attended the 3-yearly conferences of supervisors of ISS units.

From 2000 until the end of 2003 Liz Emery of the UK Branch and Rolf Widmer of the Swiss Branch, undertook the editorship of an International Newsletter for the whole organisation, with a circulation to over 130 countries.

ISSUK was involved in getting funding for development of the service in Southern Africa and Georg Stahl worked on strengthening the network capacity in South Africa. Georg Stahl also built direct links between ISSUK and the correspondents in Jamaica, Nigeria, Malawi, Kenya, Zambia, Pakistan and the Democratic Republic of Congo. This had a significant impact on the service received from these countries. ISSUK was represented at the First International Conference on Child Sex Abuse in Africa, organised by the African Network for the Prevention and Protection against Child Abuse and Neglect.

ISSUK

On 13th July 2008 the office moved to open-plan premises in a modern block at I Canterbury Court, Brixton Road – along the road from the old office.

This decade saw dramatic fluctuations in income, major changes in the Governing Body and more changes in the staff team than ever before. Yet it was a time of significant improvements in working practices and in fundraising. Because of the financial climate there was a constant tension between the pressure to raise funds for work that the staff saw as priority, and the pressure to prioritise work that was most likely to attract

163 AR 2000/1.

funding. This was also a time of Inspections and Reviews, and these are summarised later in this chapter. They demonstrate how ISSUK was willing to address problems and to use its expertise to move forward.

Governance

The status of the organisation changed again when ISSUK was registered as a Company limited by Guarantee, and set up by a Memorandum and Articles of Association, on 3rd July 2000. In March 2001 the Charity Commission agreed to the change of status, and this meant having a new registration number from the Charity Commissioners.[164] ISSUK was now an incorporated body. This meant that it was a legally separate entity, and that the Trustees were no longer personally liable for any debts that it might have. The organisation was subject to both Company Law and Charity Law in the way it reported its affairs. The Trustees were now trustees of the charity for the purposes of Charity law, and Directors for the purposes of the Companies Act.

The Objects of the Charity were more specific than those in the earlier Constitutions (Chapter 6) and were now stated to be:

"a) to assist those who, as a result of voluntary or forced migration or other social problems of an international character, have to overcome personal or family difficulties, the solution of which requires co-ordinated actions in several countries, or in some cases, action only in the country of residence of the persons concerned.

b) to study from an international standpoint the conditions and consequences of migration in relation to individual and family life and, as a result of such studies, to make recommendations or undertake any other appropriate action.

c) to contribute to the prevention of social problems linked to migration or inter-country mobility.

d) to inform professionals and the public of the needs of migrant individuals and families.

[164] AR 2000–1.

e) to assist in developing and maintaining an international network of national bodies able to meet the needs of individuals and families who require the services of ISSUK"[165]

Council/Board of Trustees

Sir Anthony Figgis became President in 2001, taking over from Sir James Weatherall, the President from 1996, who was also his predecessor as Marshall of the Diplomatic Corps. In this role they both gave important backing to the members of the diplomatic community who were central to the running of the Spring Fair. They held a reception each year at which new members of the community were introduced to the work of ISSUK. It seems that it was James Weatherall who was the catalyst for change as he saw that things could not continue in the same way that they had been drifting. But change takes time and it was his successor who saw through the changes.[166]

By 2003 the Council was under severe strain because of the chronic under-funding and the constant risk of bankruptcy. Liz Emery set up a Trust from which she hoped to raise enough money, but in the event she could not do so, and what monies she had raised were given to the office in Geneva. At the end of 2003 she resigned and Douglas Lewis took over as Chairman. He set about transforming the Council, strengthening the structure and re-positioning ISSUK in the professional arena. His new proposals were for a stronger Council, concentrating on the need to raise funds, with an Income-Generation Group focusing on fund-raising and working on a Business Plan, and a Professional Advisory Group overseeing the professional work. It was proposed that only the Chair of this Advisory Group would have a seat on Council. However, such emphasis was placed on recruiting Trustees who could contribute to the fund-raising, that all Trustees with social work backgrounds resigned in 2003, though one Trustee from the Civil Service remained. This imbalance soon began to be redressed in 2004 with the

165 Memorandum of Association of ISSUK 2000.

166 Interview with C Marshall.

recruitment of two trustees with social work experience in Local Authorities (of whom I was one, and the other a retired Director of Social Services, Robert Hutchinson), and later, another social worker who had run a voluntary adoption agency, Yvettte Gayford. Other new trustees were recruited from the business world, including Ali Sattaripour and Pam Louhichi, and the Civil Service, Liz Grimsey. A few years later new trustees, such as Tessa Brewer and Sarah Palmer and Kumari Blakey would add impetus to the fundraising. Another new trustee was a lawyer, Alex Verdan, who offered expert legal advice to both the Trustees and the social workers, which was much appreciated. The Chair of the Spring Fair Committee was an ex-officio member of the Council.

From 2004 onwards the Council was usually referred to as the Board of Trustees. This was primarily to avoid confusion with the International Council.

At that time there was no formal recruitment system for appointing new Trustees: the Chairman, President and Treasurer, as Officers of the Company, sought recommendations of suitable people from other members of the Board, staff, users and donors. New members were usually co-opted to the Board until their appointments were ratified at an Annual General Meeting. They had a brief induction, and then learned about the organisation through attending Board and sub-committee meetings, meeting the staff and becoming involved in fundraising or social work matters. From 2005 a member of the social work staff presented a case at each Board meeting, in order to demonstrate the range and complexity of the work. In 2006 the Board introduced a procedure to monitor its own progress by means of an annual appraisal, and in 2008 the induction programme was formalised.

The Board of Trustees met 5 times a year, and there were 2 extraordinary meetings, in 2005 and 2008 to discuss urgent financial matters. All the members were also involved in helping with fundraising or social work matters and/or strategic planning and governance issues. The Board of Trustees set up an Income Generating Sub-group in March 2005.

In 2006 it was agreed that ISSUK should appoint certain distinguished people as Patrons, in order to help raise awareness of the agency, and thereby increase funding. The existing Patron,

Princess Alexandra, would be called the Royal Patron. The first new Patron was Lord Laming, who was appointed in 2007. He was Vice President of the Local Government Association, and had formerly been the Chief Inspector of Social Services. He immediately became involved and gave a keynote speech at an ISSUK training seminar for social workers in June 2008, and joined staff in meetings with government departments. This gave a real boost to the organisation. In 2008 Sir Anthony Figgis and Lady Françoise Middleton were made Patrons in recognition of what they had done for ISSUK. The position of Honorary Vice-Presidents was ended.

Douglas Lewis (Doug), was an ex-naval officer who had been a Director of Personnel in the Navy, and later in all the Armed Forces. He had then been Chief Executive of a leading barristers' chambers. He had experience in marketing campaigns, especially through his long involvement with navy rugby. He was first involved with ISSUK through the Spring Fair Committee which he chaired in 2002 and 2003. He became convinced of the value of the organisation, but was concerned about the way it was being run. He was elected Chairman of the Council/Board of Trustees and proceeded to put all his energies into getting the organisation on a firmer footing. He was a "hands-on" Chairman, who was concerned for the staff and their working conditions. But his focus was improving the financial status of ISSUK, and he spent countless hours finding and encouraging new donors and trustees, and energising fundraising events. From time to time, despite positive signals from potential donors, the failure of expected funds to materialise led to disappointments when budgets could not be met. Doug was determined in the pursuit of what he believed to be best for the organisation, and ruffled some feathers, but it is undoubtedly true that, without his passion and commitment the ISSUK would have folded at several points, but particularly in 2005. He took on the role of Executive Chairman when there was no Chief Executive. He also took the lead in guiding the charity towards the change of name in 2010, and remained Chair of CFAB in its early years.

Doug Lewis was elected an individual member of the Executive Council of ISS (EXCO) in Geneva in 2008 and was Chairman of the new Governing Board from 2010 to 2014. He contributed a great deal to the international meetings, and did all he could to support successive Secretaries-General. In 2014 he was elected International President of ISS.

Staff

During this decade there were significant fluctuations in the numbers of staff. From 2000 to early 2003 there were nearly always 14 staff, comprising Director, Deputy Director, 5 social workers, Tracing and Family contact worker, 5 Administrative staff and an Events Organiser.

In spite of being seriously ill, Peter Fry struggled on as Director, but in the end he had to leave before his planned leaving date in July 2003, and he was too ill to have any formal farewells.

The Deputy Director, Heloise Kareem, retired in April 2003. Her wide-reaching contribution to the work of ISSUK over a 36-year period was immensely important in promoting the highest standards of social work.

By the end of 2003 the number of staff had dropped by almost a third to 9. Due to financial constraints, two social work posts were frozen and two other posts were made redundant.[167]

Sue Gilbert, Principal Social Worker, and social worker Marek Ganther were appointed Acting Directors in July 2003, with the Office Manager, Chris Platt, taking responsibility for the administrative and financial management of the organisation. Marek had wide experience in many areas of social work, including child care and mental health. Within a few months, the social work team included two other social workers, Georg Stahl and Leander Prifti, as well as the Tracing and Family contact worker, Lesley Austen. Georg was German. He had experience of working in various child care settings and had a Masters degree in European Social Policy from Bath University. In due course he became Principal Social Worker. Leander, an Albanian, had worked with asylum seekers in Southampton. 2 more social workers joined the team in 2004: a Ugandan, Hellen KulaZikulabe, who had experience with several agencies in Uganda before she came to London to study for an MA, after which she worked in the Children and Families team in Westminster; and a German, Nadine Schmitt, who had worked with ethnic communities in Germany before moving to the UK and working in 2 London Boroughs with unaccompanied asylum seeking children.

[167] AR2004.

The Administrative team, led by Chris Platt, included Mark Hunt as Finance and Statistical Officer, and Liz Sweeney who provided support to the project workers, and was Minutes Secretary to the Board of Trustees. Throughout the decade there were been improvements to administrative systems, and in particular to IT provision. In October 2003 the first website was set up. The computer system was replaced in 2004, and upgraded a few years later.

Chris Platt joined ISSGB in 1980 as an administrative assistant, and was the Administrative Officer for the Repatriation Scheme in 1981. A year later he left to return to his previous work in the retail sector, but continued to volunteer for the ISS at the Spring Fair and as part of the Thames Area Support Committee. He rejoined ISSUK in 1990 and soon was in charge of all the administration. He oversaw many of the technical developments in the office. He held so much knowledge about the organisation that he became an invaluable resource, especially at times of change.

Adrian Hatch was appointed Chief Executive in June 2004. He came with valuable experience of running a voluntary organisation in Africa. He approached his new job with great energy and enthusiasm, and impressed everyone in the way he learned about the work. He soon had a 5-year Strategic Plan prepared. He was good at involving staff and trustees in the discussions. During his time at ISSUK more local authorities registered with ISSUK (108 in 2005).

He appointed a Human Resources (HR) firm, Peninsula Business Services, in 2005 to act as consultant on all personnel matters. In this year a Staff Handbook was produced, and a Staff Appraisal Scheme was introduced. Better systems for supervision, development and training of all staff were established. New salary scales had been introduced for all staff In March 2004, and a contributory pension scheme was offered. A limited flexi-time policy was instituted.

Adrian made dozens of applications to Government sources and Trusts, but the competition was huge – with regard to one application to a Trust, he was told that only 67 applications out of 1,500 made were successful. He could not meet the income generation targets that he had been set, and so, following the near collapse of the charity in 2005, the Chief Executive post was made redundant, and Adrian left at the end of March 2006.

At this time the pressure fell on Sue Gilbert particularly, as Principal Social worker (as noted in the Board Minutes 12.07.2006). The summer of 2006 was a low point, with annual leave for a reduced staff group resulting in very thin cover in the office in August. The staff could only deal with the most urgent cases, and caseloads were unacceptably high. In October 2006 Sue Gilbert was appointed Acting Director. It was then decided that Sue should be appointed as Director in April 2007, for a period of up to 2 years, to give some stability to the organisation. Georg Stahl became Principal Social Worker in May 2007, until he left in 2009. Sue Gilbert worked enormously hard to build up and support the staff team, including more fully the administrative staff, and to strengthen the position of ISSUK within the wider ISS network and with local authorities and NGOs. Her position as Adoption Support Manager was delegated to the social worker specialising in adoption, but that worker did not have sufficient experience to carry out this role efficiently, and this contributed to the decision to end Adoption Support work in 2008.

During these years when there was no CEO some of the Trustees played a more pro-active role in the running of ISSUK. In particular, some aspects of the Chief Executive's role were assumed by Doug Lewis as Executive Chairman, notably oversight of the fundraising. Two other Trustees with social work experience offered extra back-up to the staff. It can be difficult to settle the boundaries of such roles, when trustees move from their position as overseers to that of greater involvement in the day-to-day business, but on the whole, everyone pulled together for the sake of the organisation. One of the Trustees, Rob Hutchinson, was particularly helpful in arranging links with statutory bodies.

Due to the improved publicity and the training that had been given, the number of enquiries and referrals increased, and the need for more social workers became acute. By 2007 an American, Margaret Paton had joined the social workers. In 2008 three new social workers and a fundraiser joined the team. Dorothee Wockel, a German, Hana Najsrova a Czech-Canadian,

Laura Gomez-Roldan a Spaniard and Florence Grandvalet a French social worker; they had all had social work experience overseas, and also in Britain. Some had worked in teams with asylum-seeking children. As the staff group increased, there was a feeling of optimism and lots of ideas for possible new work projects, but there was also frustration that the funds were lacking to put these ideas into practice.

As far as fundraising staff were concerned, it was not all plain sailing. In 2004 an Events Manager was appointed but was made redundant within a year. There were few applicants for the posts, given the salaries that could be offered, but a Trust Fundraiser, Lina Santeusanio was appointed in April 2005. In 2007 Nicola Power was appointed Events and Major Donor Manager, and Lina transferred to the post of Grant and Trust Manager. Kate Nevens took the Fundraising and Marketing Assistant post, which was introduced in 2008. Darren Moses joined the team as Events and Major Donors Manager when Nicola Power left in 2009.

At the beginning of 2009 the Board agreed that the finances were in place to appoint a new CEO, and there was no doubt that this was necessary for the future of ISSUK. However, it meant that there would be no need for a Director anymore, and Sue Gilbert left.

Sue Gilbert qualified as a social worker in 1985 and spent 10 years as a Probation Officer. Wanting a new challenge, she joined VSO in 1995 and was posted to the Republic of the Maldives as their Child Rights Co-ordinator, working with the Government to co-ordinate implementation of the UN Convention on the Rights of the Child. In 1998 she moved to Romania as Regional Manager for the European Children's Trust, working with Local Government to assist them with their de-institutionalisation programme. In late 1999 she moved to Macedonia as Head of Office for the International Catholic Migration Commission, involved in the resettlement of those displaced from Kosovo. She also was a Child Rights Trainer for UNICEF there.[168]

She returned to the UK in 2001 and joined ISSUK, bringing to the job a wide knowledge and experience of international social work, and a particular expertise in Children's Rights. In her 8 years with the organisation she started as an intercountry social

[168] ISSUK Newsletter Summer 2007.

worker and became Principal Social Worker a year later. In 2003 she was appointed joint Acting Director, returning to her role as Principal Social Worker the following year until 2006, when she again became Acting Director and finally Director from April 2007. Sue was bright, energetic, imaginative and passionate about the work. She could be combative in trying to achieve what she believed was necessary. She moulded a good staff group. During her time as Director, the records show how much she achieved in terms of improving so many aspects of the work – although officially working only 4 days a week. She did more than anyone else to hold the team together during some difficult years. Sue's departure in 2009 was a real loss to ISSUK.

Changes in personnel are often stressful for an organisation. As a result of continual change in this period as ISSUK tried to re-establish itself on a sound financial footing, there were regrettable staff casualties. The loss through redundancy of Sue Gilbert, Lesley Austen, the Tracing and Contact worker, and Liz Sweeney, Administrative Assistant, all of whom were long-serving members of staff, caused a slump in staff morale. As the longest serving staff member, Chris Platt played a central role in keeping the office functioning, and Mark Hunt as Receptionist, continued to present a calm, efficient and friendly response to enquirers and visitors. The remaining social work staff, led by Georg Stahl, kept the Advice Line and casework going, although there were times when cases could not be allocated because the social workers were overloaded. This was damaging to the relationships between ISSUK and other organisations, especially Local Authorities and CAFCASS, and yet the staff had got neither the resources nor the manpower or energy to combat this effectively. It was sad to see the "can-do" attitude that had always been such a feature of ISSUK turn temporarily into a "can't-do" approach. Georg Stahl left at the end of July 2009.

A new Chief Executive, Andy Elvin, was appointed in 2009. He was a qualified social worker with local authority experience. Andy took over at one of the lowest points in the history of the organisation, but with more funds available to do something about it. Within a year there was a new social work team, and there was an emphasis on recruiting social workers who had more experience of local authority work, as well as international experience. At last a Personal Assistant to the CEO was appointed, and Andy was able to assume full responsibility for operational matters, so that the Chairman could stand back from the day-to-day management issues. Due to all these factors, the morale improved and the whole organisation was re-energised.

Students

From the 1990s ISSUK had provided placements for students on social work training courses. From 2004 Georg Stahl built up this work and also gave training to students at the University of East Anglia, Brunel University and the University of Hull. A few students were from other countries, such as Denmark, and it was possible that some of them might become correspondents for ISS one day. Providing good quality student placements requires an investment of time on the part of the supervisors, and Georg made sure that the students with ISSUK were given a useful and enjoyable experience.

Strategic Plans/ Business Plans

It is likely that there were several medium to long-term plans drawn up during the 55 years covered by this history but, unfortunately, the records no longer exist to show any plans before the last decade.

1. The first Development Plan that is recorded was in 2000, as a result of an inspection by the Department of Health (DOH). It incorporated changes recommended by the DOH.

2. The Strategic Plan 2005–8 identified 6 key strategic aims. These were:

"• To offer a first class social work service to our clients
- To develop our profile and capacity in order to inform and influence UK policy and practice in our field of work.
- To play an active role in the development and strengthening of the international network
- To ensure that staff support, development and welfare is integral to ISSUK to the benefit of our clients.
- To achieve and maintain the highest standards of good governance

- To develop a sustainable and diverse financial base."[169]

3. In 2008 Sue Gilbert and the staff produced a new three-year Strategic Plan "Towards a National Intercountry Resource Centre" (ISSUK's Strategic Plan 2008–2010). This plan made clear "the need to re-position the charity vis-à-vis its statutory and private business and funding partners".[170] It focused on sharing expertise in order to train practitioners to deal more effectively with intercountry cases, and to influence the work nationally and internationally. While stressing the need to strengthen the capacity of ISSUK, the plan also emphasises the need to establish a comprehensive monitoring and evaluation system. This plan was overtaken by subsequent changes and was only partially put into effect.

4. Business Plan. In October 2008 an emergency meeting of the Board was called to consider the impact of the economic crisis on ISSUK. It was agreed that the status quo was unsustainable and, as a result of this, Yvette Gayford was commissioned to prepare a new draft Business Plan. She stood down as Trustee for the time that this consultancy took. She addressed the serious concern that there was too great a dependence on fundraising through events.

Her report made several recommendations. She proposed: "that ISSUK must begin to limit the amount of work which did not attract funding, and concentrate on developing services which the organisation was uniquely equipped to do and which would attract fees or funding".[171] The only service that ISSUK should give free of charge was casework to the ISS network. The service to Local Authorities and other statutory bodies should be fully covered by charges to those bodies. As a result of this plan and the CSCI inspection, it was decided to stop the Post Adoption Support work and Tracing. The report also recommended that a CEO should be appointed as soon as possible.

The next Business Plan 2009–12 had much the same strategic objects as previous plans; to strengthen internal capacity, to limit the work that was not fee producing, to simplify the fee structure,

169 ISSUK Strategic Plan 2005–8.

170 Report by S Gilbert to Trustees 2008.

171 Business Plan by Y Gayford 2008.

to improve relations with CAFCASS, to develop work with unaccompanied minors, to develop mediation services for separated children, to develop intercountry child protection work, to develop partnerships with other agencies and to develop specific projects to develop the network. In relation to funding of the organisation, the plan recommended rebranding the charity and building on previous fundraising strategies to establish a mixed income stream.

Risk assessment and Board management

In 2007 the Charity Commission put out improved guidelines regarding the role and preparation of Trustees. At the same time the Board recognised the need to strengthen and broaden the membership of the Board, especially from legal and fundraising perspectives.

It had been a requirement of Boards of Charities that they should review regularly a system of risk assessment. In ISS this mainly related to insurance matters, until 2007, when Liz Grimsey, a Trustee and a Civil Servant in the Ministry of Justice, was asked to review the whole area of Risk Assessment and Monitoring. A group of trustees and staff worked for some time to develop a more precise scheme of assessing and managing risk. All aspects of the agency's work was scored under 2 headings: the level of risk to the charity's operation should an event occur, and the likelihood of such an event occurring. Events that scored highly were to be monitored carefully and reviewed regularly. The main areas of risk were identified under operational, financial and external headings. Some of the main risks were tied to the variable financial situation, and to sudden withdrawal of income streams, and also to major loss of staff or trustees. External risks, such as problems within the wider ISS network, or changes to legislation were, on the whole, beyond the control of the Board of Trustees, but their possible impact needed to be recognised. The risk of collapse of the organisation was very real at times. Preoccupation with survival meant that sometimes insufficient time was given to long-term strategies, but when Strategic Plans were developed, there was not the funding to carry them out fully.

Advisors, inspections and reviews

Throughout this decade the Trustees and Staff were supported by a whole range of advisors, some of whom just undertook a one-off review, whilst others offered longer term support. The agency was also subject to a number of external inspections. The recommendations from all these were crucial to the development of the work.

As part of the drive for greater financial security, a number of reviews of the organisation took place. It was recognised that there needed to be better co-ordination of fundraising, improvement of the profile of the organisation, changes to the work as a result of outside influences, such as changes in laws and regulations, and modernisation of systems to maximise efficiency, and adapt to new technology. There was almost continuous internal review of these issues, but in addition there were several external reviews and inspections. The Charity was regulated by the Social Services Inspectorate, the Care Standards Commission and the Charity Commission.

In addition, from 2003 all social work staff had to be registered with the General Social Care Council (GSCC) in order to practise as social workers. Registration had to be renewed every 3 years.

As well as the following list of main events, there were many instances of individuals giving valued advice and support to both staff and trustees on a wide range of topics. Their contributions can only be acknowledged here. They were greatly appreciated.

Advisors:	Professional Advisory Group 2004–7
Inspections:	Dept of Health Inspection of Adoption Services in 2000
	National Care Standards Agency Inspection of Adoption in 2003
	Charity Commission Inspection in 2004
	Commission for Social Care Inspection of Adoption Services in 2007
Reviews:	Review of fundraising in 2006 by Emma Low
	Review of Administrative Support in 2007 by Steve Dixon
	Review of fundraising in 2009 by Bernie McDermott

Advisors

The advisors came from a variety of backgrounds and helped with every aspect of the work. Many Trustees gave advice – notably the Treasurers and the Legal Advisors. From time to time, fundraising committees were set up. But it was in relation to the social work that a longer term advisory group was set up.

Professional Advisory Group (PAG)

The first PAG was set up in 1994 but had ceased to function by early 2003, due to other priorities for the staff. In 2004 the Trustees set up a new Professional Advisory Group, to be chaired by a Trustee who had a social work background. The group included both trustees and independent members, all of whom had experience in social work, central government service or law.

The Terms of Reference of the group were to:

> "form a supportive link between the Council (who remain finally accountable in law for all the work of ISS) and the professional staff. It is to help ensure both that the Council's confidence may be maintained at all times in ISS's professional work, and reciprocally, that the staff may feel properly supported by Council. For working purposes, the group will:
>
> 1. Provide a forum where social work issues of current importance can be discussed fully.
>
> 2. Help the staff to develop the social work strategy for the organisation.
>
> 3. Scrutinise and discuss draft policy papers, and papers on any matters requiring decision by the Trustees.
>
> 4. Provide support for the staff.
>
> 5. Contribute to regular evaluations of the work of ISSUK."[172]

Over the next 3 years there were fifteen meetings of the group. Issues discussed included cases presenting dilemmas for the staff,

[172] Terms of Reference of PAG 1994.

new developments in the work and changes to policies. A constant theme was about the boundaries of the work. There were many questions about how far to go in certain cases, and whether there were areas of work that were not essential for ISSUK to do. Some cases highlighted questions about the role of ISSUK: what should be done in situations where families' safety might be endangered by the intervention of British social workers, from ISSUK or local authorities or CAFCASS. The new Data Protection Act threw up questions about the confidentiality of material being passed between agencies.

Staff were working on reviewing all the policies of the organisation, and these were brought to the PAG for scrutiny before being presented to the Board of Trustees for approval. These included policies related to the philosophy of ISS, such as Equal Opportunities Policy; related to the casework, such as Child Protection Policy and Policy on Tracing, and several policies concerning staff matters. Most of the policies also had accompanying Procedures.

Although individual social workers appreciated the opportunity to discuss difficult case issues with the group, there was frustration that it had not proved possible to recruit a wide enough range of advisors. It proved more useful to set up links with individual lawyers, for example, than to expect a lawyer to give up time to attend the PAG meetings.

At Board meetings, the Trustees from the PAG were in a position to support recommendations that had been discussed by the group, such as requests for more staff, new policy documents, and ideas for new projects. The PAG instigated improved links between the trustees and staff. Not only did staff members and the Trustees on the PAG get to know each other, but also one member of staff introduced a case at each Board meeting, and staff and trustees met for lunch periodically.

The PAG was disbanded in 2007, because there was now a social worker as Director. But its demise left a gap between the staff and Board of Trustees, in that there was no longer an official route ensuring that policies and social work matters, such as proposals for new work, had been sufficiently scrutinised before being put before the Board of Trustees for approval.

Inspections

Department Of Health (DOH) inspection in 2000

It was necessary that ISSUK be inspected by the DOH in order to be registered as a Voluntary Adoption Agency (VAA), under the terms of the Adoption Act 1976, in order to provide counselling for people who had been adopted before 1976. (It is not clear why this had not been done years earlier, and indeed, it seems that the registration as an Adoption Agency had been cancelled some time in the 1970s.) There was a thorough six-day inspection of the whole office. "The resulting report was generally very positive about the organisation, its work and the manner in which it was conducted. It was described as unique and recognised as providing an important service. Suggestions were made for improving some elements of it, such as publicising it more among potential users. It was acknowledged that such improvements would have resource implications."[173] Following this inspection no action appears to have been taken until the next inspection.

National Care Standards Agency inspection in 2003

Following the implementation of the Adoption Act 2002 the agency was inspected by the NCSA, who concluded that the services provided by ISSUK did not require registration as a Voluntary Adoption Agency (VAA), but that, when new regulations came in, in December 2005, ISSUK would have to register as an Adoption Support Agency (ASA) in order to offer tracing and support services to those whose adoption concerned more than one country. So ISSUK was duly registered as an ASA in 2007.

Charity Commission Inspection 2004

A Review Visit was made by 2 members of the Charity Commission in June 2004.

[173] AR 2000–1.

The review was based on their new document: "The Hallmarks of an Effective Charity". These 6 hallmarks stated that an effective charity:

"1 Considers the impact that it want to have and actually has on the people who benefit from it, is clear about its objects, vision, mission and values, and how it will achieve them.

2 Has the structure, policies and procedures to enable it to achieve its mission and aims and deliver its services efficiently.

3 Is run by a trustee body that has the right balance of skills and expedient to run the charity effectively, acts in the best interests of the charity and its beneficiaries, understands its responsibilities and has system in place to exercise them effectively.

4 Manages and uses its resources so as to optimise its potential.

5 Is accountable to the public and other stakeholders in a way that is transparent and understandable.

6 Is flexible enough to influence and adapt to changes in the environment in which it works in order to meet the changing needs of those who use its services."[174]

The review was on the whole positive, and the Commission found that most aspects of the running of ISSUK were compliant with the requirements of the Commission, but there was a reminder that the charity must restrict its activities both in relation to the casework and the fundraising, to be consistent with its Objects. The Commissioners recommended a review of the Memorandum and Articles of Association. Another recommendation was that the trustees should draw up a formal business plan – which led to the Strategic Plan of 2005.

Commission for Social Care Inspection (CSCI) in 2007

In July 2006 an independent inspection by Peter Wood, social care consultant, was undertaken in preparation for the CSCI Inspection. He identified the main problems as the unsatisfactory

[174] The Hallmarks of an Effective Charity 2004.

management situation, with the lack of a CEO, and the need to deal with the current caseload, given existing resources.

The subsequent inspection of the ISS Adoption Support Service by the CSCI concluded that "overall your service provides good outcomes for the people who use it… the agency provides a sensitive, personal and professional service, which meets the needs of service users… . The agency is well managed by a committed, well-informed and enthusiastic Acting Director, who has provided stability and focus during a period of considerable change… .The Tracing and Contact worker is experienced and knowledgeable, and service users are provided with a thoughtful and sensitive service… . There is good supervision of staff and professional development is valued… . The agency is seen as a supportive and caring employer, who is genuinely concerned for the welfare of its staff… the arrangements for the financial monitoring of the agency are now on a sound footing. Fundraising has become more professional and organised."[175] However, shortcomings were identified, in relation to compliance with regulations. The most serious one was the rule that only qualified staff should carry out birth records counselling.

As a result of this CSCI inspection, and a recognition that ISSUK had no suitably experienced adoption workers, the registration as an Adoption Support Agency was cancelled, and subsequently Lesley Austen, the Tracing and Family Contact Worker, was made redundant, along with the social worker who had been dealing with other adoption cases. This was a sad moment for ISSUK, which had contributed so much to developments in intercountry adoption, but it was recognised that there were other post-adoption agencies who could offer a similar service. The ISSUK was still able to give information about intercountry adoption, and pass on referrals requiring information from other countries.

[175] CSCI Report 1st May 2007.

Reviews

Review of Fundraising and Income Generation in 2006: by Emma Low

Emma Low was brought in as a fundraising consultant. As a result of her review, a Fundraising Strategy was established, which set out a more proactive approach to fundraising, with the aim of strengthening, developing and diversifying current income streams. A target was set of an income of £1million within three years, and this was actually achieved by 2009. Another outcome of this review was the appointment of a Trusts and Grants Co-Ordinator and an Events and Major Donor Manager.

Review of Administrative Support in 2007

An independent review of the administrative functioning of ISSUK office in May 2007 was set up to: "identify efficiency gains through improving working practices, reducing duplication of effort and extending the use of new technology".[176] The fact that the three administrative staff were the longest serving members of staff meant that they held much of the knowledge about how the organisation worked, and provided stability during periods of change. The review process went well and Steve Dixon, the reviewer from Portsmouth City Council, said: "I am hugely impressed at the way they have responded, they are self-motivated and not resistant to change, and they are keen to learn and utilise new technical tools. They are a close knit group and work well together."[177]

The resulting report recognised several excellent support services, notably: "the recent investment in IT and effective back-up system; the budget plan and monthly monitoring facility; the effective and welcoming web-site and the comprehensive HR Handbook."[178] Nevertheless, it produced recommendations to tighten procedures and monitoring by clarifying specific responsibilities, roles and tasks. The rapid increase in electronic record-keeping necessitated a thorough overhaul of the

176 Report by S Dixon 2007.
177 Ibid.
178 Ibid.

management of records of casework and finances. A major recommendation was that there should be "a cultural change, to ensure that the administrative team are, and are seen and treated, as an equal, valued and fully integrated part of the whole ISS team, with specific skills, competencies and tasks, and with the same opportunities for professional development and input into the operation and development of ISSUK."[179] Procedures and practices were updated and improved supervision and training introduced.

Review of Fundraising Strategy in 2009

Bernie McDermott, an independent consultant, undertook a 6-month review of fundraising in April 2009. As a result of this review, a Fundraising Development Board was set up, chaired by Harvey McGrath and consisting of some trustees and outside members. Its brief was to establish a diverse and sustainable funding base.

Finances and fundraising

Funding sources

- Central Government grants: At the beginning of the decade, ISSUK received a grant for General Funds from the Department of Health for the core funding of the organisation. (This was due to the efforts of Tom Luce, a senior Civil Servant at the Ministry, and a trustee of ISSUK.) But in 2004 the Government withdrew all funding for ISSUK core work, only keeping funding for special projects; the Home Office Travel Assistance Scheme; the Unaccompanied Young Persons Fund; the Child Migrants Support Fund and the Refugee Benefit Fund. In 2008 the Department of Children, Schools and Families gave a 3-year grant to develop the advice, information and training services. Part of this was used to set up a client database.
- Agency registration fees: In 2004 over 100 Local Authorities registered with ISSUK under a new scheme which gave them

[179] Ibid.

access to its information services, although they had to pay additional fees for all cases referred. In 2006 the annual Registration fee increased from £500 to £750 for each Local Authority. This resulted in a slight reduction in the number of Local Authorities registering.

- Service User fees, for all work undertaken, were charged to individuals and all unregistered agencies. The fees were revised every few years, with major revisions in 2003 and 2006. The service remained free to members of the ISS network.
- Grants from Trust Funds and other bodies, such as the Henry Smith Charity grant of over £60,000 to cover the costs for dealing with children who had been trafficked, were asylum seekers or in private foster care. A grant was obtained for a new computer system in 2005, and for the setting up of the database.
- Donations from individuals. In 2006 a booklet to encourage legacies was produced.
- Monies from fundraising events. These continued to provide a very substantial part of the income.

The balance between these different funding streams altered from year to year. This chart shows how the incoming money into general or unrestricted funds was divided, during four sample years in the decade:

Unrestricted income	2000/1	2004/5	2007/8	2008/9
Grants	65,000	0	0	0
Fees and user payments	53,112	128,627	133,357	107,419
Fundraising events	188,688	171,828	216,969	343,461
Donations and legacies	2,606	75,255	105,384	307,954
Bank interest and sundry income	6,222	879	6,295	1,493
Total unrestricted income	£315,628	£376,589	£462,005	£760,327
Restricted funds:				
Grants and donations	£604,696	£141,745	£200,461	£287,254
Total income:	**£920,324**	**£518,344**	**£662,466**	**£1,047,581**

In 2004/5 the organisation's expenditure was made up of: direct charitable expenditure 76.4%, fundraising costs 14% and administration costs 9.6%.

There were problems almost every year in relation to balancing the books. It is obvious from the figures that there was still an over-reliance on events and donations. As is the case with many charities, the Budget each year had to be drawn up without a firm commitment of funds to cover the items in it. Budgets were based on projected grants and anticipated fundraising, and these could never be accurate. Sometimes, a lower figure in one category could be balanced by a higher amount in another. For example, in 2004 the Spring Fair brought in less than budgeted, but the Local Authority user fees were higher than anticipated. There was nearly always a cash flow problem in the autumn, because the money from a lot of the major events, and Local Authority Registration fees came in during the winter. An enormous amount of time and energy was invested by all those involved in fundraising and many individuals and trusts were approached. But in a period of retrenchment, particularly of state welfare services, many charities in the health and welfare fields were looking for funding from the same sources.

Over-optimism about anticipated funds, whether from Trust Funds or events, sometimes encouraged staff to plan for continuation or expansion of services before the funding for them could be guaranteed. There was no easy answer to this, and it was sometimes the cause of tensions between staff and Trustees. But it also led to more professionalism of fundraising. In the autumn of 2005 the Treasurer, Charles Marshall, warned that there was only enough money to keep going for 3 months. He stressed the need to raise funds before making spending plans. An emergency meeting of the Board was called: "to decide if ISSUK was legally or technically insolvent".[180] £90,000 was needed by the end of December, and £120,000 by the end of the financial year. It was only due to substantial loans from individual trustees that the charity survived at that point. The situation was so grave that a plan had been drawn up for the "orderly liquidation of the company should the loan fail".[181]

In 2006 some money from the Hobson Trust was used to employ a Fundraising Consultant.

180 Minutes of Emergency Meeting of the Board of Trustees on 6.10.05.

181 Ibid.

Given the ongoing parlous state of the finances, the Board concentrated on the strategy of putting on high income events, such as the grand receptions and dinners that had been introduced very successfully during previous years, and letting go of some of the ways of fundraising that produced less income but still required a lot of organisation, for example the Annual Alexandra Rose Day collection.

Each event was organised by one or more Trustees, assisted by a committee of volunteers. It became apparent that the core of volunteers, many of them Trustees, were turning again and again to the same group of friends and supporters, and efforts were made to widen this group.

The first reception at the Mansion House had been organised by Liz Emery in 2000, and subsequent dinners were held there in 2006. It raised £18,000. The Embassy of Kuwait were particularly generous hosts – a Cartier show in November 2000, a Reception in March 2001 and a Dinner in 2005. In 2005 there were also dinners at Marlborough House in 2005, in 2006 at the Russian Embassy, in 2007 at the Egyptian Embassy and in 2009 at the French Embassy. For the 80th Anniversary of ISS worldwide in 2004 Françoise Middleton arranged a Gala Charity Concert at the French Embassy in 2004. In 2007 the first annual Child Protection Dinner was held at the Guildhall, and raised £90,000. The following year the dinner raised over £140,000.

In 2000 Dr Ali Sattaripour organised the first Celebrity Golf Tournament. Subsequently, these took place every two years, and each raised a large amount of money. The first one, in aid of the programme to help young people from Kosovo, made £24,000, and the four subsequent ones between them raised £257,000.

Reserves: the Trustees adopted a policy that they should maintain reserves of not more than six months anticipated expenditure, and that there should be adequate funds to ensure that the charity was "able to meet all current and known future liabilities."[182]

182 AR2000.

Once again, the charity was helped by receiving a substantial legacy in 2008, much of which was used to replenish the reserves. So the financial year 2008/9 ended with a total income in excess of £1million for the first time.

Publicity

At the beginning of 2000 a video was produced by two Trustees, John Wheeler and Adrian Gregory. It featured people who had been helped by the ISS who told their stories.

In 2004 and 2005, as part of the drive to improve the profile of the organisation, several actions took place to improve publicity. New promotional literature was professionally produced; the Annual Report and Review was produced as a colour booklet rather than an A4 document; the website was developed and kept up to date. In 2004 a Core Document about the work was produced for professional social work and legal agencies, and a new Referral Guide was produced for use by social workers. It contained the Case Summary format developed by the GS and used by all ISS units. From 2004 the Newsletter to supporters and users of the service was produced quarterly, and from 2007 it was printed in colour. Also, from 2007 ISSUK made available free to all registered local authorities access to the material provided by the IRC at ISS in Geneva.

Publicity material displayed the Vision, Mission Statement and Strapline of the organisation. Perhaps it is useful here to differentiate between them.

The Vision is what the agency aspires to achieve, and gives it a sense of purpose. The ISSUK Vision Statement was "A world where every child, parent and family member has the right to enjoy a family relationship in a secure environment, free from exploitation and international legal barriers."[183]

The Mission Statement defines the core purpose of an organisation – why it exists and what it does. The ISSUK Mission Statement was:

[183] ISSUK Strategic Plan "Meeting an Increased Need", 2005–8.

"ISSUK is an independent charity and part of an international network, which acts to promote and protect the rights and welfare of children, adults and families whose personal circumstances require inter-country liaison."[184]

A strapline is an advertising slogan attached to a brand name. Its purpose is to emphasise a phrase that the company wishes to be remembered by, especially for fundraising purposes. In 2007 a new strapline was introduced. It was: "Protecting children and uniting families across borders."[185] This one was used on all subsequent publicity material and reports.

Links with other organisations, international and local

During times of low staffing, it was not possible to maintain all the links with other agencies as actively as staff would have liked, but as the staffing situation improved after 2003, much was done to improve relations with government and other agencies. For example, Georg Stahl liaised with the International Social Care Group at the DfES. There were good relations with BAAF, and ISSUK joined the new Consortium of Adoption Support Agencies and the South East Post Adoption Network in 2007. Staff were attending many external meetings and had renewed links with other relevant bodies. In 2007 Members of staff made presentations at a Child Protection conference in Germany, a BAAF conference and a Law Society meeting in London.

Training

Training for local authority staff was resumed in September 2005. In 2007 Nadine Schmitt ran a workshop for postgraduate students at the University of East Anglia, and in 2008 she organised London training events; one on Welfare and Immigration and one on Children in Care. From 2008 the staff were able to offer seminars on International Child Protection Training in Peterborough and Leeds in 2009.

184 Ibid.

185 Minutes of Board of Trustees 21.3.07.

It was always necessary for staff to keep up to date by receiving training themselves, and various workers attended seminars on topics such as Justice for Children, Trafficking, Refugees and so on.

Casework

In spite of the limitations of resources, the vision for ISSUK remained ambitious. It was:

> "to become the specialist and expert agency aiming to promote children's rights across borders by:
>
> - Providing intercountry social work services through intercountry liaison with authorities overseas;
> - Providing advice on intercountry social work issues in the UK;
> - Campaigning for the rights of those affected by migration and globalisation and being formally recognised as such by authorities and NGOs alike."[186]

Whilst ISSUK continued to refer cases overseas, there were difficulties in finding anyone to deal with the cases referred from overseas units to the UK, although this was an integral part of the role of ISSUK within ISS. In the year from April 2003 to March 2004 there had been a total of 349 new cases referred, of which 138 were cases from overseas. In 2004 CAFCASS announced that its social workers could no longer take on this work, because there was no funding for it. ISSUK staff took on some cases themselves, and began to charge some of the other Branches, such as Australia, so that independent social workers or voluntary agencies could be paid for the work. But this still left other cases that could not be dealt with.

In relation to taking on work from UK agencies,, it was sometimes necessary to prioritise the cases that could be accepted during the times of greatest pressure on staff. For example, in the summer of 2006 the agreed criteria for accepting cases was:

[186] UK Newsletter Summer 2007.

- Child Protection cases/ any case where an individual was at risk
- Mandatory cases, requested by the Courts
- Cases referred by registered Local Authorities
- Cases which were feasible to deal with, within appropriate time-frames.

It was usually only necessary to operate a priority system for short periods.

In 2004 ISS staff had a constructive meeting with Dame Elizabeth Butler-Sloss, President of the Family Division of the High Court of Justice, and staff from the Foreign and Commonwealth Office (FCO) and CAFCASS to discuss concerns about the overlong timescales and poor quality of some reports from ISS units overseas. For their part, the ISS staff acknowledged the problem, and described efforts to improve the network, but they also pointed out that many referrals were made late in the process of Court proceedings, and if they were to be made earlier on, better timescales could be met.

National Advice and Information Helpline

The Advice Line was developed by Georg Stahl from the existing Duty System, which had been flagging due to staff shortages. He established a highly efficient system for dealing with at least 1,500 enquiries a year. Enquiries come from private individuals or professionals in the fields of social work, law, criminal justice, education, health, or other agencies. "ISSUK has a unique global perspective; expert knowledge of international conventions and comparative policies and services; cultural and legal awareness, casework experience and a cross national network. Using this expertise the advisors can inform the enquirer of the options available to address the issue and advise on the pros, cons, risks and likelihood of successful outcomes using different practices."[187] In 2007 a grant by the DCSF guaranteed the future of the Advice Line for 3 years. In the last complete accounting

[187] Newsletter Winter 2008.

year of ISSUK, 2008/9 1,592 enquiries were made to the line. In July 2009 the Advice Line had the busiest ever month.

On a typical day the Advice Line service might receive enquiries about:

"• A young person being picked up by the police, who discover she has been trafficked into the country and forced into prostitution
- A local authority seeking an assessment on a family member overseas
- A local authority wishing to pass on child protection information regarding a child who has travelled abroad
- A parent calling to report that their child has been abducted by the other parent and taken abroad, seeking help in establishing that the child is okay, and wanting to instigate contact."[188]

All these examples are of situations that would require follow-up work, but in addition there are requests for information that can be given quickly, or after some research. Some enquirers are referred elsewhere to a more appropriate agency.

Child protection

Children who have been identified as being at risk of harm of one sort or another can be protected to some extent under British Law. But if they are removed from the jurisdiction, then they are no longer protected. One such group is those children whose names are on At Risk Registers of their local authorities, but who are taken out of the country by adults seeking to avoid official oversight. For example, in 2008 alone there were 18 cases referred to ISS Spain because of concerns about the welfare and safety of children. Sometimes children are taken by known abusers. When ISSUK is notified by local authorities that this has happened, and as long as there is some idea of which country the child might be in, the authorities in that country will be notified. This will be in addition to any notification of police, ports etc. Although some children disappear without trace, there

188 AR 2009.

are many who are found, and the local welfare agency can check how they are, and remove them if there are legal grounds to do so. Sometimes there are disagreements about which jurisdiction takes precedence, if people in two countries have some legal claim on a child.

An additional feature of the child protection work was the increase in cases of actual or alleged sexual abuse. "In 2001/2 12 such cases were referred to us. Over the last 15 years, with the recognition of the possibility of such abuse of children within a family, such allegations have been reflected in an increased number of referrals where a family may have separated and a parent has gone to another country. They sometimes occur in custody hearings. A child may make an allegation about a parent, after the family has split up. Courts and other statutory bodies take the allegations seriously, and may ask for overseas notification when an alleged perpetrator has gone abroad. Such allegations are handled differently in different states. It is ISS's responsibility to ensure that cases are handled with discretion. Children wherever they are, have to be protected, but if an allegation is unfounded or malicious it is necessary that an alleged abuser does not suffer."[189]

As ISSUK workers dealt with an increasing number of these cases, it became apparent that there were great variations in the responses of local authorities when children deemed to be at risk were taken out of the jurisdiction. Social workers were unaware of the options available to them. Questionnaires were sent to 167 Guardians of Child Protection Registers in England and Wales, asking for protocols and procedures regarding children on the Register who were removed from the jurisdiction. At one extreme they found children being de-registered on leaving the country, without any follow-up at all. Many others said that they would refer the matter to ISSUK, or contact the relevant local authority or embassy or Consulate in the other country. Some said they would seek legal advice or go to the police. Several replied that they had no procedures in place. At the other extreme, a few took action even when the removal was temporary; one authority asked for a child to be monitored on a

[189] AR2000/1.

short trip to Disneyland with a responsible grandparent. In 2007 they set up a series of training events, which were attended by social workers from a large number of local authorities. ISSUK also pressed the government to issue a Protocol and guidelines for such cases.

Case examples

A Local Authority had reports of alleged sexual abuse of two young sisters, Zoe and Tracy, and at a Case Conference it was decided that the girls should be removed from the home. But, before any action could be taken, the family disappeared. Neighbours said that they had gone to Spain without leaving any contact details, but they were believed to be in the region of Malaga. In co-operation with ISS Spain, the family was traced and the relevant Spanish authority was notified.

ISSUK received a call from a local authority who were concerned about a Pakistani woman who was expecting her second child. Her first child had been removed from the parents at one month old with multiple fractures. It had been deemed too risky to return the baby to her parents and she had been placed for adoption. A Case Conference had placed the unborn child on the Child Protection Register because of the likely risks. But the mother returned to Pakistan just before the birth. The authorities in Pakistan were alerted, but there was no response, and so regrettably nothing more could be done.

A Local Authority social worker reported that a family, with whom they had been working because of concerns about possible abuse of the 3 children, had disappeared, and were believed to have gone to Australia, which is where the father came from. The family was found and the local social workers reported that they seemed all right and that there would be no need to monitor them. The case was closed. Yet, 2 years later, another report came in saying that the children had been removed because of abuse. The Australian authorities wanted more information about what had happened in Britain, and they were put directly in contact with the local authority.

A request came from ISS in Belgium concerning Marie, an 11-year-old girl with learning difficulties, who had been taken to England by her grandmother, seemingly at her parents' request. The authorities had been helping the family for some time because the quality of care was poor. They requested ISSUK to arrange for welfare checks to be made. This request was passed to the relevant local authority, but after some time they had taken no action, and when prompted, still did not respond. This is the reverse of the problems so often encountered when correspondents overseas do not respond to referrals.

Child trafficking

In 2007 ISSUK joined ECPAT UK – End Child Prostitution and Trafficking – in urging the Government to do more to safeguard the welfare of children believed to be the victims of trafficking into the country. The Government ratified the Council of Europe Convention on Action against Trafficking in Human Beings at the end of 2008.

ISSUK had contacts with child protection authorities in many countries, and could act fast to pass information to alert the authorities as a precautionary measure, or to initiate investigations, or to activate protection measure.

Case examples

Two separate referrals were received from one European country, each requesting assessments on two of their nationals who were now living in the UK, and who had offered to care for children in institutions in their home country. These two referrals were so similar that suspicions were raised. It turned out that these couples were both involved in the trafficking of children; the older ones for marriage or prostitution and the younger ones to be trained as pickpockets. Criminal proceedings were instituted in the UK and the other country.

A young Spanish boy Carlos was picked up at a UK airport because his papers were not in order. He was travelling with a non-related man and it turned out that he was being taken to Amsterdam for employment in the sex industry there. Through ISS his parents were contacted. They had no idea what had happened to him, and were relieved to have him back home. The traffickers were not found.

Mariam was about nine years old when she came to the notice of the local Education Department, who were notified that a child was not attending school. It turned out that Mariam had been brought to the UK from the Gambia with an older woman who had taken her to live with a Gambian family. The child was being used as a servant – kept under slave-like conditions. She was removed at once and placed in a foster home. This case posed a problem for everyone – she had no papers, and the family with whom she was living denied any knowledge of her background. So there was nothing to go on except what Mariam could remember, and that was very vague. However, after extensive efforts to find out about this child, her family was found. It transpired that her parents had died and her grandmother had sold her to traffickers, on the understanding that she was to be taken to have a good education. It was decided that Mariam should remain in Britain, in a foster home, but that she should resume regular contact with her grandmother, and that further work should be done to find out if there were any relatives who could offer her a home in the Gambia.

A six-month old boy, Joseph, was handed to officials at Heathrow Airport by a woman who had brought him into the country from a West African country. She said that his parents had been killed and she had been asked by his grandmother to bring him to Britain so that he could have a better chance in life. The local authority wanted to find out the truth behind this story. But the ISS Correspondent had fled the conflict in that country and it proved impossible to verify anything.

London Boroughs Children Project 2006–09

This 3-year project was set up in 2006, sponsored by the Bridge House Trust. The aim was to identify and work with those Local

Authorities in Greater London who had the highest number of children from a non-British and/or non-white background. The increase in people of different nationalities and ethnicities in recent years, meant that Local Authorities should be considering international dimensions when deciding the best plan for many of the children in their care. Yet the evidence suggested that this was not taken into account in many cases. One of the social workers, Nadine Schmitt became the Project Manager. She wrote: "a child may have family members in another country who could provide vital background information or who could permanently look after the child if the parents no longer could do so. Furthermore, authorities in the other country may have had similar concerns in the past, and sharing this information is very important in order to make appropriate plans for the child."[190] The aim of the project was to increase awareness of possible international aspects of work with these children and their families.. It was hoped to share examples of good practice, and identify areas where a common approach might be useful. Nadine produced some useful literature. But she had difficulty in persuading enough Local Authorities to participate, and so it was decided to change the emphasis of the project, and to focus on training.

By the following year a number of training events took place and advice was given on specific cases. The Annual Report of 2008 states that "most enquiries concerned Jamaica, France, Portugal, Israel and Iran, and mainly involved children that were at risk of abuse and required protection. Other enquiries were in relation to contacting family members overseas to ascertain whether they are able to become carers for children living in the UK without their parents."[191]

Monitoring

During this decade there was more focus on performance indicators and measuring the outcomes of the work. An internal review in 2006 identified the priority areas of work would be

[190] Article in ISSUK Newsletter Summer 2007.
[191] AR2008.

Child Protection, Child Placement, Private Law, Adoption and Tracing. The review analysed each area of work, identifying the desired outcomes of each, the role of ISSUK in achieving these outcomes, identifying how efficiency could be maintained, and setting measurable indicators of performance. At the beginning of each case the preferred outcome was identified; for example, that a child separated from a parent established contact with that parent, or that successful protection measures were put in place overseas for a vulnerable child who had been removed from the UK. An analysis of outcomes showed that substantially more than half of cases recorded a successful outcome. (6-monthly Progress Report on Strategic Plan 2008–2011.) However, analysing outcomes was time consuming, and could not be done on every case in the longer term. Sue Gilbert explained that it was difficult to know precise outcomes because ISSUK was only one part of a complex equation, involving other agencies, and sometimes the final outcome was not known for some time. She recognised that donors wanted proof that ISSUK had made children's lives better but this was sometimes difficult to prove (Director's Report Nov 2008). Even if it was known, for example, that a child had been successfully placed with relatives overseas, that would not indicate whether or not the placement proved over time to be a happy one, or that it was better than an alternative placement would have been. This is, to some extent, a dilemma for all those who make decisions about people's lives, and who have to base their decisions on predicted outcomes, which in turn, are informed by accumulated knowledge, skill and experience.

In 2007 the administrative staff started a telephone monitoring system of a sample of calls to the advice line, and feedback forms were sent to all service users on completion of a case. The figures showed that there was high overall satisfaction with the advice service and a more varied response to the casework service. This reflected the problems with the network.

The aim of the monitoring was to:

"• assess how well we are doing, what has happened and why, what is and is not working, and, using what we have learned, help us to do it better.

- Demonstrate accountability, and show others what we are effective."[192]

Throughout its history, ISSUK had always striven to learn from experience and to offer the best possible service.

[192] ISSUK Business Plan 2008–11.

Epilogue

From ISSUK to CFAB – Children and Families Across Borders – the story goes on

ISSUK came to an end on 31st December 2009, and CFAB began. The question of change of name had first been suggested in 2004. The name International Social Service implied that ISSUK was a statutory body, not needing charitable funding, and so there was an argument for finding a name that would more clearly indicate what the charity did. On the other hand, it would be a major step to abandon the name International Social Service, which was used throughout the network. So it took some years to convince everyone of the need for change. Eventually, in 2009 the new name of Children and Families Across Borders was chosen, which came naturally from out of the strapline; "Protecting children and uniting families across borders." This was to be the name for everyday use, but all official documents still had to mention that CFAB was a Branch of ISS, as that remained the legal name of the organisation.

> "Although our name has changed, what has not changed is the nature of our work and our commitment to seek the best outcomes for children who are separated by international borders from their families, working at all times in the best interests of the child."[193]

Harvey McGrath had become President in 2009 and took a very active part in guiding the organisation through its big change. With his huge expertise in business and his family's example of

[193] CFAB Newsletter Winter 2010.

philanthropy, he was ideally positioned to lead the charity forward.

The first Board of Trustees of CFAB was the last Board of ISSUK, under the chairmanship of Doug Lewis. His enthusiasm for the work of the charity was undiminished, but, having got the organisation in better shape, he was able to let go of some of his responsibilities.

Andy Elvin was already in post as CEO, and by the beginning of 2010 he had recruited an Operational Manager and 3 new social workers and built up a new staff team, including social workers from several different countries. Chris Platt and Mark Hunt offered continuity of administration. More students were taken on placement, both from Brunel University and Denmark.

Plans were underway to improve the profile of the organisation, and in particular to inaugurate an annual Child Protection Lecture. Lord Laming gave the first lecture.

Improved links with governmental and other bodies began to put ISSUK back where it had been for so long, as a contributor to discussions about changes to legislation, and an organisation ready to speak out about issues that concerned the people it served. There was a smooth transition as far as the casework was concerned. The Advice Line was as busy as ever, and the range of cases coming through CFAB remained much the same as those to ISSUK. The work on Private Fostering was set to be developed further. The role of the social workers still had two main parts: to use their knowledge to solve problems and to influence good practice in international social work through practice and training.

One challenge remained constant – to find a balance between the identified need for certain social work services, with the ability to pay for such services. Should the organisation prioritise those services which no other agency was providing, or focus on projects which could attract funding? This history shows that there has always been a tension between these two.

CFAB immediately had available to it a huge amount of expertise about putting on impressive fundraising events, and a new Fundraising committee to explore the whole range of fundraising opportunities. Preparations were ready for the Spring Fair of 2010, and other funding events.

CFAB inherited the building and most of the personnel of ISSUK. The basic policies and procedures were in place, and the administrative and technical backup was good. The links with governmental institutions and other voluntary organisations had been there for many years, although some needed refreshing. The International ISS introduced a revised Constitution in 2010, which strengthened the position of the General Secretariat. The links between it and the UK Branch CFAB were once again close, as Doug Lewis became Chair of the new ISS Governing Board.

In conclusion

This history has set out some of the achievements of ISSUK, notably through the many impressive and ground-breaking projects, and the ongoing advice and casework services. This work was not possible without funding, and so it is also a record of relentless and imaginative fundraising. From small beginnings, with an income of about £1,000 in 1955, it grew into an organisation with an income topping £1 million by 2009.

Looking back over the 55 years since ISSGB was founded in 1955, it can be seen how the ISS changed in response to world events, changes in law, new clientele, changes made possible by the huge technical advances, and changing understanding of what was needed.

Sue Gilbert summed it up well in "Lessons from the past":

> "The world has changed a lot in the last half century, migration movements continue to increase, and ISS has constantly developed and adapted itself to respond to 'new' situations – children being trafficked, children seeking asylum and the private fostering of children. Yet the problems inherent in these 'new' situations are remarkably similar to problems of the past. Children: unaccompanied, in need of protection and welfare, separated from family members by international borders. Adults are also affected: caught between legal and social systems, fighting desperately to be re-united with relatives in other countries, and many, each year, wander the world as refugees.
>
> The past 50 years have also seen the development of international conventions and treaties, as well as substantial regulatory control

on immigration and social work practices. The complexity of intercountry social work has thus increased, now requiring specialist knowledge and experience. Information technology has enabled an 'armchair approach' to gaining global knowledge, but I would question whether this is enough to understand a situation overseas. The ease of access to international air travel reduces the barrier of geographical distance, but do we really believe that other barriers do not exist? Should we, therefore, send social workers from the UK to undertake social work tasks overseas, as good practice?"[194]

So this difficult issue, which was discussed in earlier chapters, was still a central concern to ISSUK as it ended, and to CFAB as it began. CFAB has taken on this debate, and will strive to forge an understanding with Courts and social workers so that the best possible service can be offered to children and families, using the knowledge and expertise of all parties, including those in the ISS network. It is unrealistic to think that Courts will not continue to demand a faster and more sophisticated service than can be provided by some ISS correspondents, and so there may be a place for a parallel system of building up the best possible service in those parts of the network where this is achievable, and, at the same time, establishing and supporting a dedicated group of social workers – in CFAB or CAFCASS or elsewhere – who are trained to do this complex area of work.

Looking back, we can see how terminology has changed over the decades: those involved with ISSGB in the early days would not recognise some of the jargon of fundraising and of social work: the talk of brands, mission statements and straplines, let alone the language of the internet and other technology. Yet the mission statement and strapline used at the end of the period would have made sense to those at the start. Procedures, policies and practices have developed, but the philosophy and principles have remained the same.

Most importantly, CFAB took on the ethos and principles of ISSUK and the wider ISS organisation. So that it can still state that it is:

194 ISSUK Newsletter 2009.

195 Equal Opportunities Policy and Procedures.

> "a non-profit making, non-political, non-governmental, non-sectarian social work organisation providing services regardless of ethnic origin, gender, sexuality, nationality or religious belief[195] [and that its purpose is] to protect children and unite families across borders."[196]

CFAB will continue to play a part in the wider ISS organisation, and will contribute to it and benefit from it. It will contribute to social work in the UK through casework, training and involvement with agencies in ensuring the best possible standards in intercountry social work. Its fundraising efforts demonstrate how much committed trustees, staff and volunteers can achieve. No one can be expert in all areas, and the organisation will always need a balance in the leadership teams of senior staff and trustees, ensuring that there is the necessary experience of the complex requirements of the social work, the fundraising and the promotion of the work of CFAB.

Whatever the future, I believe that the work will remain "an imaginative co-operation" between all those involved in it.[197]

CFAB – I wish you well.

196 From the strapline.

197 Referral Technique – imaginative co-operation, K Luce 1955.

Appendices

A. Acronyms

Those concerning ISS:

AB	Affiliated Bureau
CFAB	Children and Families Across Borders
ISS/SSI	International Social Service/ Service Sociale Internationale
ISSGB	International Social Service of Great Britain – 1955–1990
ISSUK	International Social Service of the UK – 1991–2009
EXCO	Executive Council of ISS
GS	General Secretariat (of the ISS in Geneva)
ISS/IRC	International Reference Centre for the protection of children in adoption – later International Reference Centre for the rights of children deprived of their family
PAG	Professional Advisory Group
SG	Secretary General (of the ISS in Geneva)

British:

ARE	Adoption Resource Exchange
ASA	Adoption Support Agency
BAAF	British Agencies for Adoption and Fostering
CAFCASS	Children and Families Court Advisory Service
COS	Charity Organisation Society
CSCI	Commission for Social Care Inspection
DfES	Department for Education and Science
DHSS	Department of Health and Social Services
DOH	Department of Health

ECPAT	End Child Prostitution and Trafficking
FCO	Foreign and Commonwealth Office
FWA	Family Welfare Association
GSCC	General Social Care Council
HO	Home Office
NCSA	National Care Standards Agency
VAA	Voluntary Adoption Agency International:

International

ECOSOC	Economic and Social Council of the UN
HC	Hague Conference/Hague Convention
ICEM	Intergovernmental Committee for European Migration – became
ICM	Intergovernmental Committee for Migration
ICRC	International Committee of the Red Cross
ICSW	International Council on Social Welfare
ICVA	International Council of Voluntary Agencies
IFSW	International Federation of Social Workers
ILO	International Labour Organisation
IMS	International Migration Service
IOM	International Organisation for Migration
IRO	International Refugee Organisation (predecessor of UNHCR)
IUCW	International Union of Child Welfare
UNESCO	UN Educational, Scientific and Cultural Organisation
UNHCR	UN High Commissioner for Refugees
UNICEF	UN International Children's Emergency Fund
UNRRA	UN Relief and Rehabilitation Agency
UNRWA	UN Relief and Work Agency
USEP	US Escapee Program
YWCA	Young Women's Christian Association

Footnotes in the text: AR Annual Report

B. Branches and Affliated Bureaux and Delegations

Country	Date joined – as Branch B or Affiliated Bureau AB or delegates D. After closure some Branches became a Correspondent C
Albania	1992D
Argentina	1955 D – 1985 B closed 2003
Australia	1955 B
Austria	1950 B closed in 1977 – became C
Belgium	1954 B then closed in 1973 Re-opened B in 2003
Brazil	1955 B closed 1966, became C
Canada	1958 AB – 1979 then Branch
Czechoslovakia	1924 B- closed in war and only re-opened briefly. Sometimes C
Finland	1960 AB
France	1924 B closed 2006. Then C
Germany	1924 B closed in war and re-opened afterwards
Greece	1928 B closed in war and re-opened afterwards
Hong Kong	1958 D – 1971 then Branch
Israel	1990s AB
Italy	1930s, but fully a Branch after war. Closed 2006, then C
Japan	1956 B
Korea	1955–1966 D
Netherlands	1950 B
New Zealand	1990s AB
Philippines	1995 D 2006 B
Poland	1924 – closed in war and did not re-open. Became C
Portugal	1992 AB
South Africa	2000 AB
Spain	1982 AB
Switzerland	1932 B
United Kingdom	1955 B (1953 FWA, was C)
United States of America	1924 B
Uruguay	1955–59 B
Venezuela	1955 B
Vietnam	1966–75 D

C. Countries with whom ISSUK exchanged cases

This is a representative list – showing the countries for one year in each decade.

In the earliest decades some countries, or overseas territories, were lumped together, eg as West Africa. Not all correspondent countries will be listed here, if they were not in contact with ISSUK during the year in question.

COUNTRY	1957	1967	1977	1987	1997	2007
Afghanistan						✓
Albania	✓					✓
Algeria		✓	✓	✓		
Andorra			✓			
Angola			✓		✓	
Anguilla				✓		
Argentina		✓	✓	✓		
Australia	✓	✓	✓	✓	✓	✓
Austria	✓	✓	✓	✓	✓	✓
Bahamas			✓			
Bahrain	✓		✓			
Bangladesh			✓	✓	✓	✓
Barbados			✓	✓	✓	✓
Belgium	✓	✓	✓	✓	✓	✓
Belize					✓	
Bermuda			✓		✓	✓
Bolivia			✓	✓		
Bosnia					✓	
Botswana					✓	
Brazil		✓	✓	✓	✓	✓
Brunei				✓		
Bulgaria				✓	✓	✓
Burma	✓		✓			
Cameroon			✓	✓		
Canada	✓	✓	✓	✓	✓	✓
Canary Islands	✓		✓			
Cayman Islands				✓		
Chile			✓	✓		

COUNTRY	1957	1967	1977	1987	1997	2007
China	✓			✓	✓	✓
Colombia			✓	✓		✓
Congo DRC					✓	✓
Costa Rica			✓			
Croatia					✓	
Cuba						✓
Cyprus	✓	✓	✓	✓	✓	✓
Czechoslovakia	✓	✓	✓			
Denmark		✓	✓	✓	✓	✓
Djibouti				✓		
Dominica				✓		✓
Dominican Republic					✓	
Dubai				✓		
East Africa	✓					
Ecuador			✓		✓	
Egypt	✓	✓	✓	✓		✓
El Salvador			✓			
Eritrea					✓	
Ethiopia			✓	✓	✓	✓
Fiji			✓	✓	✓	
Finland		✓		✓	✓	
France	✓	✓	✓	✓	✓	✓
Gambia		✓	✓	✓		✓
Germany	✓	✓	✓	✓	✓	✓
Ghana		✓	✓	✓	✓	✓
Gibraltar			✓	✓		✓
Greece	✓	✓	✓	✓	✓	✓
Grenada				✓		
Guatemala					✓	
Guyana		✓	✓	✓	✓	
Haiti					✓	
Hong Kong	✓	✓	✓	✓	✓	✓
Hungary			✓	✓		✓
Iceland			✓			✓
India	✓	✓	✓	✓	✓	✓
Indonesia			✓			
Iran		✓	✓	✓		✓
Iraq		✓	✓	✓		

COUNTRY	1957	1967	1977	1987	1997	2007
Ireland	✓	✓	✓	✓	✓	✓
Israel	✓	✓	✓	✓	✓	✓
Italy	✓	✓	✓	✓	✓	✓
Ivory Coast					✓	
Jamaica		✓	✓	✓	✓	✓
Japan		✓	✓	✓	✓	
Jordan		✓	✓	✓		
Kenya		✓	✓	✓	✓	✓
Korea			✓		✓	
Kosovo					✓	✓
Kuwait			✓	✓		✓
Kyrgyzia						✓
Latvia						✓
Laos				✓		
Lebanon	✓		✓	✓		✓
Liberia		✓				
Libya			✓	✓	✓	✓
Lithuania						✓
Madagascar				✓		✓
Malawi		✓			✓	✓
Malaysia	✓	✓	✓	✓	✓	✓
Malta	✓	✓	✓	✓	✓	✓
Mauritius		✓	✓	✓		✓
Mexico			✓		✓	✓
Monaco			✓			
Morocco			✓	✓		✓
Mozambique			✓			
Nepal				✓		✓
Netherlands	✓	✓	✓	✓	✓	✓
New Zealand	✓	✓	✓	✓	✓	✓
Nigeria		✓	✓	✓	✓	✓
Norway	✓	✓	✓	✓	✓	✓
Oman			✓	✓		
Pakistan	✓	✓	✓	✓	✓	✓
Papua New Guinea			✓	✓		
Paraguay						✓
Peru				✓		✓
Philippines	✓		✓	✓	✓	✓

COUNTRY	1957	1967	1977	1987	1997	2007
Poland	✓	✓	✓	✓		
Portugal		✓	✓	✓	✓	✓
Puerto Rico					✓	
Romania			✓		✓	✓
Russia					✓	✓
Saudi Arabia			✓			
Seychelles			✓	✓	✓	✓
St. Kitts				✓	✓	✓
St. Lucia				✓	✓	✓
St. Vincent				✓		
Sierra Leone		✓	✓	✓		✓
Singapore	✓	✓	✓	✓	✓	
Slovakia						✓
Somalia				✓	✓	✓
South Africa	✓	✓	✓	✓	✓	✓
South America	✓					
Spain	✓	✓	✓	✓	✓	✓
Sri Lanka			✓	✓	✓	✓
Sudan		✓		✓		✓
Swaziland				✓		
Sweden			✓	✓	✓	
Switzerland	✓	✓	✓	✓	✓	✓
Syria		✓	✓	✓		✓
Taiwan			✓			
Tanzania		✓	✓	✓	✓	✓
Thailand			✓	✓	✓	✓
Togo				✓		
Trinidad & Tobago			✓	✓	✓	✓
Tunisia		✓	✓	✓		
Turkey		✓	✓	✓	✓	✓
Uganda		✓	✓	✓	✓	✓
Ukraine						✓
United Arab Emirates			✓			✓
USA	✓	✓	✓	✓	✓	✓
USSR/Russia			✓	✓		
Venezuela		✓	✓		✓	
Vietnam			✓			
Virgin Islands			✓			✓

COUNTRY	1957	1967	1977	1987	1997	2007
West Africa	✓					
West Indies	✓	✓	✓			
Yemen (+Aden)		✓	✓	✓		✓
Yugoslavia			✓	✓		
Zaire				✓		
Zambia		✓	✓	✓	✓	✓
Zimbabwe (Rhodesia)		✓	✓	✓	✓	✓

D. Countries that took part in the Spring Fair in 2001

This year has been chosen because it was the most successful of all the Fairs.

Antigua and Barbuda
Argentina
Armenia
Australia
Austria
Bahrain
Bangladesh
Barbados
Belarus
Belgium
Bolivia
Bosnia Herzegovina
Botswana
Brazil
Brunei
Bulgaria
Chile
China
Colombia
Costa Rica
Croatia
Cuba
Cyprus
Czech Republic
Dominica
Dominican Republic
Ecuador
Egypt
Estonia
France
The Gambia
Georgia
Greece
Guatemala
Guyana
Honduras
Hungary
India
Indonesia
Iran
Italy
Jamaica
Japan
Jordan
Kazakhstan
Kenya
Korea
Kuwait
Kyrgyz Republic
Latvia
Lithuania
Luxembourg
Malawi
Malaysia
Malta
Mexico
Mongolia
Morocco
Myanmar
Netherlands
New Zealand
Nigeria
Oman
Pakistan
Panama
Paraguay
Peru
Philippines
Poland
Portugal
Qatar
Romania
Russian Federation
Saudi Arabia
Seychelles
Singapore
Slovak Republic
Slovenia
South Africa
Spain
Sri Lanka
St. Lucia
St Vincent
Sudan
Swaziland
Sweden
Switzerland
Syria
Tanzania
Thailand
Tonga
Tunisia
Turkey
Turkmenistan
Ukraine
USA
Uzbekistan
Venezuela
Yugoslavia
Zambia
Zimbabwe

TOTAL 101 countries

E. Conventions and legislation underpinning the work of ISS.

Note that this is by no means a comprehensive list, but includes the main Conventions and statutes that provide the background to the work of ISSUK.

1. Human Rights

- Universal Declaration of Human Rights 1948

INTERNATIONAL CONVENTIONS:

- European Convention for the Protection of Human Rights and Fundamental Freedoms 1950
- United Nations Convention on the Rights of the Child, 1989. Ratified by UK in 1991
- European Convention on the Exercise of Children's Rights, 1996

BRITISH STATUTES:

- Human Rights Act 1998

2. Immigration and Nationality

INTERNATIONAL CONVENTIONS:

- UN Convention relating to the status of refugees 1951
- UN Convention relating to the status of stateless persons 1954
- UN Convention on the Reduction of Statelessness 1961

BRITISH STATUTES:

- Aliens Act 1905
- Aliens Registration Act and Aliens Restriction Act 1914 and 1919

- British Nationality and Status of Aliens Act 1914 (amended in 1918, 1922, 1933, 1943)
- British Nationality Act 1948 (and 1958 and 1964)
- Commonwealth Immigrants Act 1962
- Commonwealth Immigrants Act 1968
- Immigration Act 1971. This Act finally replaced the Aliens Act of 1905 (and those of 1914, 1919).
- British Nationality Act 1981
- National Immigration and Asylum Act 2002
- Immigration, Asylum and Nationality Act 2006
- UK Borders Act 2007

3. Child Care and Child Protection

INTERNATIONAL CONVENTIONS:

- Hague Convention concerning the powers of authorities and the law applicable in respect of the protection of minors 1961
- Hague Convention on the Civil Aspects of International Child Abduction, 1980
- European Convention on Recognition and Enforcement of Declaration concerning Custody of Children and Restoration of Custody of Children.1980
- Hague Convention on Jurisdiction, Applicable Law, Recognition, Enforcement and Co-operation in Respect of Parental Responsibility and Measures for the Protection of Children, 1996 – ratified by the UK in 2008
- UN Convention against Transnational Organised Crime 2000 (and the accompanying UN Protocol to Prevent, Suppress and Punish Trafficking in persons, especially woman and children.)
- Council of Europe Convention on Action against Trafficking in Human Beings 2005

British Statutes:

- Children Act 1948
- Children and Young Persons Act 1963
- Children Act1975
- Child Care Act 1980 this was a consolidating Act, bringing together parts of other legal instruments in order to provide better protection for children.
- Children Act 1989
- Children Act 2004 (leading to "Working Together to Safeguard Children 2006")
- Children (Private Arrangements for Fostering) Regulations 2005
- Safeguarding Vulnerable Groups Act 2006

4. Adoption

International Conventions:

- Hague Convention on the Jurisdiction, Applicable Law and Recognition of Decrees Relating to Adoption, 1965
- European Convention on Adoption of Children 1967 – ratified by UK in 1968
- Hague Convention on Protection of Children and Co-operation in Respect of Intercountry Adoption, 1993 – ratified by UK in 2003

British Statutes:

- Adoption Act 1958
- Adoption Act 1976
- Adoption (Intercountry Aspects) Act 1999
- The Adoption and Children Act 2002
- Children and Adoption Act 2006

5. Other

INTERNATIONAL CONVENTIONS:

Several conventions concerning maintenance payments, plus:

- Hague Convention on the International Protection of Adults 2000

BRITISH STATUTES:

- National Health Service Act 1948
- National Assistance Act 1948
- Local Authority Social Services Act 1970
- Data Protection Act 1998
- Freedom of Information Act 2000
- Care Standards Act 2000

6. Charity Law

- Statute of Charitable Uses 1601
- Charities Act 1960 (and 1992, 1993)
- Charities Act 2006 (all earlier acts later consolidated into Charities Act 2011)

7. Company Law

- Companies Act 1985 – under which ISSUK became a Private Company
- Companies Act 2006

F. Finances

These columns give the figures from the Annual Accounts each year of the Unrestricted Income, ie General Funds, the surplus or deficit each year in the General Funds and the Assets at the end of each accounting year. The figures for surplus or deficit are the most significant, as they demonstrate the financial health of the organisation. The figures for end of year assets include all Restricted Funds that are held over, plus the monies in Reserves. The larger than usual increase in 1969 is due to the inclusion of the residual funds from World Refugee Year for the Refugee Pension Fund, and significant increases in some other years are due to legacies.

The figures for expenditure each year are not shown – they are just the figures for unrestricted income, plus or minus the deficit or surplus for the year.

Year	Total Unrestricted Income – ie General Funds	Surplus or Deficit in General Funds – ie difference between income and expenditure	Assets at end of accounting year
1955	Started with £ 850		
1955–6	2,375	£ (-101)	£ 901
56–7	2,673	+284	898
57–8	3,376	+959	2,281
58–9	5,578	+2,222	4,748
59–60	4,436	+ 50	6,546
60–1	6,782	(-601)	12,332
61–2	6,829	0	10,275
62–3	7,162	(- 849)	8,989
63–4	8,762	(-1,669)	12,044
64 (9m)	8,171	(-63)	12,410
65	12,200	(-554)	13,124
66	12,682	+85	18,637
67	13,073	+28	22,234
68	15,853	+551	20,985
69	16,444	(-335)	43,669
70	15,787	(-1,223)	42,616
71	18,428	(-73)	41,436
72	28,839	+754	46,373
73	31,663	+241	46,221

Year	Total Unrestricted Income – ie General Funds	Surplus or Deficit in General Funds – ie difference between income and expenditure	Assets at end of accounting year
74	34,038	(-1,467)	52,385
75	46,912	+3,212	60,486
76	47,786	(-2,864)	58,587
77	51,601	(-1,631)	65,105
78	57,673	+1,829	62,728
79	60,702	(-5,467)	78,919
80	77,688	+6,789	97,374
81	76,963	(-843)	113,526
82	89,593	(-6,049)	116,524
83	93,323	(-2,196)	120,774
84	122,377	+17,920	152,657
85	138,126	+9,371	174,002
86	147,141	+7,019	240,452
87	149,739	(-4,866)	244,989
88	160,541	6,602	261,394
89	188,761	+15,525	291,783
90	200,466	(-1,156)	298,569
91	242,712	(-738)	284,898
92	234,599	(-22,301)	252,415
93	235,043	(-37,620)	254,858
94	244,836	(-5,767)	266,631
95	245,393	(-47,304)	205,078
96	300,111	(-28,680)	172,677
97	326,782	(-34,424)	159,092
98–99 15months	401,718	+1,377	136,459
99–2000	298,494	(-31,877)	123,433
2000–1	315,628	+1,424	278,362
2001–2	320,758	+626	115,630
02–3	319,887	(-39,618)	82,842
03–4	332,717	+19,962	93,923
04–5	376,589	(-14,024)	75,130
05–6	404,779	(-13 6,929)	(-17,435)
06–7	416,366	+17,396	52,711
07–8	462,905	+19,974	24,889
08–9	760,327	+199,610	248,743

G. Lists of personnel – to the date that ISSUK became CFAB

INTERNATIONAL DIRECTORS/ SECRETARIES GENERAL OF ISS

1924–26	Ruth Larned	American	Director
1926–30	Mary Hurlbutt	American	Director
1930–43	George Warren	American	Director
1946–47	Roger Mastrude	American	Director
1948–51	Herbert Kunde	American	Director
1952–62	William Kirk	American	Director
1962–66	Stewart Sutton	Canadian	Director
1966–68	Edna Weber	American	Director
1968–71	Robert Menzies	British	Director
1971–78	Ingrid Gelinek	Austrian	Secretary General
1978–86	Audrey Moser	British	Secretary General
1986–89	Marcelle Brisson	Canadian	Secretary General
1989–2003	Damien Ngabonziza	Rwandan	Secretary General
2004–07	Vincent Faber	Swiss	Secretary General
2007–	Jean Ayoub	Lebanese	Secretary General

DIRECTORS/ CHIEF EXECUTIVES OF ISSGB and ISSUK

1955–67	Kathleen Luce	Secretary and then Director
1967–90	Winifred Rouse	Director
1990–94	David Harrison	Director
1994–2003	Peter Fry	Acting Director and then Director
2003–4	Susan Gilbert and Marek Ganther	Acting Directors
2004–7	Adrian Hatch	Chief Executive
2006–7 2007–9	Susan Gilbert	Acting Director and then Director
2009–	Andy Elvin	Chief Executive

PRESIDENTS OF ISSGB and ISSUK

1955–66	Angela, Countess of Limerick
1967 1968–72	Lady (Sylvia) Kilmuir – then as Sylvia, Countess de la Warr
1973–81	Sir Robert Black
1982–95	Sir Michael Palliser
1996–2001	Sir James Weatherall
2001–8	Sir Anthony Figgis
2008–	Harvey McGrath

CHAIRMEN OF COUNCIL/BOARD OF TRUSTEES

1955–63	Lady (Frieda) Wheeler
1964–73	Sir Robert Black
1973–78	Sir Stanley Tomlinson
1979–84	Sir Peter Scott
1985–89	Peter Foster
1990–93	Sir Terence Streeton
1994–2003	Lady (Elizabeth) Emery
2004–	Douglas Lewis

HONORARY TREASURERS

Michael Sadd	1955–59
Peter Ewen	1960–64
Sir Nutcombe Hume	1964–67
Sir Richard Baker Wilbraham	1968–84 and Trustee 1963–1989
Charles Marshall	1991–2008 all as Hon Treasurer
Sheila Redrupp	2008–

LEGAL ADVISORS

Louis Blom-Cooper	1957–69
Arthur Calvert-Smith	1969–89

Robert Stinson	1990–92

Arthur Calvert-Smith gave voluntary legal advice as member of Finance and General Purposes Committee from 1992–5 (no record of legal adviser for these years)

Pat Monro	1996–2000
Sinclair Taylor and Martin	2000–2003
Russell Cooke	2004 – Solicitors

HONORARY VICE-PRESIDENTS

Viscount Bearsted	1956–75
Lady Katherine Brandram	1956–92
Lady Kilmuir	1956–66
The Hon Michael Layton	1956–88
The Hon Richard Lyttlelton	1956–77
Lord Moyne	1956–92
Sir John Balfour	1960–83
Lady (Rose) Henriques	1964–72
Angela, Countess of Limerick	1968–81
Mrs Eileen Lawrence	1973–80
Lady (Helen) de Freitas	1976–98
Mrs Hanbury- Tracy-Domvile	1978–83
Miss Kathleen Luce	1983–2003
Lady (Françoise) Middleton	1983–2008
Lady (Mavis) Coulson	1988–2009
Sir Robert Black	1990–1999
Sir Michael Palliser	1995–2008
Lady Dora Pink	1995–2008
Sir Clive Bossom	1995–2008
Vice-Admiral Sir James Weatherall	2002–08
Mr John Wheeler	2004–07
Charles Gray	2008

ROYAL PATRONS

The Duchess of Kent (Marina)	1963–68
The Duchess of Kent (Katharine)	1968–2000
Princess Alexandra of Kent	2001–

OTHER PATRONS

Lord (Herbert) Laming	2007–
Sir Anthony Figgis	2008–
Lady (Françoise) Middleton	2008–

THE FIRST COMMITTEE OF TRUSTEES IN 1955

Lady (Frieda) Wheeler	Chairman
Miss Olive Hargreaves	Vice Chairman
Michael Sadd	Hon Treasurer
Mrs P Cochrane	
Miss H Davidson	
Miss Audrey Duff	
Lady (Rose) Henriques	
Miss Holmes à Court	
Miss E Houghton	
Lady Kirkpatrick	
Angela, Countess of Limerick	
Miss C Sheldon	
Mrs L Wilson	
The Hon Mrs Woodruff	

TRUSTEES WHO SERVED FOR MORE THAN 10 YEARS

Lady (Frieda) Wheeler	1955–71 Chairman from 1955–1965
Miss Olive Hargreaves	1955–65 Vice-Chairman until 1963
The Hon Mrs Woodruff	1955–66
Lady (Rose) Henriques	1955–63 Vice President 1963–72

Miss Holmes à Court	1955–68
Angela,Countess of Limerick	1955–80, Vice-President 1968–81
Louis Blom-Cooper	1957–69 Hon Legal Adviser
Lady (Sylvia) Kilmuir then as Countess de la Warr	1957–67, 68–76, President 67–72
Lady (Mavis) Coulson	1958, 1963–91 and President Spring Fair
Miss M Monkhouse	1958–81 mostly on Finance Committee
Mrs Stella Calvert-Smith	1959–92, Vice-chairman 74–79
Arthur Calvert-Smith	1969–89 Legal Adviser
Mrs Marcella Hanbury-Tracy-Domvile	1960–78, Vice-President 1978–83
Mrs Eileen Lawrence	1960–72 Trustee and social work volunteer
Sir Richard Baker Wilbraham	1963–89 – Hon Treasurer 1968–84
William Lidbury	1963–1987
John Wheeler	1963–2004 – Vice-Chairman 1964–73, 1991–2 and 97–2004
Sir Robert Black	1964–89, Chairman 1965–72, President 1973–81, Trustee 1982–9, Honorary Vice-President 1990–99
Mrs Betty Greenhalgh	1966–78
John Greenhalgh	1980–87
Miss Kathleen Luce	1966–82 after retiring as Director
Lady (Helen) de Freitas	1968–89 Vice-Chairman 70–75
Miss Mary Windsor	1970–82
Mrs Ricketts	1966–90
Sir Stanley Tomlinson	1972–83
Lady (Dora) Pink	1974–92
Peter Fry	1977–92
Sir Peter Scott	1978–90 Chairman 79–84 and Vice-Chairman 86–90
Peter Archer	1978–89

Sir Michael Palliser	1982–92
Norman Sears	1981–92 incl. 3 years as Treasurer
Lady (Françoise) Middleton	1987–2007
Lady (Liz) Emery	1990–2003 and Chairman from 1997–2003
Charles Marshall	1991–2008 all as Hon Treasurer

THE FINAL BOARD OF TRUSTEES – when ISSUK became CFAB

Douglas Lewis	2004 – Chairman
Margaret Bryer	2004–
Ali Sattaripour	2004–
Robert Hutchinson	2004–
Liz Grimsey	2005–
Pam Louhichi	2005–
Kumari Blakey	2007–
Tessa Brewer	2007–
Sarah Palmer	2007–
Alex Verdan	2007–
Yvette Gayford	2008–
Harvey McGrath	2008 – President
Sheila Redrupp	2009 – Hon Treasurer

STAFF IN POST – when ISSGB started on 1st April 1955

Kathleen Luce	1955–67	Director
Danica Adjemovic	1955–56	Social worker
Frances (Patty) Riddell Blount	1955–61	Social worker
Mrs Gullick	1955–?	Typist
Mrs Paschen	1955–?	Typist
Violetta Metaxa	1955–?	Filing clerk

LONGEST SERVING STAFF MEMBERS *– more than 10 years between 1955–2010.*

Kathleen (Kay) Luce	1946–67	Director, and then on Council until 1982
Ruth Eames	1957–80	Fair Organiser and Director's Secretary
Winifred Klingender	1959–85	Social worker, specialist in adoption
Winifred Hatfield	1962–73	Secretary
Jean Martin	1963–87	Social worker
Heloise Tindal Kareem	1967–74 1984–88 1990–2003	Social worker/Deputy Director Director
Winifred (Win)Rouse	1967–90	Director from 67–90
Judy Clark	1972–78 1981–2001	Social worker/ Tracing specialist
Essie Grives	1974–94	Social worker/ Deputy Director from 1991
Ruth Black	1975–92	Volunteer Refugee Support worker
Ruth Ellis	1977–88	Social worker
Ruth Furnival	1978–89	Social worker
David Todd	1979–91	Administrator
Jenny Jessup	1980–92	Director's Secretary
Maggie Durham	1980–92	Spring Fair Secretary
Christopher Platt	1980–2 1990 –	Administrative Assistant Chief Administrative Officer
Enid Holliday	1980–92	Secretary
Phyllis Jackson	1982–99	Social worker on Travel Assistance Scheme
Dawn Temple	1984–96	Social worker
Peter Fry	1993–2003	Director, but formerly in GS and on Council
Elizabeth Sweeney	1988–2009	Secretarial assistant
Jean Rigg	1988–2003	Administrative Assistant, Travel Assistance Scheme

Mark Hunt	1995 –	Administrative assistant/ Receptionist
Lesley Austen	1995–2009	Tracing and Family Contact worker
Marek Ganther	1999 –	Social worker/ Travel Assistance/Libya project

STAFF IN POST – when ISSUK ended on 31st December 2009 and became CFAB

	From:	
Andy Elvin	2009	Chief Executive
Christopher Platt	1980–82 & 1990	Administrative Assistant Chief Administrative Officer
Mark Hunt	1995	Administrative Assistant/ Receptionist
Marek Ganther	1999	Social worker/Travel Assistance/Libya project
Hana Najsrova	2007	Social worker
Dorothee Wockel	2007	Social worker
Darren Moses	2008	Events Manager
Florence Grandvalet	2008	Social worker
Meena Enawalla	2009	Senior social worker
Laura Gomez-Roldan	2009	Social worker
Christina Turner	2009	Personal Assistant to Chief Executive

H. The trusts that have given most money over the years

This is a list of those Trusts that have given most consistently and generously over the years. They are listed in the order in which they began to give to ISSUK, starting with the Buttle Trust in 1955.

Buttle Trust

City Parochial Foundation

Fitton Trust

Blaxhill Charity Trust

Walter Guiness Charitable Trust

Godfrey Mitchell Charitable Trust

Samuel Ansbacher and Meyer Herech Charity Trust

Whitbread Trust

Cyril Kleinwort Charitable Trust

Clover Trust

Goldsmiths' Company Charitable Donation Fund

Noel Buxton Trust

Carnwath Charitable Trust

Ormonde Charitable Trust

Schröder Charity Trust

H O Joseph Charitable Trust

Laing Trusts

Philip Fleming Charitable Trust

Merchant Taylors' Company

Baring Foundation

Ormonde Charitable Trust

Rayne Foundation

Richard Cadbury Charitable Trust

PF Charitable Trust

Henry Smith Charitable Trust

City Bridge Trust – formerly Bridge House Trust

Garfield Weston Foundation
Hobson Charitable Trust
Lloyd's TSB
Comic Relief

I. Publications

i) Those published by ISS (these are just a sample of the many publications by ISS over the years)

International Social Service – a History 1921–1955 – by Ruth Larned 1960

The story of the ISS – a Digest – by R Larned 1960

Referral Techniques – Imaginative Co-operation – by Kay Luce 1955

The Practice of Intercountry Casework by Edna Weber – Published in International Social Work journal 1959

Immigrants at London Airport – and their settlement in the community. ISSGB 1967

Unaccompanied Children in Emergencies – a Field Guide for their Care and Protection – by Jan Williamson and Audrey Moser – Published by ISS 1987

Guidelines on Procedures for Intercountry Adoption – ISS 1992

The Early History of the International Social Service of Great Britain – article by K Luce. 1992

Keeping Families Together Across Frontiers – Principle and Methods of Intercountry Casework – ISS Staff Training Seminar October 1997

The Rights of the Child in Domestic and Intercountry Adoption – Ethics and Principles, Guidelines for Practice – ISS-IRC 1999, revised 2004

ISS Manual, revised 2000

Young People in Migration – a Challenge for Social Services – ISS 75 Years Open Day – 2000

The Activities of International Social Service and their Legal Bases – ISS 2007

Unaccompanied and Separated Minors – papers from ISS International Seminar 2003

A very personal service – a history of ISS Australia's first 50 years of service 1955–2005. Dr Barbara Pertzel 2011.

ii) Other publications which were written as a result of ISS projects

Adoption of Non-White Children – the experience of a British Adoption Project – L Raynor – Published by George Allen and Unwin 1970

Adversity, adoption and afterwards – a mid-life follow-up study of women adopted from Hong-Kong – by J Feast, M Grant, A Rushton and J Simmonds – BAAF 2013.

iii) Other relevant literature, quoted in the text

A very private practice – an investigation into private fostering – T Philpot, BAAF 2001

Index

Notes: This Index contains the main references to each topic. It is not fully comprehensive, because some words are used so frequently that it would be confusing to list every reference. Whenever there is a heading on a topic the reference is in bold type. Descriptions of significant individuals are also marked in bold type.

B

C

D

E

F

G

H

I

K

L

M

N

P

T

U

V

W

Y